CW00818854

DONG GONG
DATE SELECTION

Dong Gong Date Selection

The author can be reached at:

Mastery Academy of Chinese Metaphysics Sdn. Bhd. (611143-A)
19-3, The Boulevard, Mid Valley City,
59200 Kuala Lumpur, Malaysia.
Tel   : +603-2284 8080
Fax   : +603-2284 1218
Email   : info@masteryacademy.com
Website: www.masteryacademy.com

DISCLAIMER:

Published by JY Books Sdn. Bhd. (659134-T)

INDEX

董公擇日要覽

About The Chinese Metaphysics Reference Series

Reference Series

The Chinese Metaphysics Reference Series of books are designed primarily to be used as complimentary textbooks for scholars, students, researchers, teachers and practitioners of Chinese Metaphysics.

The goal is to provide quick easy reference tables, diagrams and charts, facilitating the study and practice of various Chinese Metaphysics subjects including Feng Shui, BaZi, Yi Jing, Zi Wei, Liu Ren, Ze Ri, Ta Yi, Qi Men and Mian Xiang.

This series of books are intended as <u>reference text and educational materials</u> principally for the academic syllabuses of the **Mastery Academy of Chinese Metaphysics**. The contents have also been formatted so that Feng Shui Masters and other teachers of Chinese Metaphysics will always have a definitive source of reference at hand, when teaching or applying their art.

Because each school of Chinese Metaphysics is different, the Reference Series of books usually do not contain any specific commentaries, application methods or explanations on the theory behind the formulas presented in its contents. This is to ensure that the contents can be used freely and independently by all Feng Shui Masters and teachers of Chinese Metaphysics without conflict.

If you would like to study or learn the applications of any of the formulas presented in the Reference Series of books, we recommend that you undertake the courses offered by Joey Yap and his team of Instructors at the Mastery Academy of Chinese Metaphysics.

Titles offers in the Reference Series as of Autumn 2008:

1. The Chinese Metaphysics Compendium
2. Dong Gong Date Selection
3. Earth Study Discern Truth
4. Xuan Kong Da Gua Reference Book
5. San Yuan's Dragon Gate Eight Formation Water Method
6. 8 Killings Sha Reference Book
7. Plum Blossoms Divination Book

Preface

"Timing is everything." How many times have you heard that? Probably more times than you care to remember!

It wouldn't be said so often if it wasn't the truth. The element of time does indeed have far-reaching consequences. If you think about it, it plays into almost every decision you make. But knowing you need to pick the right time is one thing. How do you make certain that it is indeed the right time? Sometimes, finding the answer to that is akin to making a shot in the dark.

"The only reason for time is so that everything doesn't happen at once," said Albert Einstein, and there is much wisdom to be derived from that. So much wisdom, in fact, that the factor of proper timing has been an essential part of Chinese Metaphysics since the era of the Three Kingdoms.

The Art of Date Selection, or Ze Ri, grew out of a combination of astronomy, astrology, and historical observation to detect subtle energy patterns and cycles that co-relate to certain events. The logic behind Date Selection is to pick a day for a certain activity when the energies of that day are most conducive for that activity – such as, for example, a wedding, or a burial, or a life-threatening surgery. For that reason, Date Selection is an integral part of my – and any serious practitioner's – Feng Shui practice.

The Dong Gong Method of Date Selection is based on the methods of Dong De Zhang, the reputed Ming Dynasty astrologer and author who spent a lifetime meticulously looking through the 60 Jia Zi in each of the 12 Solar Months to outline the effect of each Star. His commentaries on these form the backbone of many Date Selection practices today and are an indispensable reference to any enthusiast, practitioner or teacher of Date Selection.

My goal with this Reference Series book is to make it easier for enthusiasts and students to find the information they need. Mainly it has been designed so that Masters and other teachers of Date Selection will always have a handy reference when teaching. In my early days as a student of Chinese Metaphysics, it was often hard to find a reference when I needed it – most of the available information was a jumble of facts and figures. Sifting through volumes of books took up much of my research time.

These ancient Chinese texts are written in the Chinese language, excluding many from being able to derive any knowledge from them. Even people who are comfortable reading Chinese may stumble occasionally, as these texts were written hundreds of years ago and have a distinctive style that is hard to follow.

It is my wish, therefore, that this book serves as a one-stop guide and reference for both teachers and students of Date Selection, as well as researchers. It is a labour of love that grew out of my own experiences sourcing for information, and is a collection of tables and information referred to frequently in the Dong Gong classical texts and when necessary, can also be an essential guide in the practice of BaZi, Zi Wei and other Chinese Metaphysics.

Keep in mind that although the Dong Gong Date Selection Reference Series is a compilation and organization of Chinese References, it is not meant to teach or instruct. For that purpose, you may choose to enroll in a Ze Ri class or engage a teacher with the requisite experience to better show you how these theories are applied.

The second edition of this book has an added new chapter titled "Using the Dong Gong Date Selection Reference Book." It is a quick yet comprehensive guide that shows you how to evaluate a date for auspiciousness using the Dong Gong Method. This chapter will enable anyone, especially beginners, to approach the Dong Gong Method of Date Selection methodically and with confidence.

The Dong Gong classics have never been translated into English before, and it is my belief that this Dong Gong Date Selection book will set new standards in reference books for Chinese Metaphysics.

More important, it is my hope that by making it easier to study and research Date Selection, BaZi and other Chinese Metaphysics, we are able to create a growing awareness on this valuable body of knowledge and light a spark that will create a revolutionary change in the study and practice of these subjects.

Joey Yap
May 2008
(Second Edition)

Author's personal website: www.joeyyap.com | www.fengshuilogy.com
Academy website:
www.masteryacademy.com | www.masteryjournal.com | www.maelearning.com

MASTERY ACADEMY
OF CHINESE METAPHYSICS™

At **www.masteryacademy.com**, you will find some useful tools to ascertain key information about the Feng Shui of a property or for the study of Astrology.

The Joey Yap Flying Stars Calculator can be utilised to plot your home or office Flying Stars chart. To find out your personal best directions, use the 8 Mansions Calculator. To learn more about your personal Destiny, you can use the Joey Yap BaZi Ming Pan Calculator to plot your Four Pillars of Destiny – you just need to have your date of birth (day, month, year) and time of birth.

For more information about BaZi, Xuan Kong or Flying Star Feng Shui, or if you wish to learn more about these subjects with Joey Yap, logon to the Mastery Academy of Chinese Metaphysics website at **www.masteryacademy.com.**

www.maelearning.com

Bookmark this address on your computer, and visit this newly-launched website today. With the E-Learning Center, knowledge of Chinese Metaphysics is a mere 'click' away!

Our E-Learning Center consists of 3 distinct components.

1. Online Courses
These shall comprise of 3 Programs: our Online Feng Shui Program, Online BaZi Program, and Online Mian Xiang Program. Each lesson contains a video lecture, slide presentation and downloadable course notes.

2. MA Live!
With MA Live!, Joey Yap's workshops, tutorials, courses and seminars on various Chinese Metaphysics subjects broadcasted right to your computer screen. Better still, participants will not only get to see and hear Joey talk 'live', but also get to engage themselves directly in the event and more importantly, TALK to Joey via the MA Live! interface. All the benefits of a live class, minus the hassle of actually having to attend one!

3. Video-On-Demand (VOD)
Get immediate streaming-downloads of the Mastery Academy's wide range of educational DVDs, right on your computer screen. No more shipping costs and waiting time to be incurred!

Study at your own pace, and interact with your Instructor and fellow students worldwide...at your own convenience and privacy. With our E-Learning Center, knowledge of Chinese Metaphysics is brought DIRECTLY to you in all its clarity, with illustrated presentations and comprehensive notes expediting your learning curve!

Welcome to the Mastery Academy's E-LEARNING CENTER...YOUR virtual gateway to Chinese Metaphysics mastery!

Using the Dong Gong Date Selection Reference Book

Dong Gong Date Selection is a Month-Based Date Selection Method which is essentially the culmination of Grandmaster's Dong De Zhang's (Ming Dynasty) lifetime study and analysis of the effect of Stars on each of the 60 Jia Zi days, for every Solar month in a year (according to the Chinese Solar Calendar). The Dong Gong Method is thus not only an important cross-check for experienced Date Selection practitioners, it is also a convenient reference for beginners who wish to err on the safe side when selecting suitable dates.

Hence, the crux of the Dong Gong Method is that it enables the practitioner to juxtapose the Qi present on a particular Jia Zi against the month it falls in. This empowers the practitioner to derive an accurate insight into the cosmic qi patterns taking place in the universal constellations which influence the qi and activities of each day. Date Selection is literally a reverse engineering of the selection of suitable stars and constellations to match an intended activity or endeavour!

The main components of this Dong Gong Date Selection Reference Book are the transliterations of Grandmaster Dong's commentaries/notes for every Jia Zi (ie. Day Pillar) of each Chinese Solar month. These transliterations are to be read carefully as they provide details of the positive or negative influences of each day, as well as the suitable activities (or activities to avoid). In addition, I have also included, in this Dong Gong Date Selection Reference Book, a easy-to-use rating system for quick reference, at the end of each commentary. Simply refer to the rating to determine the overall auspiciousness of a particular Jia Zi day in any month.

The following is a guide in utilising the commentaries and ratings to evaluate the auspiciousness of any date using the Dong Gong Method:

i) Refer to the appropriate chapter on the specific Chinese Solar Month containing the date in question

ii) Obtain the Jia Zi for the date

iii) Read and understand the commentary for the day in question, in particular what a specific Jia Zi day is suitable (or unsuitable) for

iv) Check the rating system to determine the overall auspiciousness (or inauspiciousness) of the Jia Zi day

For example, let's take a date for an intended activity, say the launch of a new business. Let's choose 23 October 2008. We follow the guide above to evaluate the suitability of the day in question:

i)   23 October falls in the ninth month (ie. Dog or Xu (戌) month) of the Chinese Solar Calendar. Turn to corresponding chapter of the Dog month which begins on **Page 114**

ii) Next, we need to find out the Jia Zi (Day Pillar) of 23 October 2008. For this, you will need to refer to Joey Yap's Ten Thousand Year Calendar or any Tong Shu for 2008. We find that the Jia Zi of 23 October 2008 is Bing Shen (丙申).

iii) Turn to the page containing the commentary for the Shen Monkey (申) day of the Dog Xu (戌) month, which is on **Page 125** of this book. Read the commentary carefully. From the commentary, we can establish that while a Bing Shen day is not as auspicious as the Wu Shen or Jia Shen days, it is still regarded as a good day (while Geng Shen (庚申) day is clearly an inauspicious one).

iv) From the rating system at the bottom of the page, we can also see that a Bing Shen (丙申) day is "Auspicious". As such, based on Grandmaster Dong's assessment, we can surmise that 23 October 2008 is a usable day for a business launch.

In addition to the commentaries and rating system, you will notice that each chapter of each month opens with supplementary information for Date Selection practitioners eg. additional benevolent stars based on the Heavenly Stem or Earthly Branch, 24 Solar Seasons, Monthly Three Killings etc.

The Dong Gong Date Selection Method is best complemented with a sound understanding of the 12 Day Office Method of Date Selection. The 12 Day Officer Method is based on the concept that each day of the month is governed by one of 12 "Guardian Stars" (or "Guardian Officers") which determine the types of suitable activities for each of 12 types of days. For a beginners' reference to the 12 Day Officer Method, refer to Joey Yap's Personal Date Selection, of The Art of Date Selection Series.

In addition, we advise you to seek the tutelage or advice of a qualified teacher if you wish to benefit fully from understanding or utilising the Dong Gong Method. This is because the transliterations of the commentaries herein are designed for practitioners who are already fairly proficient in the study of Chinese Metaphysics. Furthermore, while this book includes other reference material for Date Selection practitioners (eg. Auxiliary Stars, Purple White Annual Star Diagrams etc), there is NO explanation or elucidation of these additional references.

First Month 正月

February 4th – March 5th

Tiger 寅 (Yin) Month

February 4th – March 5th
Tiger 寅 (Yin) Month

月德丙、月恩丙，母倉亥子，天德合壬。

For the Tiger 寅 (Yin) Month, the positive Monthly Virtue and Monthly Benevolence Stars can be found on Bing 丙 Days. Pig 亥 (Hai) and Rat 子 (Zi) Days are also accompanied by the presence of the auspicious Motherly Storage 母倉 Star. In addition, the Qi brought about by the Heavenly Virtue 天德 Star supports Ren 壬 Days.

立春：立春前一日爲四絕。

The 'Coming of Spring' 立春 (Li Chun)

One day before of Li Chun (Coming of Spring) is called the Four Extinction 四絕 Day.

雨水：立春後,三煞在北,亥、子、丑方,忌修造、動土。

'Rain Water' 雨水 (Yu Shui)

Upon the Coming (Commencement) of Spring, the Three Killings 三煞 (San Sha) Affliction will occupy the Northwest 3 亥 (Hai – NW3), North 2 子 (Zi – N2) and Northeast 1 丑 (Chou - NE1) sectors of the home or workplace. As such, refrain from renovating or digging the ground in these sectors, to prevent unleashing the harmful energies of the Three Killings.

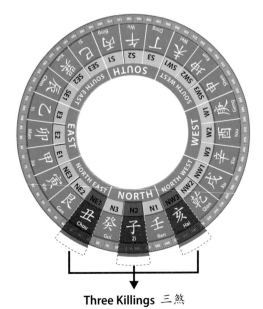

Three Killings 三煞

十二值神 12 Day Officers	十二地支 Animal Sign of the Day	董公擇日解說 Dong Gong Description
建 *Jian* **Establish**	寅 *Yin* **Tiger** Yang Wood	往亡日。不利起造、結婚姻、納采，主家長病、招官司犯之主六十日、一百二十日內損小口，一年內見重喪，百事不宜。 This is known as an Emptiness Day 往亡日. It is therefore not ideal to be used to begin construction works, for marriage or to sign contracts. Using this day for such endeavors will result in elderly family members falling ill or the advent of legal entanglements. Once violated, the adverse effects of the Emptiness Day will be felt within 60 to 120 days, during which small children run the risk of being hurt or injured. Furthermore, there might also be a death in the family. As such, this day is unsuitable for any important activities or endeavors.

董公擇日要覽

寅
Tiger

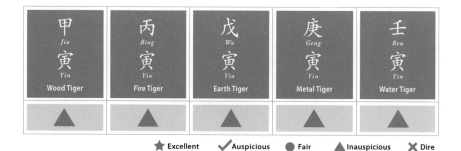

甲 *Jia* 寅 *Yin* **Wood Tiger**	丙 *Bing* 寅 *Yin* **Fire Tiger**	戊 *Wu* 寅 *Yin* **Earth Tiger**	庚 *Geng* 寅 *Yin* **Metal Tiger**	壬 *Ren* 寅 *Yin* **Water Tiger**
▲	▲	▲	▲	▲

★ Excellent ✓ Auspicious ● Fair ▲ Inauspicious ✗ Dire

董公擇日要覽

Rabbit

十二值神 12 Day Officers	十二地支 Animal Sign of the Day	董公擇日解說 Dong Gong Description
除 *Chu* **Remove**	卯 *Mao* **Rabbit** **Yin Wood**	不宜起造、婚姻,犯之主六十日内損家長、招官司。三五年内見凶冷退,主兄弟不義、各業分散、惡人相逢、生離死別。 This is not a suitable day for renovation or marriage. If used, elderly family members will be prone to injuries or ailments and legal problems may surface within a period of 60 Days. Disharmony, separation or a rift between siblings may be expected within 3 to 5 years' time. The family will also be threatened by bandits, robbers or hostile people, and a permanent separation caused by death will also occur.

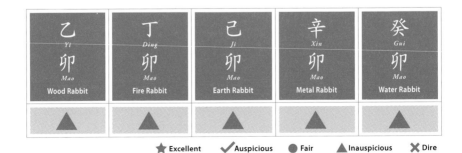

乙 *Yi* 卯 *Mao* Wood Rabbit	丁 *Ding* 卯 *Mao* Fire Rabbit	己 *Ji* 卯 *Mao* Earth Rabbit	辛 *Xin* 卯 *Mao* Metal Rabbit	癸 *Gui* 卯 *Mao* Water Rabbit
▲	▲	▲	▲	▲

★ Excellent   ✔ Auspicious   ● Fair   ▲ Inauspicious   ✗ Dire

十二值神 12 Day Officers	十二地支 Animal Sign of the Day	董公擇日解説 Dong Gong Description
滿 *Man* **Full**	辰 *Chen* **Dragon** Yang Earth 	天富、天賊、天羅星臨。甲辰雖有氣，與戊辰同，煞集中宮，百事皆忌，犯之主殺人、退財，大凶。餘辰日亦不吉。 The Heavenly Fortune 天富, Heavenly Thief 天賊 and Heavenly Spiral 天羅 stars arrive on this day. The Jia Chen 甲辰 and Wu Chen 戊辰 pillars will not possess sufficient strength, and this situation is further compounded by the presence of Sha (Killing) Qi in the Central Palace. This day is therefore unsuitable for most activities or endeavors, for if used, it may bring about physical harm and loss of wealth. The other Chen 辰 (Dragon) days are not as inauspicious, but still not ideal enough to be used, and are best avoided where possible.

甲 *Jia* 辰 *Chen* Wood Dragon	丙 *Bing* 辰 *Chen* Fire Dragon	戊 *Wu* 辰 *Chen* Earth Dragon	庚 *Geng* 辰 *Chen* Metal Dragon	壬 *Ren* 辰 *Chen* Water Dragon
✖	▲	✖	▲	▲

★ Excellent   ✔ Auspicious   ● Fair   ▲ Inauspicious   ✖ Dire

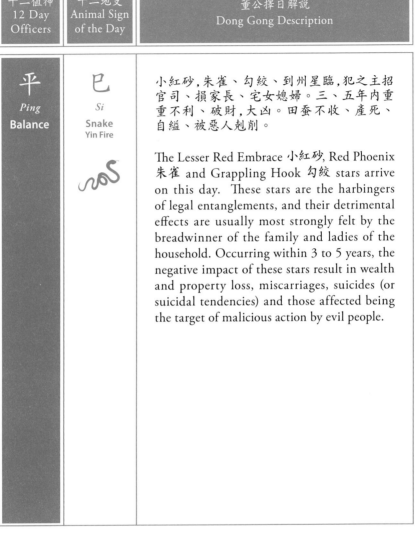

十二值神 12 Day Officers	十二地支 Animal Sign of the Day	董公擇日解説 Dong Gong Description
平 *Ping* **Balance**	巳 *Si* Snake Yin Fire	小紅砂,朱雀、勾絞、到州星臨,犯之主招官司、損家長、宅女媳婦。三、五年內重重不利、破財,大凶。田蠶不收、產死、自縊、被惡人剋削。 The Lesser Red Embrace 小紅砂, Red Phoenix 朱雀 and Grappling Hook 勾絞 stars arrive on this day. These stars are the harbingers of legal entanglements, and their detrimental effects are usually most strongly felt by the breadwinner of the family and ladies of the household. Occurring within 3 to 5 years, the negative impact of these stars result in wealth and property loss, miscarriages, suicides (or suicidal tendencies) and those affected being the target of malicious action by evil people.

董公擇日要覽

Snake

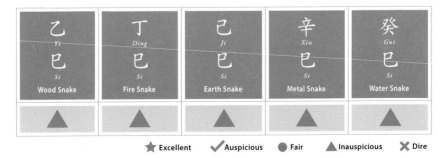

乙 *Yi* 巳 *Si* Wood Snake	丁 *Ding* 巳 *Si* Fire Snake	己 *Ji* 巳 *Si* Earth Snake	辛 *Xin* 巳 *Si* Metal Snake	癸 *Gui* 巳 *Si* Water Snake
▲	▲	▲	▲	▲

★ Excellent　✓ Auspicious　● Fair　▲ Inauspicious　✗ Dire

董公擇日要覽

十二值神 12 Day Officers	十二地支 Animal Sign of the Day	董公擇日解説 Dong Gong Description
定 *Ding* **Stable**	午 *Wu* Horse Yang Fire 	黃砂日,有黃羅、紫檀、天皇、地皇、金銀庫樓、田塘、月財庫、貯星,諸吉星蓋照,宜起造、安葬、移徙、開張、出行、婚姻,主六十日、一百二十日內進橫財、田產,或因附寄成家,大作大發、小作小發,主田蠶大收獲,金銀滿庫。 This is a Yellow Embrace Day 黃砂日, due to the presence of the Yellow Spiral 黃羅, Purple Sandalwood 紫檀, Heavenly Emperor 天皇, Earthly Emperor 地皇、Golden Wealth Storage 金銀庫樓, Property Embankment Star 田塘, Monthly Wealth Storage 月財庫 and Storage 貯 stars on this day. As such, this is an auspicious day for renovations, burial, moving house, opening a business, travel and marriage. If used, one will see an improvement in one financial standing or an increase in property assets within 60 to 120 days. Endeavors or activities that are undertaken on a large scale will also reap considerable returns, while smaller-scale undertakings will enjoy correspondingly proportional returns.

午
Horse

甲 *Jia* 午 *Wu* Wood Horse	丙 *Bing* 午 *Wu* Fire Horse	戊 *Wu* 午 *Wu* Earth Horse	庚 *Geng* 午 *Wu* Metal Horse	壬 *Ren* 午 *Wu* Water Horse
✔	★	✔	✔	✔

★ Excellent ✔ Auspicious ● Fair ▲ Inauspicious ✖ Dire

十二值神 12 Day Officers	十二地支 Animal Sign of the Day	董公擇日解説 Dong Gong Description
執 *Zhi* **Initiate**	未 *Wei* Goat Yin Earth 	天賊、朱雀、勾絞星臨。六十日、一百二十日內損六畜、傷騾馬、成惡疾。乙未煞集中宮,更忌起造、入宅、婚姻、開張、修整等事。 The negative Heavenly Thief 天賊, Red Phoenix 朱雀 and Grappling Hook 勾絞 stars arrive on this day. The animals or pets in the household will be adversely affected within 60 to 120 days if any (important) activity or endeavor is undertaken on this day, and human occupants will also be susceptible or prone to ailments. The worst of the Wei 未 (Goat) Days is the Yi Wei 乙未 Day, when Sha (Killing) Qi enters the Central Palace of a home or office. As such, avoid moving house, getting married or starting a business on these days.

Goat

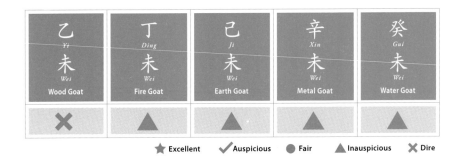

乙 *Yi* 未 *Wei* Wood Goat	丁 *Ding* 未 *Wei* Fire Goat	己 *Ji* 未 *Wei* Earth Goat	辛 *Xin* 未 *Wei* Metal Goat	癸 *Gui* 未 *Wei* Water Goat
✖	▲	▲	▲	▲

★ Excellent ✔ Auspicious ● Fair ▲ Inauspicious ✖ Dire

董公擇日要覽

Monkey

十二值神 12 Day Officers	十二地支 Animal Sign of the Day	董公擇日解說 Dong Gong Description
破 *Po* **Destruction**	申 *Shen* Monkey Yang Metal 	遇朱雀、勾絞星，主招官司、口舌、退牲 財，三、五年內見寡婦、醜事。庚申正四 廢，更凶。 Negative stars such as the Red Phoenix 朱雀 and Grappling Hook 勾絞 govern this day. Hence, such a day is the harbinger of legal entanglements, malicious gossips and rumors, arguments and loss of wealth. According to this ancient text, the detrimental effects of these stars will produce widows or scandals within 3 to 5 years, which makes this day a particularly inauspicious one for the patriarch of the family. Of all the bad days in this group, the Geng Shen 庚申 Day is the worst, as it is also known as a Four Abandonment Day 四廢 .

甲 *Jia* 申 *Shen* Wood Monkey	丙 *Bing* 申 *Shen* Fire Monkey	戊 *Wu* 申 *Shen* Earth Monkey	庚 *Geng* 申 *Shen* Metal Monkey	壬 *Ren* 申 *Shen* Water Monkey
▲	▲	▲	✖	▲

★ Excellent ✔ Auspicious ● Fair ▲ Inauspicious ✖ Dire

十二值神 12 Day Officers	十二地支 Animal Sign of the Day	董公擇日解説 Dong Gong Description
危 *Wei* **Danger**	酉 *You* Rooster Yin Metal 	辛酉正四廢，不宜用事。惟丁酉有天德福星蓋照，宜安葬、還福愿、出行、開張、參官、見貴吉。只不宜起造、婚姻、嫁娶等事，乃比和之日也。餘酉日均不可用。 The Xin You 辛酉 Day is one of the Four Abandonment Days, and therefore unsuitable for activities of any sort. However, the Heavenly Virtue 天德 and Prosperity 福星 stars are present on the Ding You 丁酉 Day, making it a good day for burial, business travel, opening a new business, debt-collection or meeting with high officials. In any case, the Ding You Day is not suitable for beginning construction or marriage, while the remaining You 酉 (Rooster) Days should not be used for important endeavors or activities.

董公擇日要覽

酉
Rooster

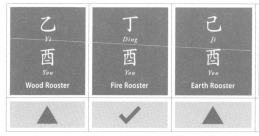

乙 *Yi* 酉 *You* Wood Rooster	丁 *Ding* 酉 *You* Fire Rooster	己 *Ji* 酉 *You* Earth Rooster	辛 *Xin* 酉 *You* Metal Rooster	癸 *Gui* 酉 *You* Water Rooster
▲	✓	▲	✗	▲

★ Excellent   ✓ Auspicious   ● Fair   ▲ Inauspicious   ✗ Dire

董公擇日要覽

戌
Dog

十二值神 12 Day Officers	十二地支 Animal Sign of the Day	董公擇日解説 Dong Gong Description
成 *Cheng* **Success**	戌 *Xu* Dog Yang Earth 	天喜、地網星同臨,不宜犯之。主家長病、人口不義、冷退。丙戌、戊戌、庚戌、壬戌,煞集中宮,犯之主首殺人、兄弟不義、死別生離,尤忌起造、婚姻、入宅、修作。 The Sky Happiness 天喜 and Earthly Web 地網 stars rule this day, and their effects do not augur well for endeavors or undertakings of any sort. It is best to avoid using this day, as it will result in family members falling ill and the possibility of a death in the family. In particular, there will be Sha (Killing) Qi in the Central Palace on Bing Xu 丙戌, Wu Xu 戊戌, Geng Xu 庚戌 and Ren Xu 壬戌 Days. Hence, disturbing the Central Palace on these days will result in discord amongst siblings or separation caused by a death in the family. Do not begin construction, get married or move into a new house on this day, under any circumstances.

甲 *Jia* 戌 *Xu* Wood Dog	丙 *Bing* 戌 *Xu* Fire Dog	戊 *Wu* 戌 *Xu* Earth Dog	庚 *Geng* 戌 *Xu* Metal Dog	壬 *Ren* 戌 *Xu* Water Dog
✕	▲	✕	▲	✕

★ Excellent   ✓ Auspicious   ● Fair   ▲ Inauspicious   ✕ Dire

董公擇日要覽

亥
Pig

十二值神 12 Day Officers	十二地支 Animal Sign of the Day	董公擇日解說 Dong Gong Description
收 *Shou* **Receive**	亥 *Hai* Pig Yin Water 	有勾絞不宜用事。犯之損家長、害子孫。六十日、一百二十日內主南方白衣刑害、男女多災，大凶。惟平日地支與月建陰陽合德者次吉。 The negative Grappling Hook 勾絞 star governs this day. Unleashing its energies will only result in the elders or grandchildren in the family being prone to injuries. One will also receive the tragic news of a death from the South within 60 to 120 days. The children in the family will also encounter plenty of hassles and hindrances in their course of life.

乙 *Yi* 亥 *Hai* Wood Pig	丁 *Ding* 亥 *Hai* Fire Pig	己 *Ji* 亥 *Hai* Earth Pig	辛 *Xin* 亥 *Hai* Metal Pig	癸 *Gui* 亥 *Hai* Water Pig
▲	▲	▲	▲	▲

 ★ Excellent ✔ Auspicious ● Fair ▲ Inauspicious ✘ Dire

十二值神 12 Day Officers	十二地支 Animal Sign of the Day	董公擇日解説 Dong Gong Description
開 *Kai* **Open**	子 *Zi* Rat Yang Water 	甲子自死之金,五行陰忌之日。壬子木打寶瓶,終是北方沐浴之地,不宜起造、婚姻、入宅、開張等事。戊子、丙子、庚子三日,水土生人用之大吉。內有黃羅、紫檀、天皇、地皇、金銀寶藏、財庫貯、聯珠眾星蓋照,主六十日、一百二十日內得大財、貴人接引、職祿、謀事大吉,旺六畜、益財產、亦宜安葬。 On a Jia Zi 甲子 (Wood Rat) Day, the Metal Element (Qi) self-enters into Death. This is known as a Five Element Yin Negative Day. On a Ren Zi 壬子 (Water Rat) Day, the Wood 木 Qi is unstable and fickle. This is considered the North's Bath Water 沐浴 sector. Neither of the days mentioned above is suitable to begin construction, get married, move into a new house or open a new business. Persons whose self-element is either Water or Earth will benefit the most from Wu Zi 戊子 (Earth Rat), Bing Zi 丙子 (Fire Rat) and Geng Zi 庚子(Metal Rat) Days, due to the presence of the auspicious Yellow Spiral 黃羅, Purple Sandalwood 紫檀, Heavenly Emperor 天皇 and Earthly Emperor 地皇 stars on these days. Used well, one will enjoy a significant influx of wealth within 60 to 120 days, as well as the assistance of noble people, especially in times of need.

Rat

甲 *Jia* 子 *Zi* Wood Rat	丙 *Bing* 子 *Zi* Fire Rat	戊 *Wu* 子 *Zi* Earth Rat	庚 *Geng* 子 *Zi* Metal Rat	壬 *Ren* 子 *Zi* Water Rat
▲	✔	✔	✔	▲

★ Excellent   ✔ Auspicious   ● Fair   ▲ Inauspicious   ✘ Dire

十二值神 12 Day Officers	十二地支 Animal Sign of the Day	董公擇日解説 Dong Gong Description
閉 *Bi* **Close**	丑 *Chou* Ox Yin Earth 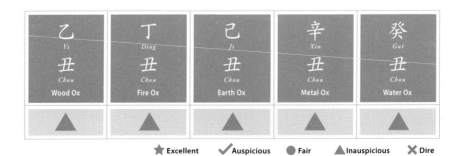	不利婚姻、起造,防虎蛇傷、騾馬踢、成惡疾貧病,大凶. This is not a suitable day to get married or begin construction works. One should also guard against being attacked by a tiger or venomous tiger. This is an extremely inauspicious day, when Winged Horse kicks. The risk of being plagued by an illness is very high on this day.

乙 *Yi* 丑 *Chou* Wood Ox	丁 *Ding* 丑 *Chou* Fire Ox	己 *Ji* 丑 *Chou* Earth Ox	辛 *Xin* 丑 *Chou* Metal Ox	癸 *Gui* 丑 *Chou* Water Ox
▲	▲	▲	▲	▲

★ Excellent   ✓ Auspicious   ● Fair   ▲ Inauspicious   ✗ Dire

Second Month 二月

March 6th – April 4th

Rabbit 卯 (Mao) Month

March 6th – April 4th
Rabbit 卯 (Mao) Month

月德甲、月恩丁，母倉亥子，天德合己。

During the Rabbit 卯 (Mao) Month, the auspicious Monthly Virtue 月德 Star presides over Jia 甲 Days, the Monthly Benevolence 月恩 Star is present on Ding 丁 Days, while the Motherly Storage 母倉 Star accompanies Pig 亥 (Hai) and Rat 子 (Zi) Days. In addition, the positive energies of the Heavenly Virtue 天德 Star support Wu 己 Days.

驚蟄：春分前一日爲四離。

The 'Awakening of Worms' 驚蟄 (Jing Zhi)

The 'Awakening of Worms' is the term used to identify the day before the Spring Equinox 春分 sets in. One day before the Spring Equinox also known as the Four Separating 四離 Day.

春分：驚蟄後，三煞在西，申、酉、戌方，忌修造、動土。

The 'Spring Equinox' 春分 (Chun Fen)

After the advent of Jing Zhi 驚蟄, the Three Killings (San Sha) Affliction is found in the West; namely the Southwest 3 申 (Shen – SW3), West 2 酉 (You – W2) and Northwest 1 戌 (Xu –NW1) sectors. It would therefore be advisable to avoid commencing any construction work, or physically digging the ground of these particular sectors.

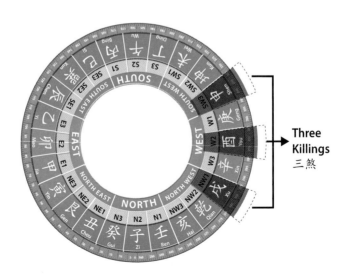

Three Killings 三煞

董公擇日要覽

十二值神 12 Day Officers	十二地支 Animal Sign of the Day	董公擇日解說 Dong Gong Description
 建 *Jian* **Establish**	 **卯** *Mao* **Rabbit** Yin Wood 	不宜用事,犯之損家長,及少房子孫,遭瘟疫,貧苦、哭泣重重。三、五年或遲至九年,橫訟敗亡。二月建卯日,爲天地轉煞之日也。 This day is unsuitable for activities of any sort, for if violated, its harmful energies will wreck havoc on your loved ones at home – both young and old. They will be particularly susceptible to poor health and financial losses, with many other unfortunate events following suit. Worse still, the malevolent effects can last to a minimum of 3 years and a maximum of 9 years; with the possibility of even fatal accidents threatening domestic happiness. The Establish 建 (Jian) Day of the 2nd Month is an especially inauspicious day; also known as the `Heaven & Earth Rotating' Sha (Killing) 天地轉煞 (Killing).

卯
Rabbit

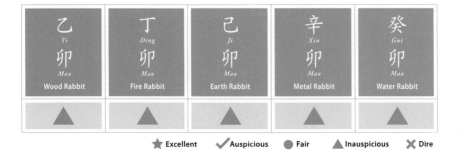

乙 *Yi* 卯 *Mao* Wood Rabbit	丁 *Ding* 卯 *Mao* Fire Rabbit	己 *Ji* 卯 *Mao* Earth Rabbit	辛 *Xin* 卯 *Mao* Metal Rabbit	癸 *Gui* 卯 *Mao* Water Rabbit
▲	▲	▲	▲	▲

★ Excellent   ✓ Auspicious   ● Fair   ▲ Inauspicious   ✗ Dire

董公擇日要覽

Dragon

十二值神 12 Day Officers	十二地支 Animal Sign of the Day	董公擇日解説 Dong Gong Description
除 *Chu* **Remove**	辰 *Chen* Dragon Yang Earth	不利移居、入宅、婚姻、開張、一切營爲等事。犯之六十日至一百二十日内主招官司,損財敗田蠶,失產業。甲辰戊辰殺集中當更凶。主三年内亡宅長、舊物作怪、火盜侵欺。 Avoid moving house (or moving into a new residence), tying the marital knot or launching a new commercial venture on this day. Violating this rule will result in lawsuits arising, as well as leakage of wealth and other material assets (including property) within a timeframe of 60 to 120 days. Avoid the Jia Chen甲辰 and Wu Chen 戊辰 days in particular, as their effects are the worst. After all, you certainly do not wish to see a death of a beloved elderly member in your household, or a fire or armed robbery threatening the tranquility of your loved ones.

甲 *Jia* 辰 *Chen* Wood Dragon	丙 *Bing* 辰 *Chen* Fire Dragon	戊 *Wu* 辰 *Chen* Earth Dragon	庚 *Geng* 辰 *Chen* Metal Dragon	壬 *Ren* 辰 *Chen* Water Dragon
✖	▲	✖	▲	▲

★ Excellent ✔ Auspicious ● Fair ▲ Inauspicious ✖ Dire

十二值神 12 Day Officers	十二地支 Animal Sign of the Day	董公擇日解說 Dong Gong Description
滿 *Man* **Full**	巳 *Si* Snake Yin Fire	天空、往亡日，不宜動土。如修造，百事俱吉，若在乾巽二宮起造皆吉，出行、開張、婚姻、入宅，內有黃羅、紫檀、田塘、庫貯，星蓋照，主年內家生貴子，田蠶興旺，永代吉昌。 This is a Sky Emptiness 天空 and therefore, Void Day. It is unsuitable to be used for groundbreaking ceremonies, although simple renovation works or adjustments will bear auspicious results. Similarly, any endeavors undertaken on the Qian 乾 and Xun 巽 palaces will yield positive outcomes. Certainly, by all means, go ahead and travel, launch a business, get married or move into your new residence, as these activities will enjoy the positive energies of the Yellow Spiral 黃羅, Purple Sandalwood 紫檀, Field 田塘 and Wealth Storage 庫貯 Stars. In addition, couples that are trying to conceive will find the ladies producing noble offspring within a year, and there will also be an increment in material assets such as property.

巳
Snake

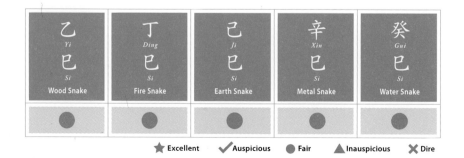

乙 *Yi* 巳 *Si* Wood Snake	丁 *Ding* 巳 *Si* Fire Snake	己 *Ji* 巳 *Si* Earth Snake	辛 *Xin* 巳 *Si* Metal Snake	癸 *Gui* 巳 *Si* Water Snake
●	●	●	●	●

★ Excellent ✔ Auspicious ● Fair ▲ Inauspicious ✘ Dire

Horse

十二值神 12 Day Officers	十二地支 Animal Sign of the Day	董公擇日解説 Dong Gong Description
平 *Ping* **Balance**	午 *Wu* Horse Yang Fire 	只宜作生基、如婚姻、修造。用之六十日、一百二十日內招官司、損人口,三、六、九年冷退。生基即壽木及生基也。 Such a date is only suitable to be applied to Yang Tombs 生基. It is unsuitable for marriages or renovation works. Activating the energies of this day will only result in lawsuits and legal entanglements arising within 60 to 120 days. More tragically, there might also be a decrease amongst your family members within the space of 3 to 6 years.

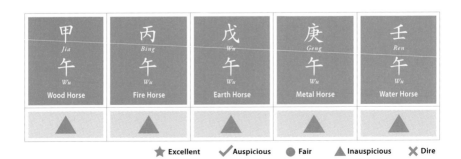

甲 *Jia* 午 *Wu* Wood Horse	丙 *Bing* 午 *Wu* Fire Horse	戊 *Wu* 午 *Wu* Earth Horse	庚 *Geng* 午 *Wu* Metal Horse	壬 *Ren* 午 *Wu* Water Horse
▲	▲	▲	▲	▲

★ Excellent ✓ Auspicious ● Fair ▲ Inauspicious ✕ Dire

十二值神 12 Day Officers	十二地支 Animal Sign of the Day	董公擇日解説 Dong Gong Description
定 *Ding* **Stable**	未 *Wei* **Goat** Yin Earth 	不利婚姻、起造,是陰宮主事,不宜向家内動作,一切屋外修爲不防。乙未乃白虎入中宮,更凶,犯之損人口。是月惟癸未一日乃水入秦州,因癸水當長生,相旺之際,内有黃羅、紫檀、天皇、地皇星蓋照,利人眷、添子孫、進田地、大吉。餘未日俱不利。 Marriages, construction works or internal renovations should be avoided at all costs, when it comes to using this day. You may, however, engage in external renovations to your property. This date is also not suitable to undertake any significant private domestic affairs. Of all the inauspicious days, the Yi Wei 乙未 Day is the most detrimental, as it harbors the ominous White Tiger Star. The wellbeing of a property occupants will be adversely affected if this particular day is violated. However, the Gui Wei Day is actually an auspicious day as it enjoys the protection of the Yellow Spiral 黃羅、Purple sandalwood 紫檀、Heavenly Emperor 天皇 and Earthly Emperor 地皇 stars. Put simply, such a day augurs well for the residents of a household, descendent luck as well as asset and property gains. Do note however that the other Wei 未 (Goat) days are not auspicious.

Goat

乙 *Yi* 未 *Wei* Wood Goat	丁 *Ding* 未 *Wei* Fire Goat	己 *Ji* 未 *Wei* Earth Goat	辛 *Xin* 未 *Wei* Metal Goat	癸 *Gui* 未 *Wei* Water Goat
✖	▲	▲	▲	✔

★ Excellent　✔ Auspicious　● Fair　▲ Inauspicious　✖ Dire

董公擇日要覽

Monkey

十二值神 12 Day Officers	十二地支 Animal Sign of the Day	董公擇日解説 Dong Gong Description
執 *Zhi* **Initiate**	申 *Shen* Monkey Yang Metal 	有天、月二德,宜修造、動土、埋葬、婚姻、開張、入宅、出行等事。並有黃羅、紫檀、金銀庫樓、寶藏星蓋照,三、六、九年內大旺,添人口、生貴子、置田產,大吉。庚申日乃春正四廢,百事皆忌。 The Heavenly 天德 and Monthly Virtue 月德 Stars guard over this day, therefore making it a positive one to commence renovation or groundbreaking works, undertake burials, get married, launch a new business, move into a new residence or even travel. The auspicious bevy of stars governing this day include the Yellow Spiral 黃羅, Purple Sandalwood 紫檀, Gold & Silver Storage 金銀庫樓 and Precious Treasure 寶藏 stars, which bring about fantastic prosperity, an increase in the population, the birth of a noble child and tremendous material gains. In short, the recipient will enjoy affluence (in whatever perceived form) within 3, 6 or 9 years. However, the Geng Shen 庚申 Day is not a useable one since it is a Four Direct Day 正四廢.

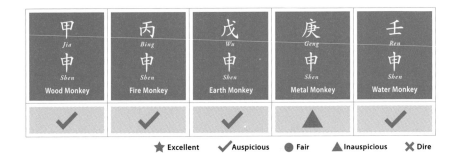

甲 *Jia* 申 *Shen* **Wood Monkey**	丙 *Bing* 申 *Shen* **Fire Monkey**	戊 *Wu* 申 *Shen* **Earth Monkey**	庚 *Geng* 申 *Shen* **Metal Monkey**	壬 *Ren* 申 *Shen* **Water Monkey**
✔	✔	✔	▲	✔

★ Excellent ✔ Auspicious ● Fair ▲ Inauspicious ✘ Dire

董公擇日要覽

十二值神 12 Day Officers	十二地支 Animal Sign of the Day	董公擇日解説 Dong Gong Description
破 *Po* **Destruction**	酉 *You* Rooster Yin Metal 	小紅砂、天賊星臨，不利婚姻、修造等事,犯之六十日、一百二十日內招官司、口舌、陰人劫、耗小口、疾病。辛酉正四廢,更凶,此日乃月破大凶之日。 The inauspicious Lesser Red Embrace 小紅砂 and Heavenly Thief Stars 天賊 are present on this day, rendering it unsuitable to tie the knot or renovate the house. Do not violate the harmful energies of these stars, as they are the harbingers of legal entanglements, disputes, robberies, people falling ill, children being endangered or even evil spirits and phantoms. In particular, look out for the Xin You 辛酉 Day, which is one of the Four Direct Days at its worst.

酉
Rooster

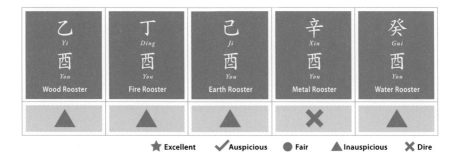

乙 *Yi* 酉 *You* Wood Rooster	丁 *Ding* 酉 *You* Fire Rooster	己 *Ji* 酉 *You* Earth Rooster	辛 *Xin* 酉 *You* Metal Rooster	癸 *Gui* 酉 *You* Water Rooster
▲	▲	▲	✖	▲

★ Excellent ✔ Auspicious ● Fair ▲ Inauspicious ✖ Dire

十二值神 12 Day Officers	十二地支 Animal Sign of the Day	董公擇日解説 Dong Gong Description
危 *Wei* **Danger**	戌 *Xu* Dog Yang Earth 	宜合板作生基。如修造、會親、婚姻，不利長房，先退田地、火盜侵欺。又云丙戌、壬戌，煞入中宮，更凶。 By all means, go ahead and make a Yang Tomb 生基 on this day. Refrain from renovating your property, proposing marriage or tying the knot on this day, though. If you happen to inadvertently activate its negative energies and also happen to be the 'eldest' in seniority of any kind within a household, be warned that a fire risk threatens your property. The worst days are the Bing Xu 丙戌 and Ren Xu 壬戌.

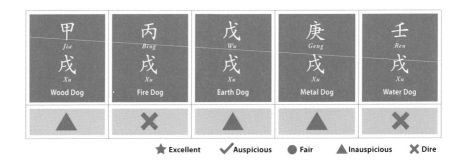

甲 *Jia* 戌 *Xu* Wood Dog	丙 *Bing* 戌 *Xu* Fire Dog	戊 *Wu* 戌 *Xu* Earth Dog	庚 *Geng* 戌 *Xu* Metal Dog	壬 *Ren* 戌 *Xu* Water Dog
▲	✖	▲	▲	✖

★ Excellent　✔ Auspicious　● Fair　▲ Inauspicious　✖ Dire

董公擇日要覽

亥
Pig

十二值神 12 Day Officers	十二地支 Animal Sign of the Day	董公擇日解説 Dong Gong Description
成 *Cheng* **Success**	亥 *Hai* **Pig** **Yin Water** 	天喜,有天皇、地皇、黃羅、紫檀、玉堂、聚寶星蓋照,宜婚姻、開張、入宅、出行、起造、安葬、定拴架,六十日、一百二十日内進財、貴人接引、謀事大吉。是月之辛亥、癸亥上吉。 The Sky Happiness 天喜, Heavenly Emperor 天皇, Earthly Emperor 地皇, Yellow Spiral 黃羅, Purple Sandlewood 紫檀, Jade Hall 玉堂 and 聚寶 Precious Convergence stars rule over this day, and their combined positive energies augur well for any endeavor. Hence, such days are good for marriages, launching a new business, moving house, travel, building a new residence and even burial services. With plenty of hard work, recipients will reap substantial returns-on-investment within 60 to 120 days, as well as assistance in times of need from noble people. Furthermore, nothing will remain bad or undesirable for a long time. Make the most of the Xin Hai 辛亥 and Gui Hai 癸亥 Days, as they are the best ones to have.

乙 *Yi* 亥 *Hai* Wood Pig	丁 *Ding* 亥 *Hai* Fire Pig	己 *Ji* 亥 *Hai* Earth Pig	辛 *Xin* 亥 *Hai* Metal Pig	癸 *Gui* 亥 *Hai* Water Pig
✔	✔	✔	★	★

★ Excellent ✔ Auspicious ● Fair ▲ Inauspicious ✖ Dire

董公擇日要覽

Rat

十二值神 12 Day Officers	十二地支 Animal Sign of the Day	董公擇日解説 Dong Gong Description
收 *Shou* **Receive**	子 *Zi* Rat Yang Water	忌婚姻、起造、入宅、開張，犯之三年內必 退財、無進益，主是非、官訟、產業虛耗。 Do not get married, commence construction on a development, move into a new house or start a business on this day. Violating its harmful energies will only result in your wealth deteriorating and your loved ones pursuits proving to be futile over the next 3 years. Worse still, you will tend to attract gossip and legal problems as well as lose your material assets (such as properties) wherever you go and whatever you do.

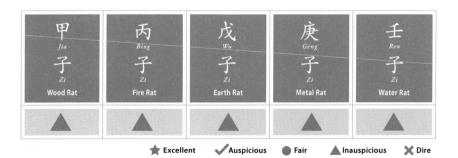

十二值神 12 Day Officers	十二地支 Animal Sign of the Day	董公擇日解説 Dong Gong Description
開 *Kai* Open	丑 *Chou* Ox Yin Earth 	不利造作、裝修、婚姻、會親，犯之主田蠶不收、室有產厄、湯火之災。丁丑、癸丑，煞入中宮更凶，主官非、損人口、小人侵害。 A most unsuitable day for renovation or construction works, marriages or even meeting your future in-laws, as well as relatives. In addition, you also risk losing your house, investments, loved ones, wealth or even literally suffer fire-caused burns. Pay particular attention to the Ding Chou 丁丑 and Gui Chou 癸丑 days, as they herald the entry of negative stars into the Central Palace and hence Qi at its worst. In real-life situations, these pertain to lawsuits, physical injuries to residents and the interference of malicious, petty-minded people.

丑
Ox

乙 *Yi* 丑 *Chou* Wood Ox	丁 *Ding* 丑 *Chou* Fire Ox	己 *Ji* 丑 *Chou* Earth Ox	辛 *Xin* 丑 *Chou* Metal Ox	癸 *Gui* 丑 *Chou* Water Ox
▲	✕	▲	▲	✕

★ Excellent ✓ Auspicious ● Fair ▲ Inauspicious ✕ Dire

Tiger

十二值神 12 Day Officers	十二地支 Animal Sign of the Day	董公擇日解説 Dong Gong Description
閉 *Bi* **Close**	寅 *Yin* **Tiger** **Yang Wood** 	黃砂,活曜星臨。宜合板、作生基。但不利修造、動土、婚姻、入宅、開張等事。是日乃五行無氣,平常之用則可,雖無大害,不用爲妙。 With the presence of the Yellow Embrace 黃砂 Star, this is a suitable day for preparing a Yang Tomb. It is however unsuitable for to carry out renovation or groundbreaking work, tie the matrimonial knot, enter a new house or launch a business. As this day does not have any Qi present within the Five Elements, use it for only unimportant events, and you will find any potential negative effects reduced to a minimum. In plain terms, this is neither a harmful nor beneficial day.

甲 *Jia* 寅 *Yin* **Wood Tiger**	丙 *Bing* 寅 *Yin* **Fire Tiger**	戊 *Wu* 寅 *Yin* **Earth Tiger**	庚 *Geng* 寅 *Yin* **Metal Tiger**	壬 *Ren* 寅 *Yin* **Water Tiger**
▲	▲	▲	▲	▲

★ Excellent   ✔ Auspicious   ● Fair   ▲ Inauspicious   ✖ Dire

Third Month 三月

April 5th – May 5th

Dragon 辰 (Chen) Month

April 5th – May 5th
Dragon 辰 (Chen) Month

月德壬、月恩庚，母倉亥子，天德合丁。

For the Dragon 辰 (Chen) Month, the positive Monthly Virtue 月德 Star is present on Ren 壬 Days, the Monthly Benevolence 月恩 Star presides over Geng 庚 Days, while the Motherly Storage 母倉 Star accompanies Pig 亥 (Hai) and Rat 子 (Zi) Days. In addition, the Qi of the Heavenly Virtue 天德 Star enhances and supports Ding 丁 Days.

清明：清明後，三煞在南。

'Clear & Bright' 清明 (Qing Ming)

After Qing Ming, the Three Killings (San Sha) is in the South.

穀雨：巳、午、未方忌修造、動土。

'Grain Rain' 穀雨 (Gu Yu)

At the advent of 'Grain Rain', refrain from undertaking any construction, renovation or groundbreaking works in the Southeast 3 巳 (Si – SE3), South 2 午 (Wu – S2) and Southwest 1 未 (Wei –SW1) sectors.

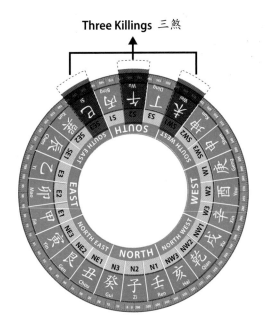

Three Killings 三煞

董公擇日要覽

十二值神 12 Day Officers	十二地支 Animal Sign of the Day	董公擇日解説 Dong Gong Description
建 *Jian* **Establish**	辰 *Chen* **Dragon** **Yang Earth** 	有地網、勾絞,不利修造、安葬、婚姻、開張等事犯之主湯火驚傷,縱生男生女皆醜拙,惡陋無益。甲辰、戊辰,煞入中宮,更凶,主三年內家破人亡。 The negative Earth Net 地網 and Grappling Hook 勾絞 Stars lord over the day – making it unsuitable for renovation, a marriage, burial or even launching a business. Once violated, these Stars spell disaster in the form of fire hazards, strained relationships and plain bad fortune. Avoid the particularly inauspicious Jia Chen 甲辰 and Wu Chen 戊辰 days, lest they cause domestic discord or a death in the family within 3 years.

辰
Dragon

甲 *Jia* 辰 *Chen* **Wood Dragon** ✖	丙 *Bing* 辰 *Chen* **Fire Dragon** ▲	戊 *Wu* 辰 *Chen* **Earth Dragon** ✖	庚 *Geng* 辰 *Chen* **Metal Dragon** ▲	壬 *Ren* 辰 *Chen* **Water Dragon** ▲

★ Excellent　✔ Auspicious　● Fair　▲ Inauspicious　✖ Dire

十二值神 12 Day Officers	十二地支 Animal Sign of the Day	董公擇日解説 Dong Gong Description
除 *Chu* **Remove**	巳 *Si* Snake Yin Fire	丁巳宜修造、入宅、移居、動土、作用、婚姻等事,大吉。己巳造作、入宅等事亦吉,如埋葬、犯重喪不利用。乙巳有十惡凶。辛巳雖有火星,卻有猖鬼、敗亡,又是十惡伐日不宜用。癸巳天上空亡,又犯土鬼,亦不宜用。此皆必應之事也。 Use the Ding Si 丁巳 Day for renovation, moving house, groundbreaking ceremonies, marriages or other important events. The Ji Si 己巳 Day is particularly good to move into a new residence, but unsuitable for burials or groundbreaking ceremonies. The Yi Si 乙巳 Day contains the Ten Ferocious 十惡 Stars and is therefore unusable for any sort of activity. Be particularly mindful of the Xin Si 辛巳 Day, which contains the Fire Star 火星, Mad Ghost 猖鬼, Void Loss 敗亡 and also the Ten Ferocious Stars. They are especially inauspicious stars, and any day that heralds their presence should not be used. The Gui Si 癸巳 Day also harbors negative stars such as the Heavenly Void 天上空亡 and Earth Ghost 土鬼 and should therefore not be utilized for any purpose whatsoever.

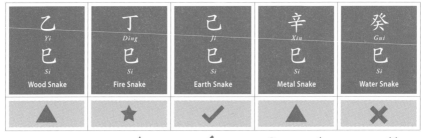

乙 *Yi* 巳 *Si* Wood Snake	丁 *Ding* 巳 *Si* Fire Snake	己 *Ji* 巳 *Si* Earth Snake	辛 *Xin* 巳 *Si* Metal Snake	癸 *Gui* 巳 *Si* Water Snake
▲	★	✔	▲	✖

★ Excellent   ✔ Auspicious   ● Fair   ▲ Inauspicious   ✖ Dire

十二值神 12 Day Officers	十二地支 Animal Sign of the Day	董公擇日解説 Dong Gong Description
滿 *Man* **Full**	午 *Wu* Horse Yang Fire 	天富,甲午有土鬼。丙午平常,不能見吉。戊午有猖鬼、敗亡,並犯重喪,即安葬亦屬不宜。庚午十惡日,不可用。壬午天、月二德,用之次吉。 The Heavenly Fortune 天富 Star is present but since it coincides with a Jia Wu 甲午 Day, the negative Earth Ghost 土鬼 Star is present as well. Luck on a Bing Wu 丙午 Day is average, as it is not supported by any auspicious stars. Its Wu Wu 戊午 counterpart is ruled by the inauspicious Mad Ghost 猖鬼 and Void Loss 敗亡 Stars – both premonitions of death within the family and also unsuitable for burial days. Similarly, a Geng Wu 庚午 Day is considered one of the Ten Ferocious Days 十惡日, thereby making it unusable. Only the Ren Wu 壬午 Day enjoys the positive energies of the Heaven & Monthly Virtue Stars 天月二德, which make it an auspicious day.

Horse

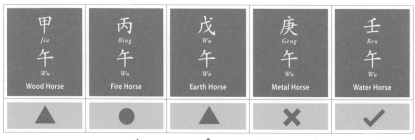

甲 *Jia* 午 *Wu* Wood Horse	丙 *Bing* 午 *Wu* Fire Horse	戊 *Wu* 午 *Wu* Earth Horse	庚 *Geng* 午 *Wu* Metal Horse	壬 *Ren* 午 *Wu* Water Horse
▲	●	▲	✖	✔

★ Excellent　✔ Auspicious　● Fair　▲ Inauspicious　✖ Dire

Third Month 三月

董公擇日要覽

Goat

十二值神 12 Day Officers	十二地支 Animal Sign of the Day	董公擇日解説 Dong Gong Description
平 *Ping* **Balance**	 *Wei* **Goat** **Yin Earth** 	與正五月相似,不宜用事,即小小營爲亦不利。若乙未更加凶險,蓋數值天。犯凶絞朱雀也。 This day is unsuitable for all major or important activities. The Yi Wei 乙未 Day is the worst of all such days, since it is accompanied by negative stars.

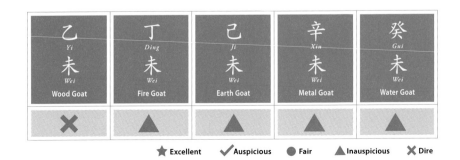

★ Excellent ✓ Auspicious ● Fair ▲ Inauspicious ✗ Dire

十二值神 12 Day Officers	十二地支 Animal Sign of the Day	董公擇日解説 Dong Gong Description
定 *Ding* **Stable**	申 *Shen* Monkey Yang Metal	甲申、丙申,宜斬草、破土、定磉、拴架、安葬,大吉。二、三年内益子孫、進財祿。壬申有天、月二德,黃羅、紫檀、天皇、地皇、金銀庫樓星蓋照,是日十全大吉大利。戊申天罡、空亡、猖鬼、敗亡,凶。庚申正四廢,亦凶,申日又屬往亡日,出行、出軍、赴任不宜取此也。 The Jia Shen 甲申 and Bing Shen 丙申 Days are particularly suitable for gardening, construction (piling), groundbreaking or burial activities. In fact, the positive effects from undertaking such activities on these days will be seen in 2 to 3 years' time, where either your offspring will benefit or your personal wealth will increase. A Ren Shen 壬申 Day that is already blessed with the Heaven and Monthly Virtue Stars - coupled with the auspicious Yellow Spiral 黃羅, Purple Sandalwood 紫檀, Heavenly Emperor 天皇, Earthly Emperor 地皇 and Gold & Silver Storage 金銀庫樓 Stars - will see all endeavors producing highly positive outcomes! However, a Wu Shen 戊申 Day harbors the inauspicious Sky Chief 天罡, Void & Emptiness 空亡, Mad Ghost 猖鬼 and Void Loss 敗亡 Stars and should not be used for any sort of activity. The same principle applies to a Geng Shen 庚申 Day, which is one of the Four Direct Days 正四廢. Such a day is generally unsuitable for traveling, dispatching troops or assuming official duties.

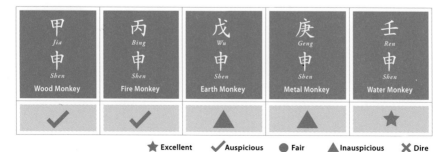

甲 *Jia* 申 *Shen* Wood Monkey	丙 *Bing* 申 *Shen* Fire Monkey	戊 *Wu* 申 *Shen* Earth Monkey	庚 *Geng* 申 *Shen* Metal Monkey	壬 *Ren* 申 *Shen* Water Monkey
✔	✔	▲	▲	★

★ Excellent   ✔ Auspicious   ● Fair   ▲ Inauspicious   ✗ Dire

董公擇日要覽

Rooster

十二值神 12 Day Officers	十二地支 Animal Sign of the Day	董公擇日解説 Dong Gong Description
執 *Zhi* **Initiate**	酉 *You* **Rooster** Yin Metal 	乙酉宜修造、入宅、婚姻、開張、出行等事。癸酉安葬大吉,丁酉安葬次吉。己酉有九土鬼,辛酉正四廢不宜用。 A Yi You 乙酉 Day is recommended to commence renovation works, enter a new house, get married, start a business or travel. Similarly, a Gui You 癸酉 Day is highly befitting for a burial service. If the burial cannot be done on a Gui You Day, then select a Ding You丁酉 Day, which is the next-best option in the list of good burial days. Do note, however, that a Ji You 己酉 Day harbors the Nine Earth Ghost 九土鬼 Star while the Xin You 辛酉 Day is considered a Four Direct Day 正四廢 and therefore unusable.

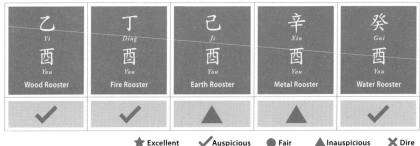

乙 *Yi* 酉 *You* Wood Rooster	丁 *Ding* 酉 *You* Fire Rooster	己 *Ji* 酉 *You* Earth Rooster	辛 *Xin* 酉 *You* Metal Rooster	癸 *Gui* 酉 *You* Water Rooster
✔	✔	▲	▲	✔

★ Excellent　✔ Auspicious　● Fair　▲ Inauspicious　✖ Dire

董公擇日要覽

戌
Dog

十二值神 12 Day Officers	十二地支 Animal Sign of the Day	董公擇日解説 Dong Gong Description
破 *Po* **Destruction**	戌 *Xu* **Dog** **Yang Earth**	值月建沖破,諸事不宜。丙戌、壬戌,煞入中宮,更凶。 This day clashes with the Month Branch. As such, avoid undertaking any important activities on such a day, especially Bing Xu 丙戌 and Ren Xu 壬戌 Days; which are the worst of such days.

甲 *Jia* 戌 *Xu* Wood Dog	丙 *Bing* 戌 *Xu* Fire Dog	戊 *Wu* 戌 *Xu* Earth Dog	庚 *Geng* 戌 *Xu* Metal Dog	壬 *Ren* 戌 *Xu* Water Dog
▲	✖	▲	▲	✖

★ Excellent　✔ Auspicious　● Fair　▲ Inauspicious　✖ Dire

董公擇日要覽

亥
Pig

十二值神 12 Day Officers	十二地支 Animal Sign of the Day	董公擇日解説 Dong Gong Description
危 *Wei* **Danger**	亥 *Hai* Pig Yin Water	天成，有凶暴。己亥，火星有文昌星蓋照，上學大吉，餘事次吉；乙亥用之亦次吉。辛亥婦人之金，陰府決遣之期，陰氣全盛，非陽間所宜。丁亥又值黑煞，癸亥六甲窮日，五行無氣，主絕人，又受死事，不可用。 The Heavenly Success 天成 and Violent Danger 凶暴 Stars govern this day, simultaneously. In addition, a Ji Hai 己亥 Day is influenced by both the auspicious Fire Star 火星 and Literary Arts 文昌 Stars. Accordingly, such circumstances make this Ji Hai Day a good day to start a pupil s studies at a new school. Other endeavors will also reap positive rewards. If it is not possible to begin such an endeavor on a Ji Hai 己亥 Day, then select the next best choice a Yi Hai 乙亥 Day. Do note, however, that the Qi of a Xin Hai 辛亥 Day is overly Yin in nature. Likewise, a Ding Hai 丁亥 Day contains the ominous Black Sha 黑煞 while a Gui Hai 癸亥 Day is a Six Jia Weakness Day 六甲窮日. Accordingly, the Qi of the Elements present during these days are weak and insufficient. Worse still, such Qi denote death and failing health. Avoid using these days at all costs.

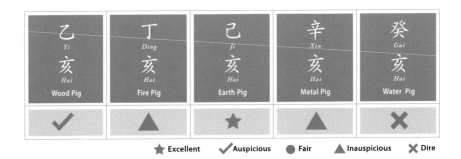

乙 *Yi* 亥 *Hai* Wood Pig	丁 *Ding* 亥 *Hai* Fire Pig	己 *Ji* 亥 *Hai* Earth Pig	辛 *Xin* 亥 *Hai* Metal Pig	癸 *Gui* 亥 *Hai* Water Pig
✔	▲	★	▲	✖

★ Excellent　✔ Auspicious　● Fair　▲ Inauspicious　✖ Dire

董公擇日要覽

Rat

十二值神 12 Day Officers	十二地支 Animal Sign of the Day	董公擇日解說 Dong Gong Description
成 *Cheng* **Success**	子 *Zi* Rat Yang Water 	黃砂,天喜,壬子雖有天、月二德,乃一白主事,木打寶瓶,終是北方沐浴之地,五行無氣,福力減淺,但小小營爲則可。若開張、出行、入宅、修理及婚姻等項,用之就見凶敗、禍害、災傷,是日謂之瓦解冰消。 The Yellow Embrace 黃砂 and Sky Happiness 天喜 stars preside over this day. But before celebrating, you might want to know that the Ren Zi 壬子 Day has the Northern Mu Yu Bath location – where Elemental Qi is very weak and prosperous Qi minimal – alongside the Heavenly 天德 and Monthly Virtue月德 Noble Stars! This is by no means anything ominous or inauspicious; it merely means that the Ren Zi Day can still be used for activities of less importance. Just don't use this day for significant activities, due to its inadequate Qi. If you choose to ignore this advice, then be prepared for water-related hazards threatening your family. Likewise, embarking on major events such as the launching of a new business, travel, moving into a new house and getting married will result in the day (and possibly, the event) ending on a very sour note!

甲子 *Jia* *Zi* Wood Rat ✔ | 丙子 *Bing* *Zi* Fire Rat ✔ | 戊子 *Wu* *Zi* Earth Rat ✔ | 庚子 *Geng* *Zi* Metal Rat ✔ | 壬子 *Ren* *Zi* Water Rat ●

★ Excellent ✔ Auspicious ● Fair ▲ Inauspicious ✗ Dire

Ox

十二值神 12 Day Officers	十二地支 Animal Sign of the Day	董公擇日解説 Dong Gong Description
收 *Shou* **Receive**	丑 *Chou* Ox Yin Earth	小紅砂、天賊，丁丑、癸丑，煞入中宮，不利修造、婚姻、入宅等事，犯之主退財、疾病、爭訟、是非，凶。餘丑亦不吉，防小人刑害。 The Lesser Red Embrace 小紅砂 and Heavenly Thief 天賊 stars going this day. Avoid Ding Chou 丁丑 and Gui Chou 癸丑 Days when it comes to renovation, tying the knot or entering a house for the first time. Breaking this rule will lead to a loss in wealth, ailments and legal entanglements. The other Chou 丑 (Ox) days are not that inauspicious, but they are still powerful enough to attract malicious, petty-minded people.

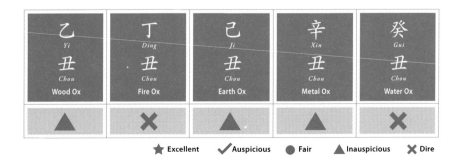

乙 *Yi* 丑 *Chou* Wood Ox	丁 *Ding* 丑 *Chou* Fire Ox	己 *Ji* 丑 *Chou* Earth Ox	辛 *Xin* 丑 *Chou* Metal Ox	癸 *Gui* 丑 *Chou* Water Ox
▲	✖	▲	▲	✖

★ Excellent   ✔ Auspicious   ● Fair   ▲ Inauspicious   ✖ Dire

董公擇日要覽

Tiger

十二值神 12 Day Officers	十二地支 Animal Sign of the Day	董公擇日解説 Dong Gong Description
開 *Kai* **Open**	寅 *Yin* **Tiger** **Yang Wood** 	天賊。戊寅，天赦用之吉。壬寅有天、月二德，只宜埋葬，及合板作生基，用之益子孫、進田地、生貴子、陞官職，上吉。其餘寅日次吉，但有六不成六不合之疑，用之終屬不利，宜慎之。 Heavenly Thief 天賊 star present. The Wu Yin 戊寅 Star is an auspicious one, containing the Heavenly Pardon 天赦 star, and can therefore be used for significant events and activities. Similarly, a Ren Yin 壬寅 Day contains the Heavenly and Monthly Virtue 天月二德 stars is a good one, which promises material and property gains, the birth of a noble son and even a promotion. However, the other Tiger 寅 (Yin) days do not share the same potential as the Ren Yin 壬寅 Day.

甲 *Jia* 寅 *Yin* **Wood Tiger**	丙 *Bing* 寅 *Yin* **Fire Tiger**	戊 *Wu* 寅 *Yin* **Earth Tiger**	庚 *Geng* 寅 *Yin* **Metal Tiger**	壬 *Ren* 寅 *Yin* **Water Tiger**
●	●	★	●	★

★ Excellent   ✓ Auspicious   ● Fair   ▲ Inauspicious   ✗ Dire

董公擇日要覽

Rabbit

十二值神 12 Day Officers	十二地支 Animal Sign of the Day	董公擇日解說 Dong Gong Description
閉 *Bi* Close	卯 *Mao* Rabbit Yin Wood 	不宜造作、婚姻、埋墓、入宅等事。犯之損傷疾痛今退凶。百事不宜。不宜造作、婚姻、埋葬、入宅等事,犯之損傷、疾痛、冷退,凶,百事不宜。 This day is unsuitable for renovations, marriages, burials or moving into a new residence. Violating this protocol will only result in family members and loved ones getting injured or falling ill.

乙 *Yi* 卯 *Mao* Wood Rabbit	丁 *Ding* 卯 *Mao* Fire Rabbit	己 *Ji* 卯 *Mao* Earth Rabbit	辛 *Xin* 卯 *Mao* Metal Rabbit	癸 *Gui* 卯 *Mao* Water Rabbit
▲	▲	▲	▲	▲

 ★ Excellent ✓ Auspicious ● Fair ▲ Inauspicious ✗ Dire

Fourth Month 四月

May 6th – June 5th

Snake 巳 (Si) Month

May 6th – June 5th
Snake 巳 (Si) Month

月德庚、月恩巳，天德合丙。

During the Snake 巳 (Si) Month, Geng 庚 Days are accompanied by the Monthly Virtue 月德 Star, and Snake 巳 (Si) Days are accompanied by the Monthly Benevolence 月恩 Star. Similarly, the positive energies of the Heavenly Virtue 天德 Star enhances Bing 丙 Days.

立夏：立夏前一日爲四絕。

The 'Coming of Summer' 立夏 (Li Xia)

One day before Li Xia is called the Four Extinction 四絕 Day (Si Jue).

小滿：立夏後，三煞在東，寅、卯、辰方忌修造、動土。

Small Sprout 小滿 (Xiao Man)

Upon the Coming (Commencement) of Summer, the Three Killings 三煞 (San Sha) Affliction will occupy the Northeast 3 寅 (Yin – NE3), East 2 卯 (Mao – E2) and Southeast 1 辰 (Chen – SE1) sectors of the home or workplace. As such, refrain from renovating or digging the ground in these sectors, to prevent unleashing the harmful energies of the Three Killings.

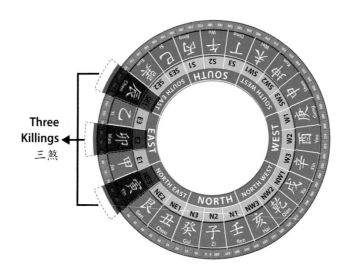

十二值神 12 Day Officers	十二地支 Animal Sign of the Day	董公擇日解說 Dong Gong Description
建 *Jian* **Establish**	巳 *Si* **Snake** Yin Fire	小紅砂日。不利出行、嫁娶、安葬、造作、入宅、開張等事,犯之主冷退、疾病、田蠶不收、客死不歸、財產破散,受死之日也。 This is known as a Lesser Red Embrace Star 小紅砂 Day. It is unsuitable for the purposes of travel, marriage, burial, commencing renovation, moving into new house or opening a business. Those who violate this rule will suffer from illness or a loss of their property assets. Their family members could also encounter fatal accidents overseas, or face bankruptcy.

董公擇日要覽

巳
Snake

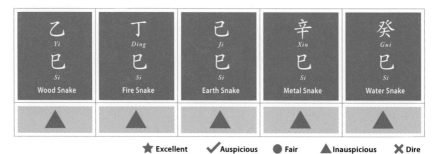

乙 *Yi* 巳 *Si* Wood Snake	丁 *Ding* 巳 *Si* Fire Snake	己 *Ji* 巳 *Si* Earth Snake	辛 *Xin* 巳 *Si* Metal Snake	癸 *Gui* 巳 *Si* Water Snake
▲	▲	▲	▲	▲

★ Excellent   ✓ Auspicious   ● Fair   ▲ Inauspicious   ✗ Dire

十二值神 12 Day Officers	十二地支 Animal Sign of the Day	董公擇日解説 Dong Gong Description

除

Chu
Remove

午

Wu

Horse
Yang Fire

黃砂。庚午月德,惟甲午、壬午,有黃羅、紫檀、天皇、地皇星蓋照,宜修造、婚姻、開張、出行、入宅等事。六十日、一百二十日內增田地、進人口、生貴子,大旺。丙午、戊午,天地轉煞,用之凶。

The Yellow Embrace 黃砂 Star governs this day. Consequently, a Geng Wu 庚午 Day is supported by the positive energies of the Monthly Virtue Star, while Jia Wu 甲午 and Ren Wu 壬午 Days are similarly enhanced by the positive energies of the auspicious Yellow Spiral 黃羅, Purple Sandalwood 紫檀, Heavenly Emperor 天皇 and Earthly Emperor 地皇 Stars; making these days suitable to undertake important activities or endeavors such as renovation and repairs, get married, open a business, travel, embark on a new academic pursuit and move into new house. Those who use these auspicious days for such activities will result in an increase in wealth and material assets (such as properties) within 60 to 120 days. They will also see their family growing bigger, with the birth of noble children. Will increase population in family, giving birth to noble child. However, Bing Wu 丙午 and Wu Wu 戊午 Days are accompanied by the negative Heaven and Earth Drilling Sha 天地轉煞 Star, which renders them unsuitable for activities or endeavors of any sort.

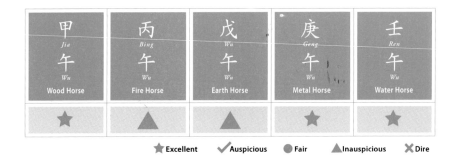

甲 *Jia* 午 *Wu* Wood Horse	丙 *Bing* 午 *Wu* Fire Horse	戊 *Wu* 午 *Wu* Earth Horse	庚 *Geng* 午 *Wu* Metal Horse	壬 *Ren* 午 *Wu* Water Horse
★	▲	▲	★	★

★ **Excellent** ✓ **Auspicious** ● **Fair** ▲ **Inauspicious** ✕ **Dire**

十二值神 12 Day Officers	十二地支 Animal Sign of the Day	董公擇日解説 Dong Gong Description
滿 *Man* **Full**	未 *Wei* Goat Yin Earth 	天富、天賊・辛未有天、月二德,己未有火星,均次吉,宜定碌、造架、埋葬,但婚姻、起造二事不載又修造,曆云是日白虎入中宮,用之非不利,須查是年月日,如有吉星與命宮相合方可。是月厭、天賊犯之,主凶、冷退。 The Sky Pledge 天當 and Sky Thief 天賊 Stars preside over this day, although the Xin Wei 辛未 Day is supported by the positive energies of the Heavenly 天德 and Monthly Virtue 月德 Stars. Its counterpart, the Ji Wei 己未 Day is accompanied by the presence of the Fire Star and is therefore considered to be secondarily auspicious. While this day may be used for fixing sculptural structures such as pedestal columns and frames, or for burial, it would be unsuitable to use it for marriage and the official commencement of construction works on a building. Do note as well that the other Wei 未 (Goat) Days are not auspicious, as the White Tiger 白虎 Star is present on these days.

Goat

乙 *Yi* 未 *Wei* Wood Goat	丁 *Ding* 未 *Wei* Fire Goat	己 *Ji* 未 *Wei* Earth Goat	辛 *Xin* 未 *Wei* Metal Goat	癸 *Gui* 未 *Wei* Water Goat
▲	▲	✔	✔	▲

★ Excellent ✔ Auspicious ● Fair ▲ Inauspicious ✘ Dire

Fourth Month 四月

十二值神 12 Day Officers	十二地支 Animal Sign of the Day	董公擇日解説 Dong Gong Description
平 *Ping* **Balance**	申 *Shen* Monkey Yang Metal 	朱雀、勾絞星臨,不利起造、出行、安葬、婚姻、入宅,主招官司、口舌、小口生災。甲申、庚申,煞入中宮,更凶,必主小人牽連、禍事、破財、生子醜怪、有水火災厄。 The Red Phoenix 朱雀 and Grappling Hook 勾絞 Stars govern this day, making it unsuitable for starting renovation works, travel, burial, marriage or moving into a new house. Ignoring this precautionary advice will only lead to legal entanglements, disputes and young children being harmed. In particular, the Jia Shen 甲申 and Geng Shen 庚申 Days are the worst of the lot, as they are the harbingers of malicious action by jealous or petty-minded people, accidents and mishaps, loss of wealth, giving birth to a abnormal or handicapped child or being threatened by fire or water hazards.

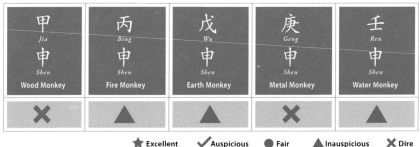

甲 *Jia* 申 *Shen* Wood Monkey	丙 *Bing* 申 *Shen* Fire Monkey	戊 *Wu* 申 *Shen* Earth Monkey	庚 *Geng* 申 *Shen* Metal Monkey	壬 *Ren* 申 *Shen* Water Monkey
✘	▲	▲	✘	▲

★ **Excellent**   ✔ **Auspicious**   ● **Fair**   ▲ **Inauspicious**   ✘ **Dire**

董公擇日要覽

十二值神 12 Day Officers	十二地支 Animal Sign of the Day	董公擇日解説 Dong Gong Description
定 *Ding* **Stable**	酉 *You* Rooster Yin Metal 	雖有九土鬼,不宜動土、安葬,若小小營爲在四月,酉爲次吉之日。如婚姻、入宅、修造,斷不可用,主凶。 The inauspicious Nine Earth Ghost 九土鬼 Star dominates this day, rendering it unsuitable for activities that involve groundbreaking or 'disturbing' the earth, such as burial. Minor activities or endeavors may however be undertaken, and will in fact reap correspondingly minor gains. This day should not be utilized for major, important activities such as marriage, moving into a new house or commencing renovation works.

酉
Rooster

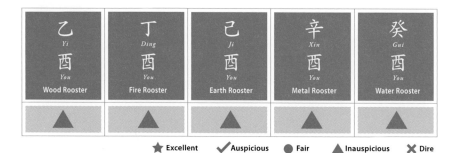

乙 *Yi* 酉 *You* Wood Rooster	丁 *Ding* 酉 *You* Fire Rooster	己 *Ji* 酉 *You* Earth Rooster	辛 *Xin* 酉 *You* Metal Rooster	癸 *Gui* 酉 *You* Water Rooster
▲	▲	▲	▲	▲

★ Excellent ✓ Auspicious ● Fair ▲ Inauspicious ✕ Dire

十二值神 12 Day Officers	十二地支 Animal Sign of the Day	董公擇日解説 Dong Gong Description
執 *Zhi* **Initiate**	 戌 *Xu* **Dog** **Yang Earth** 	有勾絞,丙戌、壬戌,煞入中宮,百事大凶。甲戌,小小營爲次吉。二十四向諸煞朝天,偷修則可,婚姻、安葬、入宅、開張,非所宜,用之主損宅長、傷手足、耗錢財,大凶。 This day is marked by the presence of the Grappling Hook 勾絞 Star. Hence, Sha Qi predominates over Bing Xu丙戌 and Ren Xu 壬戌 Days, in particular – making them unsuitable days to execute important matters on. A Jia Xu 甲戌 Day is more suitable for less important activities, although it must be noted that the other days are inauspicious as they harbor Sha Qi in all 24 Directions (Mountains). As such, significant endeavors or activities like the commencing of renovation and construction works, marriage, burial, moving into a new house, opening of a new business must be avoided at all costs. Violating this warning will only result in elderly family members being injured, the limbs of the protagonists being more prone to injury or wealth being lost. Be warned that these are greatly inauspicious days.

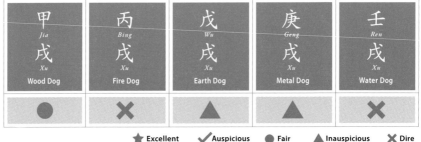

甲 *Jia* 戌 *Xu* Wood Dog	丙 *Bing* 戌 *Xu* Fire Dog	戊 *Wu* 戌 *Xu* Earth Dog	庚 *Geng* 戌 *Xu* Metal Dog	壬 *Ren* 戌 *Xu* Water Dog
●	✖	▲	▲	✖

 ★ Excellent   ✔ Auspicious   ● Fair ▲ Inauspicious   ✖ Dire

十二值神 12 Day Officers	十二地支 Animal Sign of the Day	董公擇日解説 Dong Gong Description
破 *Po* **Destruction**	亥 *Hai* **Pig** **Yin Water**	往亡,朱雀、勾絞,招官司、小人啾唧之災,主損錢財、染疾病。癸亥正四廢,更凶,是月亥日諸事忌之。 This is known as an Emptiness 往亡 Day, marked by the presence of the Red Phoenix 朱雀 and Grappling Hook 勾絞 Stars, which indicate the propensity to attract petty-minded people and legal problems. Such a combination also denotes loss of wealth and the threat of illnesses. The Gui Mao 癸亥 Day is the worst of such days, as it is also a Direct Abandonment Day 正四廢. Avoid undertaking any activities or endeavors of importance on this day.

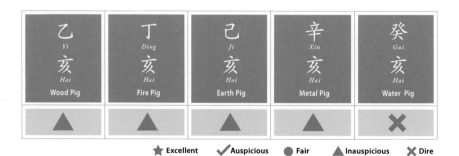

乙 *Yi* 亥 *Hai* Wood Pig	丁 *Ding* 亥 *Hai* Fire Pig	己 *Ji* 亥 *Hai* Earth Pig	辛 *Xin* 亥 *Hai* Metal Pig	癸 *Gui* 亥 *Hai* Water Pig
▲	▲	▲	▲	✖

★ Excellent　✔ Auspicious　● Fair　▲ Inauspicious　✖ Dire

十二值神 12 Day Officers	十二地支 Animal Sign of the Day	董公擇日解説 Dong Gong Description
危 *Wei* **Danger**	子 *Zi* Rat Yang Water	庚子月德、丙子、戊子,起造、婚姻、興工、動土、出行、開張、移徒,進人口、益子孫、旺田蠶、增財產、大作大發、小作小發。甲子是自死之金,五行無氣,壬子木打寶瓶,北方沐浴之地,福力甚薄,又是四正廢,用之損人口,主冷退,大凶。甲子、壬子二日用之,立見蕭索損破。 The Geng Zi 庚子 Day enjoys the positive energies of the Monthly Virtue 月德 Star. Meanwhile, Bing Zi 丙子 and Wu Zi 戊子 Days are ideal for renovation, marriage, starting work, groundbreaking, traveling, opening a business and migrating. Those who tap into the useful energies of these days will be blessed with an expanding family, good descendent luck and an increase in material wealth and assets. In fact, the more significant the undertaking, the greater the returns or outcomes. However, the Qi is weak on Jia Zi 甲子 Day and Ren Zi 壬子 Day, as they are also known as the Four Direct Abandonment Days 四正廢, and hence unsuitable for use. Using such days will only result in family members being prone to injuries, domestic discord and deteriorating fortunes in terms of family wealth.

甲 *Jia* 子 *Zi* Wood Rat	丙 *Bing* 子 *Zi* Fire Rat	戊 *Wu* 子 *Zi* Earth Rat	庚 *Geng* 子 *Zi* Metal Rat	壬 *Ren* 子 *Zi* Water Rat
▲	✔	✔	★	▲

★ **Excellent**　✔ **Auspicious**　● **Fair**　▲ **Inauspicious**　✖ **Dire**

董公擇日要覽

十二值神 12 Day Officers	十二地支 Animal Sign of the Day	董公擇日解説 Dong Gong Description
成 *Cheng* **Success**	丑 *Chou* Ox Yin Earth	天喜、天成,欲犯朱雀、勾絞,用之招官司、口舌、小人、肆誣妄毀。丁丑、癸丑,煞入宮,更凶,此數日犯空亡、破財、小人陷害。 Despite this day being accompanied by the presence of the Sky Happiness 天喜 and Heavenly Success 天成 Stars, the simultaneous presence of the inauspicious Red Phoenix 朱雀 and Grappling Hook 勾絞 Stars unfortunately negate any positive effects that would otherwise benefit endeavors. Consequently, using this day will only result in legal entanglements and disputes arising, as well as indicate the interference of petty-minded people. The Ding Chou 丁丑 and Gui Chou 癸丑 Days are the worst, as they also violate the Death and Emptiness 空亡 rule; thereby indicating loss of wealth and acts of sabotage by malicious people.

丑
Ox

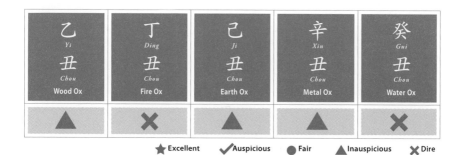

乙 *Yi* 丑 *Chou* Wood Ox	丁 *Ding* 丑 *Chou* Fire Ox	己 *Ji* 丑 *Chou* Earth Ox	辛 *Xin* 丑 *Chou* Metal Ox	癸 *Gui* 丑 *Chou* Water Ox
▲	✖	▲	▲	✖

★ Excellent   ✔ Auspicious   ● Fair   ▲ Inauspicious   ✖ Dire

十二值神 12 Day Officers	十二地支 Animal Sign of the Day	董公擇日解說 Dong Gong Description
收 *Shou* **Receive**	寅 *Yin* **Tiger** Yang Wood 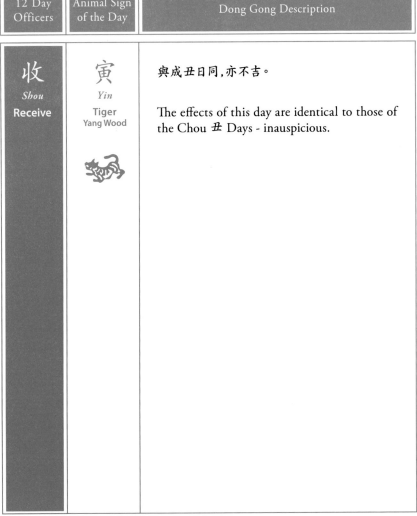	與成丑日同，亦不吉。 The effects of this day are identical to those of the Chou 丑 Days - inauspicious.

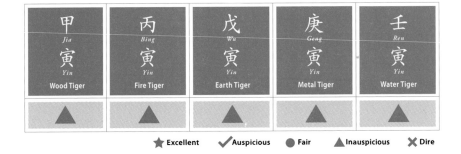

甲 *Jia* 寅 *Yin* Wood Tiger	丙 *Bing* 寅 *Yin* Fire Tiger	戊 *Wu* 寅 *Yin* Earth Tiger	庚 *Geng* 寅 *Yin* Metal Tiger	壬 *Ren* 寅 *Yin* Water Tiger
▲	▲	▲	▲	▲

★ Excellent　✔ Auspicious　● Fair　▲ Inauspicious　✗ Dire

董公擇日要覽

Rabbit

十二值神 12 Day Officers	十二地支 Animal Sign of the Day	董公擇日解説 Dong Gong Description
開 *Kai* **Open**	卯 *Mao* **Rabbit** Yin Wood 	辛卯天德、癸卯、己卯，有黃羅、紫檀、天皇、地皇星蓋照，出行、婚葬、造作、開張、入宅等事，大吉，主謀事享通、貴人接引、進財祿。餘卯次吉。 The Xin Mao 辛卯 Day has the 天德 Heavenly Virtue present, while the Gui Mao 癸卯 and Ji Mao 己卯 Days are supported by the positive energies of the Yellow Spiral 黃羅, Purple Sandalwood紫檀, Heavenly Emperor 天皇 and Earthly Emperor 地皇 Stars. As such, these days are suitable for traveling, marriage, renovation, opening a business and moving into a new house. All endeavors undertaken will enjoy auspicious outcomes, with a possibility of an increase in wealth and help from noble people where necessary. Furthermore, the other Mao 卯 Days are also favorable.

乙 *Yi* 卯 *Mao* Wood Rabbit	丁 *Ding* 卯 *Mao* Fire Rabbit	己 *Ji* 卯 *Mao* Earth Rabbit	辛 *Xin* 卯 *Mao* Metal Rabbit	癸 *Gui* 卯 *Mao* Water Rabbit
✔	✔	★	★	★

★ **Excellent** ✔ **Auspicious** ● **Fair** ▲ **Inauspicious** ✗ **Dire**

董公擇日要覽

辰
Dragon

十二值神 12 Day Officers	十二地支 Animal Sign of the Day	董公擇日解說 Dong Gong Description
閉 *Bi* **Close**	辰 *Chen* **Dragon** **Yang Earth** 	戊辰、甲辰，煞入中宮，不利婚姻、修造、開張、入宅、安葬，犯之財產有失、損人口、六畜不旺。庚辰雖值月德，卻有天地轉煞之疑。丙辰、壬辰火星，小小營爲則可，不宜婚姻、起造、移徒、開張大用也。 Negative stars govern Wu Chen 戊辰 and Jia Chen 甲辰 Days, rendering them unsuitable for marriage, renovation works, opening a business, moving into a new house or burial. Violating this warning will result in the young children of the household being prone to injury; and even the domestic pet animals will also be susceptible to illness. Furthermore, financial fortunes will take a turn for the worse. The Geng Chen 庚辰 Day has the Monthly Virtue Star present, while Bing Chen 丙辰 and Ren Chen 壬辰 Days are accompanied by the presence of the Fire Star. This makes such days usable for small-scale matters of significance. Nevertheless, they should not be utilized for important events or endeavors such as marriage, commencing construction works, migration or opening a business.

甲 *Jia* 辰 *Chen* Wood Dragon	丙 *Bing* 辰 *Chen* Fire Dragon	戊 *Wu* 辰 *Chen* Earth Dragon	庚 *Geng* 辰 *Chen* Metal Dragon	壬 *Ren* 辰 *Chen* Water Dragon
✖	●	✖	●	●

★ Excellent　✔ Auspicious　● Fair　▲ Inauspicious　✖ Dire

Fifth Month 五月

June 6th – July 6th

Horse 午 (Wu) Month

June 6th – July 6th
Horse 午 (Wu) Month

月德丙、月恩戊，母倉寅卯，天德合寅。

In the Horse 午 (Wu) Month, Bing 丙 Days are supported by the energies of the Monthly Virtue 月德 Star, Wu 戊 Days are accompanied by the Monthly Benevolence 月恩 Star, while the Motherly Storage 母倉 Star exerts its positive influence on Tiger 寅 (Yin) and Rabbit 卯 (Mao) Days. Similarly, the Qi of the Heavenly Virtue 天德 Star combines with the Qi on Tiger 寅 (Yin) Days to bring about positive effects.

夏至：夏至前一日爲四離。

'Summer Solstice' 夏至 (Xia Zhi)

The day before the beginning of the Summer Solstice is called the 4 Separation 四離 Day.

芒種：芒種後，三煞在北，亥、子、丑方忌修造、動土。

The 'Planting of Thorny Crops' 芒種 (Mang Zhong)

After the 'Planting of Thorny Crops', the Three Killings 三煞 (San Sha) Affliction resides in the North sector. As such, avoid 'disturbing' the ground in the Northwest 3 亥 (Hai – NW3), North 2 子 (Zi – N2) and Northeast 1 丑 (Chou – NE1) directions.

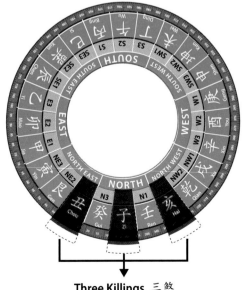

Three Killings 三煞

十二值神 12 Day Officers	十二地支 Animal Sign of the Day	董公擇日解説 Dong Gong Description
建 *Jian* **Establish**	午 *Wu* Horse Yang Fire 	甲午天赦,雖是轉煞,埋葬用之次吉。餘午日埋葬亦不利。若別事用,主招官司、口舌、孤寡、窮病,蓋五月逢午,皆係天地轉煞也。 In the Fifth 未 (Wei) Month, all Wu 午 (Horse) days are adversely affected by the Heaven and Earth Drilling Sha 天地轉煞. However, the Jia Wu 甲午 Day is accompanied by the Heavenly Pardon Star, and hence may be used as a slightly favorable day for burial. All the other Wu Days, of course, remain unusable, as they are the harbingers of legal problems, gossips and rumors, loneliness and sickness.

Horse

甲 *Jia* 午 *Wu* Wood Horse	丙 *Bing* 午 *Wu* Fire Horse	戊 *Wu* 午 *Wu* Earth Horse	庚 *Geng* 午 *Wu* Metal Horse	壬 *Ren* 午 *Wu* Water Horse
✔	▲	▲	▲	▲

★ Excellent ✔ Auspicious ● Fair ▲ Inauspicious ✘ Dire

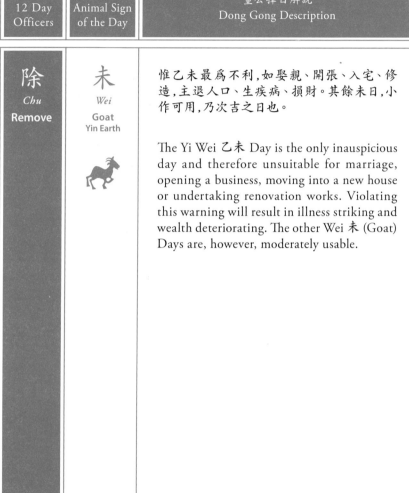

十二值神 12 Day Officers	十二地支 Animal Sign of the Day	董公擇日解説 Dong Gong Description
除 *Chu* **Remove**	未 *Wei* Goat Yin Earth	惟乙未最爲不利，如娶親、開張、入宅、修造，主退人口、生疾病、損財。其餘未日，小作可用，乃次吉之日也。 The Yi Wei 乙未 Day is the only inauspicious day and therefore unsuitable for marriage, opening a business, moving into a new house or undertaking renovation works. Violating this warning will result in illness striking and wealth deteriorating. The other Wei 未 (Goat) Days are, however, moderately usable.

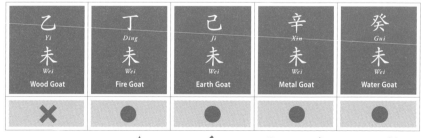

乙未 *Yi Wei* Wood Goat	丁未 *Ding Wei* Fire Goat	己未 *Ji Wei* Earth Goat	辛未 *Xin Wei* Metal Goat	癸未 *Gui Wei* Water Goat
✖	●	●	●	●

★ Excellent ✔ Auspicious ● Fair ▲ Inauspicious ✖ Dire

十二值神 12 Day Officers	十二地支 Animal Sign of the Day	董公擇日解説 Dong Gong Description
滿 *Man* **Full**	申 *Shen* Monkey Yang Metal 	天富、天喜,甲申、丙申、戊申,宜安葬、起造、婚姻、入宅、開張、出行次吉。不宜動土。庚申只宜安葬,不宜修造、入宅。壬申西沉之日,五行無氣,不可用,雖是葬日,但月令不利。 The positive Heavenly Fortune 天富 and Sky Happiness 天喜 Stars are present on this day, lending impetus to its auspiciousness. Jia Shen 甲申, Bing Shen 丙申 and Wu Shen 戊申 Days are considered 'secondary' favorable days, and therefore suitable for burial, marriage, moving into a new residence, opening a business and traveling. Do note, however, that these days are not suitable for groundbreaking. A Geng Shen 庚申 Day is only suitable for burial, but should not be used for renovation or moving into a new house. Similarly, the Qi on a Ren Shen 壬申 Day is extremely weak; hence such a date should not be used for activities or endeavors of any sort.

甲 *Jia* 申 *Shen* Wood Monkey	丙 *Bing* 申 *Shen* Fire Monkey	戊 *Wu* 申 *Shen* Earth Monkey	庚 *Geng* 申 *Shen* Metal Monkey	壬 *Ren* 申 *Shen* Water Monkey
✔	✔	✔	●	▲

★ Excellent　✔ Auspicious　● Fair　▲ Inauspicious　✘ Dire

十二值神 12 Day Officers	十二地支 Animal Sign of the Day	董公擇日解説 Dong Gong Description
平 *Ping* **Balance**	酉 *You* Rooster Yin Metal	小紅砂,有朱雀、勾絞、到州星,招官司、損長幼、家下伶仃、百事不宜,犯之大凶。 The Lesser Red Embrace 小紅砂 Star governs the day, accompanied by the arrival of the Red Phoenix 朱雀 and Grappling Hook 勾絞 Stars. These stars are the harbingers of legal entanglements, and also do not augur well for the safety and health of the eldest and youngest occupants in a household. They are highly inauspicious and equally unsuitable for important endeavors or activities. Families who unwittingly unleash the harmful energies of these stars will not grow or expand.

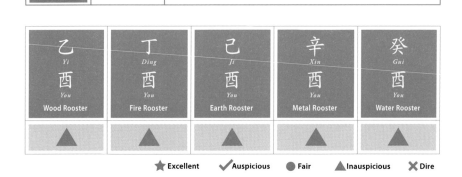

乙 *Yi* 酉 *You* Wood Rooster	丁 *Ding* 酉 *You* Fire Rooster	己 *Ji* 酉 *You* Earth Rooster	辛 *Xin* 酉 *You* Metal Rooster	癸 *Gui* 酉 *You* Water Rooster
▲	▲	▲	▲	▲

★ Excellent ✔ Auspicious ● Fair ▲ Inauspicious ✘ Dire

十二值神 12 Day Officers	十二地支 Animal Sign of the Day	董公擇日解説 Dong Gong Description
定 *Ding* **Stable**	戌 *Xu* Dog Yang Earth 	甲戌、戊戌、庚戌,有黃羅、紫檀、天皇、地皇、金銀,寶藏,田塘、庫珠、聚祿、駕馬,御聖遊頑星蓋照,大吉。如起造、興工、動土、入宅、開張、婚姻、埋葬諸事,加官進爵、生貴子、益橫財。惟丙戌、壬戌二日,煞入中宮,雖有吉星相解,終難受益。 The Jia Xu 甲戌, Wu Xu 戊戌 and Geng Xu 庚戌 Days are supported by the positive energies of the auspicious Yellow Spiral 黃羅, Purple Sandalwood 紫檀, Heavenly Emperor 天皇, Earthly Emperor 地皇、 Golden Ingot Star 金銀, Precious Treasure 寶藏、 Field Embankment 田塘, Pearl Storage 庫珠、Prosperity Gathering 聚祿 and Valiant Horse 駕馬 Stars; making them highly auspicious days. They can therefore by suitably used for renovation, ground-digging, commencing renovations or work, moving into a new house, opening a business, marriage and burial. Their positive effects will bring about promotion prospects, the birth of noble children and an increase in wealth. Do note however that Bing Xu 丙戌 and Ren Xu 壬戌 Days harbor Sha (Killing) Qi; so even with the presence of auspicious stars, the resultant Qi will not be so beneficial.

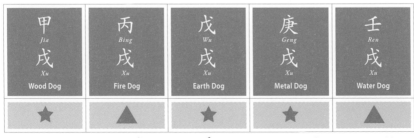

甲 *Jia* 戌 *Xu* Wood Dog	丙 *Bing* 戌 *Xu* Fire Dog	戊 *Wu* 戌 *Xu* Earth Dog	庚 *Geng* 戌 *Xu* Metal Dog	壬 *Ren* 戌 *Xu* Water Dog
★	▲	★	★	▲

★ **Excellent** ✓ **Auspicious** ● **Fair** ▲ **Inauspicious** ✗ **Dire**

十二值神 12 Day Officers	十二地支 Animal Sign of the Day	董公擇日解説 Dong Gong Description
執 *Zhi* **Initiate**	亥 *Hai* Pig Yin Water 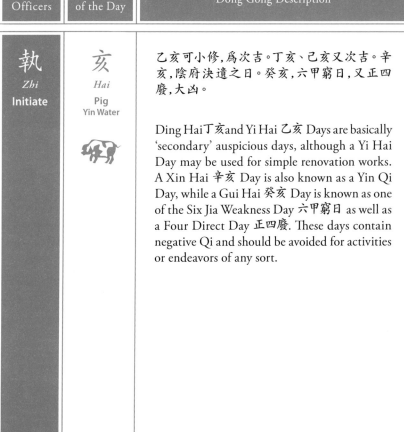	乙亥可小修，爲次吉。丁亥、己亥又次吉。辛亥，陰府决遗之日。癸亥，六甲窮日，又正四廢，大凶。 Ding Hai 丁亥 and Yi Hai 乙亥 Days are basically 'secondary' auspicious days, although a Yi Hai Day may be used for simple renovation works. A Xin Hai 辛亥 Day is also known as a Yin Qi Day, while a Gui Hai 癸亥 Day is known as one of the Six Jia Weakness Day 六甲窮日 as well as a Four Direct Day 正四廢. These days contain negative Qi and should be avoided for activities or endeavors of any sort.

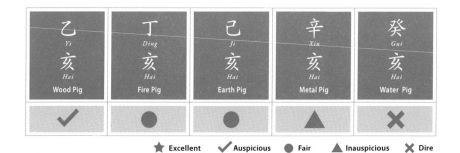

乙 *Yi* 亥 *Hai* Wood Pig	丁 *Ding* 亥 *Hai* Fire Pig	己 *Ji* 亥 *Hai* Earth Pig	辛 *Xin* 亥 *Hai* Metal Pig	癸 *Gui* 亥 *Hai* Water Pig
✔	●	●	▲	✖

★ **Excellent**   ✔ **Auspicious**   ● **Fair**   ▲ **Inauspicious**   ✖ **Dire**

十二值神 12 Day Officers	十二地支 Animal Sign of the Day	董公擇日解説 Dong Gong Description
破 *Po* **Destruction**	子 *Zi* Rat Yang Water 	天賊,不宜娶親、造作、安葬、入宅等事,犯之招官司,損六畜,田產不收,大凶。壬子,正四廢,更凶,此日百事不利,犯之受死。 Due to the presence of the negative Heavenly Thief 天賊 Star, this is a very inauspicious day and therefore not suitable to get married, undertake renovation works, enter a new house, or for burials. Violating this rule will only bring about legal issues, livestock being hurt or affected, or properties being lost. The Ren Zi 壬子 Day, also known as a Four Direct Day 正四廢 brings about even worse outcomes. Avoid undertaking any important activities on this day.

子
Rat

甲 *Jia* 子 *Zi* Wood Rat	丙 *Bing* 子 *Zi* Fire Rat	戊 *Wu* 子 *Zi* Earth Rat	庚 *Geng* 子 *Zi* Metal Rat	壬 *Ren* 子 *Zi* Water Rat
▲	▲	▲	▲	✖

★ Excellent ✔ Auspicious ● Fair ▲ Inauspicious ✖ Dire

十二值神 12 Day Officers	十二地支 Animal Sign of the Day	董公擇日解説 Dong Gong Description
危 *Wei* **Danger**	丑 *Chou* Ox Yin Earth 	丁丑、癸丑不宜娶親、造作、安葬、入宅，犯之田產不收、財物失脫、虎咬蛇傷，多凶。餘丑亦不吉，損六畜、招官司，諸事不宜。 Ding Chou 丁丑 and Gui Chou 癸丑 Days are unsuitable for marriage, renovation or moving into a new house. They cause severe loss of property, wealth, and other material belongings, or cause people to be the victim of an attack by a tiger or serpent. The other Chou 丑 (Ox) Days are also inauspicious, as they cause damage to livestock or attract legal issues. Avoid these days for all important activities or endeavors.

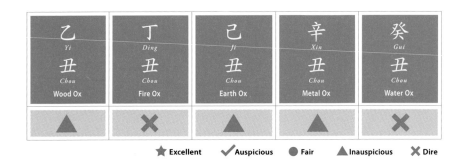

乙 *Yi* 丑 *Chou* Wood Ox	丁 *Ding* 丑 *Chou* Fire Ox	己 *Ji* 丑 *Chou* Earth Ox	辛 *Xin* 丑 *Chou* Metal Ox	癸 *Gui* 丑 *Chou* Water Ox
▲	✖	▲	▲	✖

★ **Excellent**　✔ **Auspicious**　● **Fair**　▲ **Inauspicious**　✖ **Dire**

董公擇日要覽

寅
Tiger

十二值神 12 Day Officers	十二地支 Animal Sign of the Day	董公擇日解説 Dong Gong Description

成
Cheng
Success

寅
Yin
Tiger
Yang Wood

黃砂、天喜,丙寅天、月二德、庚寅、戊寅、甲寅,有黃羅、紫檀、天皇、地皇、金銀庫樓、玉堂寶藏、吉星相照、興工動土、定磉拴架、入宅、開張,六十日一百二十日內益財增喜,家門從此富盛,世道愈見安康,大吉也。是月壬寅雖有吉星相照,內中稍有煞星相剋,次吉。

The auspicious Yellow Embrace 黃砂 and Sky Happiness 天喜, preside over this day. The Bing Yin 丙寅 Day enjoys the positive energies of the Heavenly and Monthly Virtue 天月二德 Star. Similarly, Geng Yin 庚寅, Wu Yin 戊寅 and Jia Yin 甲寅 Days are simultaneously enhanced by the useful energies of the Yellow Spiral 黃羅, Purple Sandalwood 柴檀, Heavenly Emperor 天皇, Earthly Emperor 地皇, Golden Ingot 金銀, Storage Tower Stage 庫樓, Jade Hall 玉堂 and Precious Treasure 寶藏 Stars. This makes such days especially suitable to start work and for ground-digging, to build or move into a new house, launch a business or for couples to even try to conceive. The positive effects of tapping into the useful energies of such days may be seen within 60 to 120 days, with wealth-gain and good health the more obvious outcomes. The only exception however lies in the Ren Yin 壬寅 Day, for although it is accompanied by positive stars, there is also Sha (Killing) Qi present on that day. As such, this day is only considered to be 'secondarily' auspicious.

甲 *Jia* 寅 *Yin* Wood Tiger	丙 *Bing* 寅 *Yin* Fire Tiger	戊 *Wu* 寅 *Yin* Earth Tiger	庚 *Geng* 寅 *Yin* Metal Tiger	壬 *Ren* 寅 *Yin* Water Tiger
★	★	★	★	✓

★ Excellent　✓ Auspicious　● Fair　▲ Inauspicious　✗ Dire

十二值神 12 Day Officers	十二地支 Animal Sign of the Day	董公擇日解説 Dong Gong Description
收 *Shou* **Receive**	卯 *Mao* **Rabbit** Yin Wood 	往亡,有朱雀、勾絞,小人刑害、禍患纏綿、官司、口舌、損六畜,百事不宜,大凶。 This is known as an Emptiness Day 往亡, where the presence of the inauspicious Red Phoenix 朱雀 and Grappling Hook 勾絞 Stars exert their negative influence over the day. This results in the interference of petty-minded people, as well as legal problems and disputes arising. In addition, the pet animals of the household will also be harmed or suffer. Avoid using this day for any important activities or endeavors.

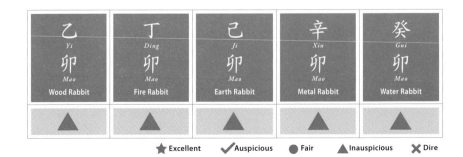

乙 *Yi* 卯 *Mao* **Wood Rabbit**	丁 *Ding* 卯 *Mao* **Fire Rabbit**	己 *Ji* 卯 *Mao* **Earth Rabbit**	辛 *Xin* 卯 *Mao* **Metal Rabbit**	癸 *Gui* 卯 *Mao* **Water Rabbit**
▲	▲	▲	▲	▲

★ Excellent　✓ Auspicious　● Fair　▲ Inauspicious　✗ Dire

十二值神 12 Day Officers	十二地支 Animal Sign of the Day	董公擇日解説 Dong Gong Description
開 *Kai* **Open**	辰 *Chen* **Dragon** **Yang Earth** 	天成、丙辰,有月德;庚辰、壬辰,有黃羅、紫檀吉星蓋照,用之增田產、六畜興旺、生貴子,百事大吉。惟戊辰、甲辰,煞入中宮,大凶。 The auspicious Heavenly Success Star lords over this day, with the Bing Chen 丙辰 Day also supported by the positive energies of the Monthly Virtue 月德 Star. Similarly, Geng Chen 庚辰 and Ren Chen 壬辰 Days are positively enhanced by the presence of the Yellow Spiral 黃羅 and Purple Sandalwood 紫檀 Stars. These combinations herald an increase property-ownership and assets, as well as the birth of noble offspring, making the pertinent days suitable for all activities and endeavors. However, Wu Chen 戊辰 and Jia Chen甲辰 Days contain Sha (Killing) Qi, and should not be used for any important activities.

甲 *Jia* 辰 *Chen* Wood Dragon	丙 *Bing* 辰 *Chen* Fire Dragon	戊 *Wu* 辰 *Chen* Earth Dragon	庚 *Geng* 辰 *Chen* Metal Dragon	壬 *Ren* 辰 *Chen* Water Dragon
▲	★	▲	★	★

★ Excellent ✔ Auspicious ● Fair ▲ Inauspicious ✕ Dire

董公擇日要覽

Snake

十二值神 12 Day Officers	十二地支 Animal Sign of the Day	董公擇日解説 Dong Gong Description
閉 *Bi* Close	巳 *Si* Snake Yin Fire	乙巳、辛巳，有黄羅、紫檀星蓋照，興工、造作、動土、修造、池塘、倉庫、牛羊欄圈、入宅、婚姻、開張、出行、大益家門，子孫昌盛，田産倍收，人口安康，大吉。餘巳不言。 The Yi Si 乙巳 and Xin Si 辛巳 Days are accompanied by the auspicious Yellow Spiral 黄羅 and Purple Sandalwood 紫檀星 Stars; making them suitable to undertake renovation, ground-digging and pond excavation works, moving into a new house, opening a storage or containment system, marriage, launch a business and travel. Their positive energies will bring prosperity to one offspring, as well as increase one wealth and other material assets. Note though that the other Si 巳 (Snake) days are not suitable for activities of any sort.

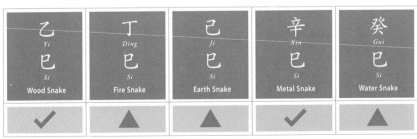

★ Excellent ✔ Auspicious ● Fair ▲ Inauspicious ✗ Dire

Sixth Month 六月

July 7th — August 7th

Goat 未 (Wei) Month

July 7th – August 7th
Goat 未 (Wei) Month

月德甲、月恩辛，母倉寅卯。天德合己。

During the Goat 未 (Wei) Month, the Monthly Virtue 月德 Star is present on Jia 甲 Days, the Monthly Benevolence 月恩 Star is present on Xin 辛 Days, while the Motherly Storage 母倉 Star exerts its auspicious influence on Tiger 寅 (Yin) and Rabbit 卯 (Mao) Days. Meanwhile, the useful energies of the Heavenly Virtue 天德 Star combine with the Qi on Ji 己 Days to bring about positive outcomes.

小暑：小暑後，三煞在西。

'Lesser Heat' 小暑 (Xiao Shu)

After the advent of Lesser Heat, the Three Killings 三煞 (San Sha) Affliction lies in the West sector.

大暑：申、酉、戌方忌修造、動土。

'Greater Heat' 大暑 **(Da Shu)**

Greater Heat follows in the wake of Lesser Heat, with the Three Killings Affliction in the West sector. As such, refrain from digging or 'disturbing' the ground in the Southwest 3 申 (Shen – SW3), West 2 酉 (You – W2) and Northwest 1 戌 (Xu – NW1) directions in particular.

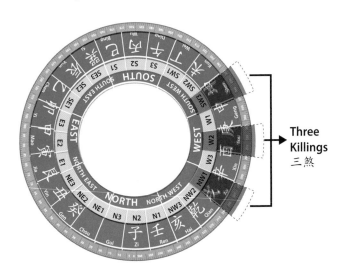

Three Killings 三煞

董公擇日要覽

Goat

十二值神 12 Day Officers	十二地支 Animal Sign of the Day	董公擇日解説 Dong Gong Description
建 *Jian* **Establish**	未 *Wei* Goat Yin Earth 	乙未，煞入中宮，不利修造、婚姻、入宅、開張、上官、諸事犯之不吉，犯之招時氣瘟疫、損人口、失財物，大凶。 On a Yi Wei 乙未 Day, Sha (Killing) Qi enters the Central Palace of a residence or workplace, making this day unsuitable to undertake renovation works, get married, move into a new house, open a business or assume a new post. Violating this rule of caution will result in chaos and all facets of life being adversely affected; from family members being hurt to wealth being lost. It is therefore best to avoid this day insofar as all important activities or endeavors are concerned.

乙 *Yi* 未 *Wei* Wood Goat	丁 *Ding* 未 *Wei* Fire Goat	己 *Ji* 未 *Wei* Earth Goat	辛 *Xin* 未 *Wei* Metal Goat	癸 *Gui* 未 *Wei* Water Goat
✖	▲	▲	▲	▲

★ Excellent   ✔ Auspicious   ● Fair   ▲ Inauspicious   ✖ Dire

十二值神 12 Day Officers	十二地支 Animal Sign of the Day	董公擇日解説 Dong Gong Description
除 *Chu* **Remove**	申 *Shen* **Monkey** Yang Metal	甲申,有天、月二德、黄羅、紫檀星蓋照,利豎造、起造、安葬、動土、開山、斬草、出行、開張,百事皆吉。餘申日亦大吉。惟丙申一日,五行無氣,不可用。庚申日慎用。 The presence of the auspicious Heavenly 天德 and Monthly Virtue 月德, as well as Yellow Spiral 黃羅 and Purple Sandalwood 紫檀 Stars lend positive support to this Jia Shen甲申 Day. It is hence a suitable and auspicious day for constructing vertical beams, renovation, burial, ground-digging, excavating mountains for development purposes, landscaping, travel and launching a business. The other Shen 申 (Monkey) days are also considered auspicious, except for the Bing Shen 丙申 Day when Qi of the Five Elements is either trapped or dead, and therefore cannot be used. In addition, one needs to be cautious if using the 庚申Day for significant activities or endeavors.

甲 *Jia* 申 *Shen* Wood Monkey	丙 *Bing* 申 *Shen* Fire Monkey	戊 *Wu* 申 *Shen* Earth Monkey	庚 *Geng* 申 *Shen* Metal Monkey	壬 *Ren* 申 *Shen* Water Monkey
✖	▲	✔	●	✔

★ Excellent ✔ Auspicious ● Fair ▲ Inauspicious ✖ Dire

十二值神 12 Day Officers	十二地支 Animal Sign of the Day	董公擇日解説 Dong Gong Description
滿 *Man* **Full**	酉 *You* Rooster Yin Metal 	天喜、天富。乙酉、辛酉,伐木、捨架、定礎、起造,乃次吉日。己酉九土鬼日;癸酉小葬日,又犯黑煞所臨,僅可備於急用。丁酉逢滿日,亦不利,此數日恐吉中有凶,終不美,用宜慎之。 The positive Sky Happiness 天喜 and Heavenly Fortune 天富 Stars are present on Yi You 乙酉 and Xin You 辛酉 Days. Even so, these days are only moderately suitable to be used for particular activities such as lumbering, fastening frames, fixing a new column or pedestal, or constructing a new house. The Ji You 己酉 Day is also known as a Nine Earth Ghost Day 九土鬼日, while the Gui You 癸酉 Day is identified as a Lesser Cremate Day 小葬日. Both these days harbor inauspiciously Black Sha (Killing) Qi and are therefore unsuitable for important activities. A Ding You 丁酉 Day appears to be initially auspicious due to the presence of positive stars but since it is also the harbinger of hidden problems, it should be avoided insofar as activities or endeavors are concerned.

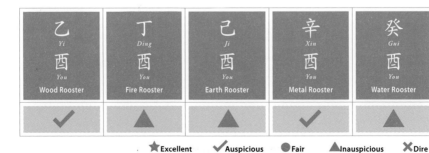

乙 *Yi* 酉 *You* Wood Rooster	丁 *Ding* 酉 *You* Fire Rooster	己 *Ji* 酉 *You* Earth Rooster	辛 *Xin* 酉 *You* Metal Rooster	癸 *Gui* 酉 *You* Water Rooster
✔	▲	▲	✔	▲

★ Excellent   ✔ Auspicious   ● Fair   ▲ Inauspicious   ✘ Dire

十二值神 12 Day Officers	十二地支 Animal Sign of the Day	董公擇日解說 Dong Gong Description
平 *Ping* **Balance**	戌 *Xu* Dog Yang Earth 	有朱雀、勾絞、又犯到州星,不利入宅、婚姻等事,犯之主招官非,損人口、退血財,大凶。惟甲戌一日,爲玄女偸修之日,八方俱白,二十四日向諸神朝天之日,有氣可用。 The presence of the negative Red Phoenix 朱雀 and Grappling Hook 勾絞 Stars make this day unsuitable for moving into a new house or getting married. Its detrimental effects include legal entanglements, family members being more prone to injuries and poor health. Only the Jia Xu 甲戌 Day contains some auspicious stars, making it usable for activities or endeavors of importance.

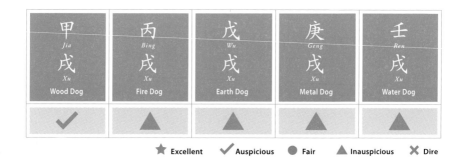

★ Excellent   ✓ Auspicious   ● Fair   ▲ Inauspicious   ✗ Dire

董公擇日要覽

亥
Pig

十二值神 12 Day Officers	十二地支 Animal Sign of the Day	董公擇日解説 Dong Gong Description
定 *Ding* **Stable**	亥 *Hai* Pig Yin Water 	己亥火星，丁亥有黄羅、紫檀、天皇、地皇星蓋照，乙亥文昌值日，宜出行、入宅、婚姻、入學、修造、動土、參官見貴，招財祿、生貴子、大作大發、小作小發。文昌乙亥在午，文昌是太陽，午宮乃太陽之位，故有文昌星值日，是以大吉。辛亥是婦人之金，陰氣全盛，癸亥六甲窮日，五行無氣，此二日不宜用。 The Ji Hai 己亥 Day is marked by the presence of the Fire Star 火星, while the Ding Hai 丁亥 Day contains the Yellow Spiral 黄羅, Purple Sandalwood 紫檀, Heavenly Emperor 天皇 and Earthly Emperor 地皇 Stars. Meanwhile, the Yi Hai 乙亥 Day is accompanied by the Literary 文昌 Star; making it a good day to embark on a journey, move into a new house, get married, commence studies at a new school, or engage in renovation or groundbreaking works or see somebody of importance. Using such a day will bring about wealth opportunities and the birth of a noble son. The more significant the activity, the more prominent the outcome. The Literary 文昌 Star present on a Yi Hai Day can be found in the Wu 午 (Horse) Palace. The literary star is akin to the Sun 太陽, which in turn is strongest when it is found in Wu Palace – thereby augmenting the Literary Arts Star's positive effects even further. However, the Qi on a Xin Hai 辛亥 Day is overly Yin in polarity, while the Gui Hai 癸亥 Day is also known as a Six Jia Exhaustion Day 六甲窮日. Neither of these two days possesses any Qi, so avoid using them for any activities or endeavors.

乙 *Yi* 亥 *Hai* Wood Pig	丁 *Ding* 亥 *Hai* Fire Pig	己 *Ji* 亥 *Hai* Earth Pig	辛 *Xin* 亥 *Hai* Metal Pig	癸 *Gui* 亥 *Hai* Water Pig
★	★	✔	▲	▲

★ Excellent　　✔ Auspicious　　● Fair　　▲ Inauspicious　　✕ Dire

十二值神 12 Day Officers	十二地支 Animal Sign of the Day	董公擇日解説 Dong Gong Description

Rat

執 *Zhi* **Initiate**	子 *Zi* Rat Yang Water 	黃砂。丙子、庚子,利起造、興工、動土、及倉庫、入宅、移徒、開張、出行。戊子次吉。甲子雖是六甲之首,在正月六月值天德、月德豈不可用,然自死之金,五行無氣,平常之人,不能當此黑煞,北方將軍之氣,壬子木打寶瓶,北方沐浴之地,又是正四廢,更忌用。 The presence of the Yellow Embrace 黃砂 Star makes Bing Zi 丙子 and Geng Zi 庚子 Days are suitable for renovation, ground-digging, opening something previously stored or contained, moving into a new house, launching a business and travel. In addition, Wu Zi 戊子 Days are considered `secondary'-choice days. However, although a Jia Zi 甲子 Day may appear to be the best of the 60 Jia Zi (Day Pillar) combinations, since it enjoys the presence of Heavenly and Monthly Virtue Stars this month, it cannot be used because Metal Qi is dead and the Five Elements are totally devoid of strength. Meanwhile, a Ren Zi 壬子 Day assumes the Bath Position 沐浴之地 in the North sector, thereby making defining it as one of the Direct Pure Days 正四廢; which should not be used for activities or endeavors of any sort.

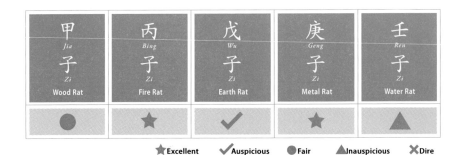

甲 *Jia* 子 *Zi* Wood Rat	丙 *Bing* 子 *Zi* Fire Rat	戊 *Wu* 子 *Zi* Earth Rat	庚 *Geng* 子 *Zi* Metal Rat	壬 *Ren* 子 *Zi* Water Rat
●	★	✔	★	▲

★Excellent　✔Auspicious　●Fair　▲Inauspicious　✗Dire

十二值神 12 Day Officers	十二地支 Animal Sign of the Day	董公擇日解說 Dong Gong Description
破 *Po* **Destruction**	丑 *Chou* Ox Yin Earth 	小紅砂。此日無吉星，不可營爲，萬不得已須擇時，僅作小小急用。若起造、開張、出行、婚姻等事，主損六畜、招官司。丁丑、癸丑，煞入中宮，犯之殺人，凶不可言。 The Lesser Red Embrace 小紅砂 Star presides over this day, which otherwise lacks the presence of auspicious stars. Hence, employ caution if you wish to select this date for a certain purpose. It is certainly unsuitable for opening a business, travel and marriage, as it spells harm for animals and livestock, as well as the advent of legal issues. The Ding Chou 丁丑 and Gui Chou 癸丑 Days are the worst, as Sha (Killing) Qi enters the Central Palace on these days. Using them will only bring about catastrophe for occupants and unwitting victims.

乙 *Yi* 丑 *Chou* Wood Ox	丁 *Ding* 丑 *Chou* Fire Ox	己 *Ji* 丑 *Chou* Earth Ox	辛 *Xin* 丑 *Chou* Metal Ox	癸 *Gui* 丑 *Chou* Water Ox
▲	✖	▲	✖	✖

★ Excellent   ✔ Auspicious   ● Fair   ▲ Inauspicious   ✖ Dire

董公擇日要覽

寅
Tiger

十二值神 12 Day Officers	十二地支 Animal Sign of the Day	董公擇日解説 Dong Gong Description
危 *Wei* **Danger**	寅 *Yin* Tiger Yang Wood 	夏爲鬼神空亡。甲寅有天月二德、黃羅、紫檀、金銀庫樓、祿馬,寶蓋,帝馭蓋星照,但不利遠行、起造、入宅、婚姻,緣有爲鬼神凶宅之疑耳。如開山、埋葬、營謀百事,六十日、一百二十日內生貴子、家業興旺、貴人接引、進產業,大吉。餘寅日次吉。 This day, also known as the Ghost and Deities Emptiness Day 鬼神空亡. 甲寅 Day, is ironically accompanied by the presence of the auspicious Heavenly and Monthly Virtue 天月二德, Yellow Spiral 黃羅, Purple Sandalwood 紫檀, Golden Ingot 金銀, Storage 庫樓 and Prosperous Treasure 祿寶 Stars. Hence, it may indeed be considered auspicious, but should still not be utilized for travel, renovation, moving into a new residence and marriage. This day is however totally unusable for Opening (Exploring) New Land 開山 or Burial. Nevertheless, used well or carefully, one will be blessed with the birth of a noble child, and an increase in material assets within 60 to 120 days. In addition, there will be no shortage of help in times of need from noble people. Do note though that the other Yin 寅 (Tiger) Days are considered 'secondary' in terms of usefulness.

甲 *Jia* 寅 *Yin* **Wood Tiger**	丙 *Bing* 寅 *Yin* **Fire Tiger**	戊 *Wu* 寅 *Yin* **Earth Tiger**	庚 *Geng* 寅 *Yin* **Metal Tiger**	壬 *Ren* 寅 *Yin* **Water Tiger**
★	✔	✔	✔	✔

★ Excellent   ✔ Auspicious   ● Fair   ▲ Inauspicious   ✕ Dire

十二值神 12 Day Officers	十二地支 Animal Sign of the Day	董公擇日解說 Dong Gong Description
成 *Cheng* **Success**	卯 *Mao* **Rabbit** Yin Wood 	天喜。乙卯、辛卯有黄羅、紫檀、鑾與寶蓋、綠蔭、馬注星蓋照,瓊玉,金寶、天帝,聚寶,諸吉星照臨,利造作、入宅、開張、出行、婚姻等事,主益子孫、旺田產、進横財、增房屋、生貴子,大吉。餘卯次吉。 In addition to the presence of the auspicious Sky Happiness 天喜 Star, Yi Mao 乙卯 and Xin Mao 辛卯 Days are also accompanied by the presence of the following positive Stars: The Yellow Spiral 黃羅, Purple Sandalwood 紫檀, Precious Cover 寶蓋, Prosperous Inheritance 祿蔭, Sky Horse 馬注星, Precious Jade 瓊玉, Golden Treasure 金寶, Heavenly King 天帝 and Converging Treasure 聚寶. This situation makes such days suitable for renovation, moving into a new house, opening a new business, travel and marriage. Used well, one will witness one's material wealth and assets increasing, as well as one's offspring prospering. Do note that the other Mao 卯 (Rabbit) Days are considered second-best options.

董公擇日要覽

Rabbit

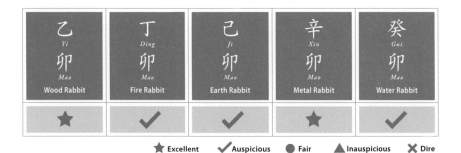

乙 *Yi* 卯 *Mao* Wood Rabbit	丁 *Ding* 卯 *Mao* Fire Rabbit	己 *Ji* 卯 *Mao* Earth Rabbit	辛 *Xin* 卯 *Mao* Metal Rabbit	癸 *Gui* 卯 *Mao* Water Rabbit
★	✔	✔	★	✔

★ Excellent   ✔ Auspicious   ● Fair   ▲ Inauspicious   ✖ Dire

董公擇日要覽

辰
Dragon

十二值神 12 Day Officers	十二地支 Animal Sign of the Day	董公擇日解説 Dong Gong Description
收 *Shou* **Receive**	辰 *Chen* **Dragon** **Yang Earth** 	甲辰天德,丙辰、壬辰三日次吉,利偷方修理,主益田産、旺六畜,亦宜安葬、營爲。庚辰爲騰蛇、朱雀,不宜用。戊辰亦不吉。 The Jia Chen 甲辰 Day is accompanied by the Heavenly Virtue 天德 Star, while Bing Chen 丙辰 and Ren Chen 壬辰 Days are considered 'secondary' auspicious days. Activities or endeavors undertaken on these days will bring about an improvement in material fortunes and an amassment of wealth and other worldly assets. Burials may also be undertaken on these days. However, the Geng Chen 庚辰 Day is rendered unusable by the presence of the Surging Snake 騰蛇 and Red Phoenix 朱雀 Stars and similarly, the Wu Chen 戊辰 Day is also unsuitable for use.

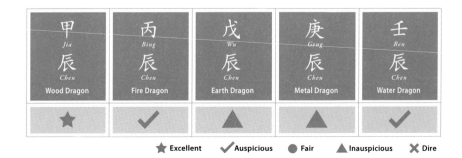

甲 *Jia* 辰 *Chen* **Wood Dragon**	丙 *Bing* 辰 *Chen* **Fire Dragon**	戊 *Wu* 辰 *Chen* **Earth Dragon**	庚 *Geng* 辰 *Chen* **Metal Dragon**	壬 *Ren* 辰 *Chen* **Water Dragon**
★	✓	▲	▲	✓

★ **Excellent**　✓ **Auspicious**　● **Fair**　▲ **Inauspicious**　✗ **Dire**

董
公
擇
日
要
覽

巳
Snake

十二值神 12 Day Officers	十二地支 Animal Sign of the Day	董公擇日解説 Dong Gong Description
開 *Kai* **Open**	巳 *Si* Snake Yin Fire	天成，天賊。福生宜結福，乙巳、癸巳，興工、動土、入宅、開張次吉。餘巳不利，犯月厭，凶。 The Heavenly Success 天成 and Heavenly Ripper 天賊 Stars govern this day, thereby facilitating the accumulation of prosperous Qi. Yi Si 乙巳 and Gui Si 癸巳 Days are the next best choice of days to commence construction, move into a new house, or launch or officiate an event. These days may hence be used if there is no other suitable substitute of days, although they should only be utilized very carefully for specific purposes.

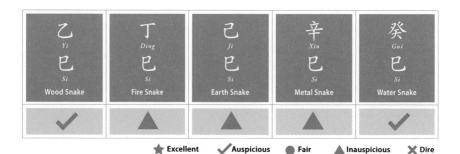

乙 *Yi* 巳 *Si* Wood Snake	丁 *Ding* 巳 *Si* Fire Snake	己 *Ji* 巳 *Si* Earth Snake	辛 *Xin* 巳 *Si* Metal Snake	癸 *Gui* 巳 *Si* Water Snake
✔	▲	▲	▲	✔

★ **Excellent**   ✔ **Auspicious**   ● **Fair**   ▲ **Inauspicious**   ✖ **Dire**

董公擇日要覽

十二值神 12 Day Officers	十二地支 Animal Sign of the Day	董公擇日解說 Dong Gong Description
閉 *Bi* **Close**	午 *Wu* **Horse** **Yang Fire** 🐎	往亡,甲午天赦,不係轉煞,又值月德,然亦只可小用,因有受死不全之氣。丙午葬日,如小小營爲亦次吉。壬午、庚午小葬次吉,餘事不宜。戊午重喪,不可用。 This day is also known as an Emptiness 往亡 Day. However, the Jia Wu 甲午 Day is accompanied by the positive Heavenly Pardon 天赦 and Monthly Virtue Stars, which act to negate or neutralize the ill-effects of the Drilling Sha 轉煞 that is also present. The Bing Wu 丙午 Day can be used for affairs of lesser significance, while Ren Wu 壬午 and Geng Wu 庚午 Days can be utilized for even more insignificant matters. Avoid using a Wu Wu 戊午 Day, though.

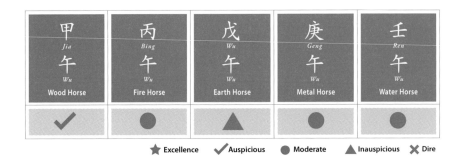

甲 *Jia* 午 *Wu* Wood Horse	丙 *Bing* 午 *Wu* Fire Horse	戊 *Wu* 午 *Wu* Earth Horse	庚 *Geng* 午 *Wu* Metal Horse	壬 *Ren* 午 *Wu* Water Horse
✔	●	▲	●	●

⭐ **Excellence**　✔ **Auspicious**　● **Moderate**　▲ **Inauspicious**　✖ **Dire**

Seventh Month 七月

August 8th – September 7th

Monkey 申 (Shen) Month

Seventh Month 七月

August 8th – September 7th
Monkey 申 (Shen) Month

月德壬、月恩壬，母倉辰戌丑未。天德合戌。

The Monthly Virtue 月德 and Monthly Benevolence 月恩 Stars preside over Ren 壬 Days, while the Motherly Storage 母倉 Star lords over Dragon 辰 (Chen), Dog 戌 (Xu), Ox 丑 (Chou) and Goat 未 (Wei) Days. Similarly, the Heavenly Virtue 天德 Star exerts its strongest influence on Wu 戊 Days to bring about positive outcomes.

立秋：立秋前一日爲四絕。

The `Coming of Autumn' 立秋 (Li Qiu)

One day before Li Qiu (Coming of Autumn) is one of the Four Extinction 四絕 Days.

處暑：立秋後三煞在南巳午未方，忌修造、動土。

'Heat Ends' 處暑 (Chu Shu)

The day after Li Qiu 立秋 (The Coming of Autumn) ends also marks the commencement of Chu Shu 處暑 (Heat Ends). Accordingly, the Three Killings 三煞 (San Sha) Affliction can be found in the South sector. Hence, refrain from digging or 'disturbing' the ground in the Southeast 3 巳 (Si – SE3), South 2 午 (Wu – S2) and Southwest 1 未 (Wei – SW1) directions, lest the harmful energies of the Three Killings is unleashed.

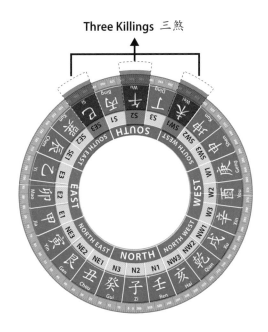

Three Killings 三煞

十二值神 12 Day Officers	十二地支 Animal Sign of the Day	董公擇日解説 Dong Gong Description
建 *Jian* **Establish**	申 *Shen* **Monkey** **Yang Metal** 	戊申爲天赦，甲申、壬申爲比和之日，只宜埋葬，然月建上凶，不可用。庚申煞入中宮，丙申五行無氣，更主凶。 The Wu Shen 戊申 Day contains the auspicious Heavenly Pardon 天赦 Star, while Jia Shen 甲申 and Ren Shen 壬申 Days are equally suitable for burials. Note, however, that Sha (Killing) Qi enters the Central Palace on a Geng Shen 庚申 Day and on a Bing Shen 丙申 Day, the Five Elements are devoid of any Qi. As such, using any of these days will only result in disappointment and catastrophe.

甲 *Jia* 申 *Shen* Wood Monkey	丙 *Bing* 申 *Shen* Fire Monkey	戊 *Wu* 申 *Shen* Earth Monkey	庚 *Geng* 申 *Shen* Metal Monkey	壬 *Ren* 申 *Shen* Water Monkey
✔	▲	★	▲	✔

★ Excellent ✔ Auspicious ● Fair ▲ Inauspicious ✘ Dire

十二值神 12 Day Officers	十二地支 Animal Sign of the Day	董公擇日解説 Dong Gong Description
除 *Chu* **Remove**	酉 *You* **Rooster** **Yin Metal** 	往亡。乙酉無凶星,開山、斬草、安葬、興工、定磉、拴架、修方、造作、出行、開張、入宅、移居,次吉。己酉九土鬼,丁酉凶敗,癸酉伏劍之金,北方黑煞將軍之氣,損傷、凶惡。辛酉天地轉煞,正四廢,凶。 This is considered an Emptiness 往亡 Day. However, there are no negative stars affecting Yi You 乙酉 Days and hence, they may be used for opening or exploring new land, quarrying works, landscaping projects, burial, starting construction work, building a new house, repairs, travel, opening a business, entering a new house or migrating. The Ji You 己酉 Day is marked by the presence of the Nine Earth Ghost 九土鬼 Star, while Ding You 丁酉 and Gui You 癸酉 Days should be avoided, especially as the latter harbors 'dulled' Metal Sword Qi. Such a combination only spells harm and disastrous outcomes. In addition, a Xin You 辛酉 Day is also known as a Pure Direct Day 正四廢, containing Heaven and Earth Drilling Sha 天地轉煞 – making it an inauspicious day for activities or endeavors.

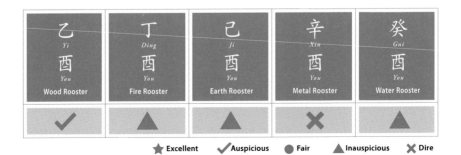

乙 *Yi* 酉 *You* Wood Rooster	丁 *Ding* 酉 *You* Fire Rooster	己 *Ji* 酉 *You* Earth Rooster	辛 *Xin* 酉 *You* Metal Rooster	癸 *Gui* 酉 *You* Water Rooster
✔	▲	▲	✖	▲

★ Excellent ✔ Auspicious ● Fair ▲ Inauspicious ✖ Dire

十二值神 12 Day Officers	十二地支 Animal Sign of the Day	董公擇日解說 Dong Gong Description
滿 *Man* **Full**	戌 *Xu* Dog Yang Earth 	天富、天賊。丙戌、壬戌，朱雀、勾絞、白虎入中宮，用之主招官司、是非、家門衰敗、損人口、疾病纏綿，一起一倒，不離床席，大凶，忌之。 While the Heavenly Fortune 天富 and Heavenly Thief 天賊 Stars are simultaneously present, Bing Xu 丙戌 and Ren Xu 壬戌 Days also harbor the negative Red Phoenix 朱雀, Grappling Hook 勾絞 and White Tiger 白虎 Stars. The presence of such stars forewarn of legal entanglements, hassles and malicious gossip, as well as worsening health amongst family members. As such, do not use these days at all costs.

戌 Dog

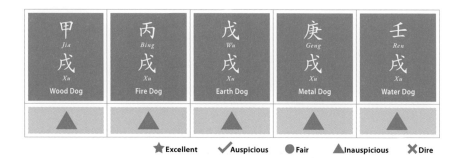

甲戌 *Jia Xu* Wood Dog	丙戌 *Bing Xu* Fire Dog	戊戌 *Wu Xu* Earth Dog	庚戌 *Geng Xu* Metal Dog	壬戌 *Ren Xu* Water Dog
▲	▲	▲	▲	▲

★Excellent ✓Auspicious ●Fair ▲Inauspicious ✗Dire

十二值神 12 Day Officers	十二地支 Animal Sign of the Day	董公擇日解説 Dong Gong Description
平 *Ping* **Balance**	亥 *Hai* Pig Yin Water 	螣蛇纏繞,損人口、遭官司、口舌、橫禍,凶。 The inauspicious Surging Snake 螣蛇 Star bedevils this day, resulting in family members being easily injured, legal problems arising, accidents and mishaps occurring and the interference of petty-minded people. This is a very inauspicious day and should therefore be avoided.

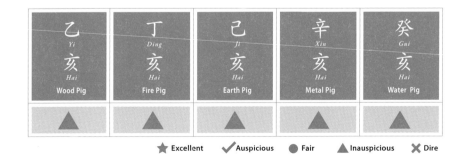

乙 *Yi* 亥 *Hai* Wood Pig	丁 *Ding* 亥 *Hai* Fire Pig	己 *Ji* 亥 *Hai* Earth Pig	辛 *Xin* 亥 *Hai* Metal Pig	癸 *Gui* 亥 *Hai* Water Pig
▲	▲	▲	▲	▲

★ Excellent   ✓ Auspicious   ● Fair   ▲ Inauspicious   ✗ Dire

董公擇日要覽

子
Rat

十二值神 12 Day Officers	十二地支 Animal Sign of the Day	董公擇日解說 Dong Gong Description
定 *Ding* **Stable**	子 *Zi* Rat Yang Water 	丙子潔淨之水，又遇旺地，值黃羅、紫檀星蓋照，宜修造、安葬、娶親、開張、出行、入宅、興工、動土，主子孫繁昌富盛，大吉。庚子、戊子次吉。壬子木打寶瓶水，不逢時，乃葉落之木。甲子自死之金，此值秋金，殺氣方盛，不宜用也。 Water Qi is pure and serene on Bing Zi 丙子 Days, therefore resulting in prosperous Qi being produced. The presence of the auspicious Yellow Spiral 黃羅 and Purple Sandalwood 紫檀 Stars enhance the positive energies of these days, making them suitable for renovation, burial, proposing marriage, opening a business, travel, moving into a new house, and ground-digging works. Used well, one's children and descendants will prosper accordingly, due to the extremely auspicious energies present. Meanwhile, Geng Zi 庚子 and Wu Zi 戊子 Days may also be considered as second-best options. However, the Qi is neither conducive nor good on Ren Zi 壬子 Days. In fact, the Qi on Jia Zi 甲子 Days is extremely weak and totally unusable.

甲 *Jia* 子 *Zi* Wood Rat	丙 *Bing* 子 *Zi* Fire Rat	戊 *Wu* 子 *Zi* Earth Rat	庚 *Geng* 子 *Zi* Metal Rat	壬 *Ren* 子 *Zi* Water Rat
▲	★ .	✔	✔	▲

★ Excellent　✔ Auspicious　● Fair　▲ Inauspicious　✘ Dire

十二值神 12 Day Officers	十二地支 Animal Sign of the Day	董公擇日解説 Dong Gong Description
執 *Zhi* **Initiate**	丑 *Chou* Ox Yin Earth 	有朱雀,勾絞螣蛇,白虎之煞不宜用事。犯之主退財、傷人口。丁丑癸丑煞入中宫,切不可用。乃受命之日也。有朱雀、勾絞、螣蛇、白虎之煞,不宜用事,犯之主退財、傷人口。丁丑、癸丑煞入中宫,尤切不可用,乃受命之日也。 The presence of the negative Red Phoenix 朱雀 and Grappling Hook 勾絞 Stars only serve to worsen the adversity of the Snake 螣蛇 and White Tiger 白虎 Sha Qi. Inadvertently tapping into such an inauspicious combination will only result in loss of wealth or worse still, a death in the family. In particular, avoid Ding Chou 丁丑 and Gui Chou 癸丑 Days for all important activities or endeavors, for their harmful energies will only cause people to be hurt or wealth to be lost.

乙 *Yi* 丑 *Chou* Wood Ox	丁 *Ding* 丑 *Chou* Fire Ox	己 *Ji* 丑 *Chou* Earth Ox	辛 *Xin* 丑 *Chou* Metal Ox	癸 *Gui* 丑 *Chou* Water Ox
▲	✕	▲	▲	✕

★ Excellent ✓ Auspicious ● Fair ▲ Inauspicious ✕ Dire

十二值神 12 Day Officers	十二地支 Animal Sign of the Day	董公擇日解説 Dong Gong Description
破 *Po* **Destruction**	寅 *Yin* **Tiger** **Yang Wood** 	甲寅正四廢,凶。庚寅、戊寅、丙寅皆不吉,諸事不宜,主官司、退財、人口啾唧。惟壬寅一日有月德,只利安葬也。 The Jia Yin 甲寅 Day is also one of the Four Direct 正四廢 Days. It is an inauspicious day, on which any important endeavors or activities should not be conducted. Furthermore, Geng Yin 庚寅, Wu Yin 戊寅 and Bing Yin 丙寅 Days are only unsuitable, as they display a tendency to attract legal issues and leakage of wealth. Only the Ren Yin 壬寅 Day, accompanied by the presence of the Monthly Virtue 月德 Star, is suitable for burials.

甲 *Jia* 寅 *Yin* **Wood Tiger**	丙 *Bing* 寅 *Yin* **Fire Tiger**	戊 *Wu* 寅 *Yin* **Earth Tiger**	庚 *Geng* 寅 *Yin* **Metal Tiger**	壬 *Ren* 寅 *Yin* **Water Tiger**
✖	▲	▲	▲	✔

★ Excellent   ✔ Auspicious   ● Fair   ▲ Inauspicious   ✖ Dire

董公擇日要覽

Rabbit

十二值神 12 Day Officers	十二地支 Animal Sign of the Day	董公擇日解説 Dong Gong Description
危 *Wei* **Danger**	卯 *Mao* **Rabbit** **Yin Wood** 	乙卯正四廢,凶。癸卯、丁卯有天德、黄羅、紫檀、金銀庫樓、玉堂聚寶星蓋照,宜起造、婚姻、嫁娶、興工、動土、定磉、拴架、開張、出行、作倉庫、牛羊欄圈、主家業昌盛,人口興旺、生貴子、進横財、富貴雍穆。餘卯日次吉。 The Yi Mao 乙卯 Day is also known as one of the Four Direct 正四廢 Days, and therefore a negative day. However, Gui Mao 癸卯 and Ding Mao 丁卯 Days enjoy the support of the auspicious Heavenly Virtue 天德, Yellow Spiral 黄羅, Purple Sandalwood 紫檀, Golden Ingot 金銀, Storage 庫樓, Jade Hall 玉堂 and Converging Treasure 聚寶 Stars. The presence of these stars makes such days suitable for renovation, marriage, ground-digging, building or moving into a new house, launching a business, travel, or appointing a new officer or supervisor. Used properly, one will see one's family expanding in numbers, with the birth of noble children as well as an increase in wealth. All the other Mao 卯 (Rabbit) days are considered to be 'secondarily' useful for important endeavors or activities.

乙 *Yi* 卯 *Mao* Wood Rabbit	丁 *Ding* 卯 *Mao* Fire Rabbit	己 *Ji* 卯 *Mao* Earth Rabbit	辛 *Xin* 卯 *Mao* Metal Rabbit	癸 *Gui* 卯 *Mao* Water Rabbit
✖	★	✔	✔	★

★ Excellent　✔ Auspicious　● Fair　▲ Inauspicious　✖ Dire

十二值神 12 Day Officers	十二地支 Animal Sign of the Day	董公擇日解說 Dong Gong Description
 成 *Cheng* **Success**	 **辰** *Chen* **Dragon** **Yang Earth** 	天喜。壬辰月德，庚辰、丙辰三日皆是葬日，次吉，俱不宜大用。戊辰、甲辰白虎入中宮，犯之三、六、九年蕭索遭凶。 With the presence of the Sky Happiness 天喜 Star, accompanied by the Monthly Virtue Noble 月德 Star, the Ren Chen 壬辰 Day is a fairly auspicious one. In fact, Geng Chen 庚辰 and Bing Chen 丙辰 Days are also reasonably auspicious days, and can be used for endeavors or activities of lesser significance. They should not, however, be used for large-scale, important activities. Wu Chen 戊辰 and Jia Chen 甲辰 Days are unfortunately accompanied by the presence of the White Tiger 白虎 Star, which renders them inauspicious if used. Ill-fortune and poor luck will befall anyone who uses these days within a period of 3, 6 or 9 years.

Dragon

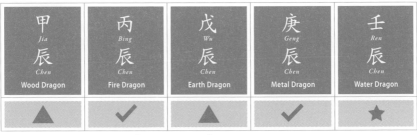

甲 *Jia* 辰 *Chen* Wood Dragon	丙 *Bing* 辰 *Chen* Fire Dragon	戊 *Wu* 辰 *Chen* Earth Dragon	庚 *Geng* 辰 *Chen* Metal Dragon	壬 *Ren* 辰 *Chen* Water Dragon
▲	✔	▲	✔	★

★ Excellent   ✔ Auspicious   ● Fair   ▲ Inauspicious   ✘ Dire

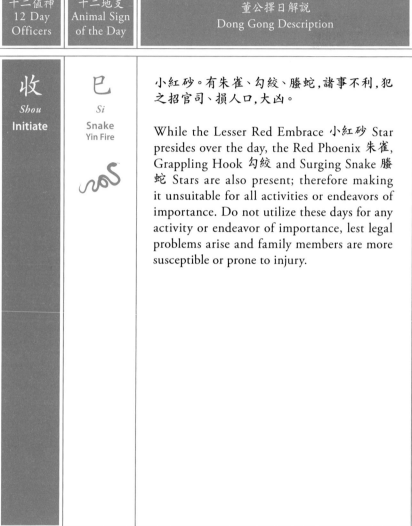

十二值神 12 Day Officers	十二地支 Animal Sign of the Day	董公擇日解説 Dong Gong Description
收 *Shou* **Initiate**	巳 *Si* Snake Yin Fire	小紅砂。有朱雀、勾絞、騰蛇，諸事不利，犯之招官司、損人口，大凶。 While the Lesser Red Embrace 小紅砂 Star presides over the day, the Red Phoenix 朱雀, Grappling Hook 勾絞 and Surging Snake 騰蛇 Stars are also present; therefore making it unsuitable for all activities or endeavors of importance. Do not utilize these days for any activity or endeavor of importance, lest legal problems arise and family members are more susceptible or prone to injury.

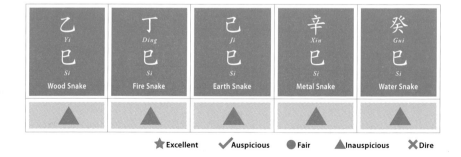

乙 *Yi* 巳 *Si* Wood Snake	丁 *Ding* 巳 *Si* Fire Snake	己 *Ji* 巳 *Si* Earth Snake	辛 *Xin* 巳 *Si* Metal Snake	癸 *Gui* 巳 *Si* Water Snake
▲	▲	▲	▲	▲

★ Excellent ✓ Auspicious ● Fair ▲ Inauspicious ✗ Dire

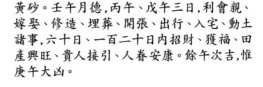

十二值神 12 Day Officers	十二地支 Animal Sign of the Day	董公擇日解説 Dong Gong Description
開 *Kai* **Open**	午 *Wu* **Horse** **Yang Fire** 	黄砂。壬午月德,丙午、戊午三日,利會親、嫁娶、修造、埋葬、開張、出行、入宅、動土諸事,六十日、一百二十日內招財、獲福、田產興旺、貴人接引、人眷安康。餘午次吉,惟庚午大凶。 While the Yellow Embrace 黃砂 Star is present, Ren Wu 壬午 Days also enjoy the positive energies of the Monthly Virtue 月德 Star, with Bing Wu 丙午 and Wu Wu 戊午 Days equally useable. Accordingly, such days are ideal for visiting relatives (customarily for proposing marriage), tying the knot, renovation, burial, business openings, travel, moving into a new house and ground-digging. The useful energies present on these days will bring about an increase in material wealth within 60 to 120 days, and there will also be no shortage of help from noble people in times of need. Jia Wu 甲午 Days may also be used, but Geng Wu 庚午 Days contain extremely inauspicious stars and should be avoided at all costs.

甲 *Jia* 午 *Wu* Wood Horse	丙 *Bing* 午 *Wu* Fire Horse	戊 *Wu* 午 *Wu* Earth Horse	庚 *Geng* 午 *Wu* Metal Horse	壬 *Ren* 午 *Wu* Water Horse
✔	★	★	▲	★

★ **Excellent**　　✔ **Auspicious**　　● **Fair**　　▲ **Inauspicious**　　✗ **Dire**

董公擇日要覽

Goat

十二值神 12 Day Officers	十二地支 Animal Sign of the Day	董公擇日解説 Dong Gong Description
閉 *Bi* **Close**	未 *Wei* **Goat** Yin Earth	天成、天賊，癸未火星天德、己未火星，宜修造、入宅、定磉、拴架、出行、開張次吉。辛未、丁未小用亦次吉。惟乙未煞入中宮，若在庭中釘丁、打物、喧嘩、吵叫等類，驚動神煞，刑於家長，損傷頭目手足，大凶，主血光湯火之厄、飛來禍事、小人侵害、官司、口舌纏綿。凡煞入中宮之日俱宜仿此選忌。 The Heavenly Success 天成 and Heavenly Thief 天賊 Stars exert their influence, and on Gui Wei 癸未 Days, the Fire Star 火星 and Heavenly Virtue 天德 Stars add their own effects. Accordingly, Ji Wei 己未 Day is ideal for renovation or moving into a new house. However, Xin Wei 辛未 and 丁未 Ding Wei Days can only be used for smaller-scale activities. Take note that on Yi Wei 乙未 Days, Sha (Killing) Qi pierces the very heart of the day, and hence such days should be avoided. Those who ignore this warning will encounter a blood-shedding disaster or worsening health, or find that elderly family members get hurt easily. From a materialistic perspective, they will also tend to lose their personal belongings more easily.

乙 *Yi* 未 *Wei* Wood Goat	丁 *Ding* 未 *Wei* Fire Goat	己 *Ji* 未 *Wei* Earth Goat	辛 *Xin* 未 *Wei* Metal Goat	癸 *Gui* 未 *Wei* Water Goat
▲	✔	★	✔	★

★ Excellent   ✔ Auspicious   ● Fair   ▲ Inauspicious   ✘ Dire

Eighth Month 八月

September 8th – October 7th

You 酉 (Rooster) Month

September 8th – October 7th
You 酉 (Rooster) Month

月德庚、月恩癸，母倉辰戌丑未。天德合亥。

The Monthly Virtue 月德 Star is present on Geng 庚 Days, the Monthly Benevolence 月恩 Star presides over Gui 癸 Days, while the Motherly Storage 母倉 Star exerts its positive influence on Dragon 辰 (Chen), Dog 戌 (Xu), Ox 丑 (Chou) and Goat 未 (Wei) Days. Similarly, the Qi of the Heavenly Virtue 天德 Star combines with the Qi on Pig 亥 (Hai) Days to bring about positive effects.

白露：秋分前一日爲四離。
'White Dew' 白露 (Bai Lu)
The period before Qiu Fen 秋分 (The Autumn Equinox) is known as Bai Lu 白露 (White Dew), and the eve of Qiu Fen is also one of the Four Separation 四離 Days.

秋分：白露後三煞在東，寅、卯、辰方忌修造、動土。
'Autumn Equinox' 秋分 (Qiu Fen)
The end of Bai Lu 白露 (White Dew) is marked by the commencement of the Autumn Equinox, during which the Three Killings 三煞 (San Sha) Affliction can be found in the East. In particular, refrain from digging or 'disturbing' the ground of the Northeast 3 寅 (Yin – NE3), East 2 卯 (Mao – E2) and Southeast 1 辰 (Chen – SE1) sectors, to prevent the harmful energies of the Three Killings from being unleashed.

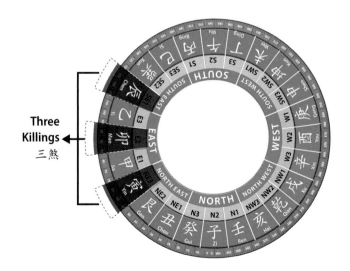

Three Killings 三煞

十二值神 12 Day Officers	十二地支 Animal Sign of the Day	董公擇日解説 Dong Gong Description
建 *Jian* **Establish**	酉 *You* Rooster Yin Metal	小紅砂、天成。乃五行自敗之時,百事招凶。兼犯天地轉煞,用之大凶,招官司、產厄、水火災厄、子孫逃散、敗家。 The presence of inauspicious stars supercedes the influence of the Lesser Red Embrace 小紅砂 and Heavenly Success 天成 Stars; resulting in the Qi of the Five Elements being weak. Avoid undertaking any important activities or endeavors on this day, more so when it also carries the Heaven and Earth Drilling Sha 天地轉煞. Such a combination only heightens the risk of lawsuits, miscarriage, as well as water and fire hazards. Worse still, one's descendents will have no affinity amongst themselves, resulting in a broken family and poor familial fortunes.

董公擇日要覽

酉 Rooster

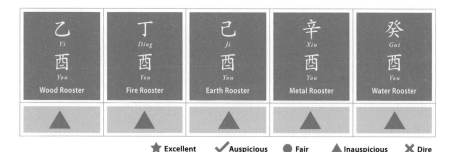

乙 *Yi* 酉 *You* Wood Rooster	丁 *Ding* 酉 *You* Fire Rooster	己 *Ji* 酉 *You* Earth Rooster	辛 *Xin* 酉 *You* Metal Rooster	癸 *Gui* 酉 *You* Water Rooster
▲	▲	▲	▲	▲

★ Excellent　✔ Auspicious　● Fair　▲ Inauspicious　✗ Dire

戌
Dog

十二值神 12 Day Officers	十二地支 Animal Sign of the Day	董公擇日解説 Dong Gong Description

除
Chu
Remove

戌
Xu
Dog
Yang Earth

庚戌,天、月二德,戊戌、甲戌,宜興工、動土、入宅、開張、婚姻等事,用之次吉。丙戌、壬戌,煞入中宮,諸事不宜,犯之主失財、冷退,大凶。

On Geng Xu 庚戌 Days, the auspicious Heavenly 天德 and Monthly Virtue 月德 Stars exert their positive influence. Furthermore, Wu Xu 戊戌 and Jia Xu 甲戌 Days are also good for commencing construction or groundbreaking works, moving into a new house, opening a new business and getting married. However, Sha (Killing) Qi renders Bing Xu 丙戌 and Ren Xu 壬戌 Days unsuitable for activities or endeavors of importance. Accordingly, loss of wealth will follow those who use such days for their endeavors.

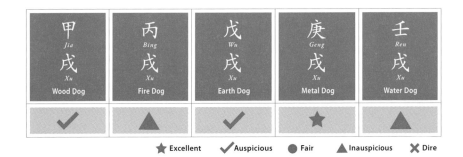

甲戌 *Jia* *Xu* Wood Dog	丙戌 *Bing* *Xu* Fire Dog	戊戌 *Wu* *Xu* Earth Dog	庚戌 *Geng* *Xu* Metal Dog	壬戌 *Ren* *Xu* Water Dog
✔	▲	✔	★	▲

★ Excellent   ✔ Auspicious   ● Fair   ▲ Inauspicious   ✘ Dire

董公擇日要覽

亥
Pig

十二值神 12 Day Officers	十二地支 Animal Sign of the Day	董公擇日解説 Dong Gong Description
滿 *Man* **Full**	亥 *Hai* Pig Yin Water	天富。乙亥、文昌,貴顯之星,丁亥、己亥有黃羅、紫檀、天皇、地皇、華彩操持、祿馬諸星蓋照,利起造、興工、動土、拴架、入宅、嫁娶、開張、出行、營爲諸事,大作大發,小作小發,六十日、一百二十日内,遲至週年便見獲財,成家生貴子、旺田產、興六畜。辛亥陰府決遺之日,非陽間所用。癸亥六甲窮日,五行無氣,不可用。 The Heavenly Fortune 天富 Star is present throughout the month, while Yi Hai 乙亥 Days are also blessed with the presence of the Literary Arts 文昌 Star. Likewise, Ding Hai 丁亥 and Ji Hai 己亥 Days are accompanied by good stars such as the Yellow Spiral 黃羅, Purple Sandalwood 紫檀, Heavenly Emperor 天皇, Magnificent Colors 華彩 and Prosperous Horse 祿馬 Stars. As such, these days are ideal for renovations, commencing construction, groundbreaking, building or moving into a new house, marriage, opening a business and travel. Activities or endeavors that are done on a large-scale will reap huge gains, while smaller-scale endeavors will enjoy gains on a corresponding scale. The positive results of using these days will be seen within 60 to 120 days, with a notable increase of wealth and assets as well as the birth of noble children. However, Xin Hai 辛亥 Days are overly Yin while a Gui Hai 癸亥 Day is also known as a Six Jia Weakness Day 六甲窮日 and is therefore devoid of Qi. Avoid using these days if possible.

乙 *Yi* 亥 *Hai* Wood Pig	丁 *Ding* 亥 *Hai* Fire Pig	己 *Ji* 亥 *Hai* Earth Pig	辛 *Xin* 亥 *Hai* Metal Pig	癸 *Gui* 亥 *Hai* Water Pig
★	★	★	▲	✖

★ Excellent ✔ Auspicious ● Fair ▲ Inauspicious ✖ Dire

十二值神 12 Day Officers	十二地支 Animal Sign of the Day	董公擇日解説 Dong Gong Description
平 *Ping* **Balance**	子 *Zi* Rat Yang Water 	往亡。朱雀、勾絞,招官司,損宅長。丙子乃水潔淨之時,庚子火星傍天、月二德,戊子等三日,利起造、嫁娶、入宅、出行、動土,用之卻吉。甲子亦有火星,但是北方黑煞之氣,壬子草木凋零之時,五行無氣,不可用。 This is known as an Emptiness Day 往亡, due to the presence of the negative Red Phoenix 朱雀 and Grappling Hook 勾絞 Stars. As such, it is the harbinger of legal issues and also causes the eldest family member to be more prone to injury. From a more positive angle, a Bing Zi 丙子 Day contains pure and serene Water Qi, while a Geng Zi 庚子 Day is marked by the presence of the auspicious Fire 火星 and Monthly Virtue 月二德 Stars. Such circumstances make these two days, including a Wu Zi 戊子 Day suitable for renovations, marriage, moving into a new house, travel or groundbreaking. However, while a Jia Zi 甲子 Day harbors the positive Fire Star, it is also adversely affected by the presence of Black Sha (Killing) Qi from the North, which renders it unsuitable for use. Lastly, the Qi of the Five Elements on a Ren Zi 壬子 Day is weak and therefore useless as well.

甲 *Jia* 子 *Zi* Wood Rat	丙 *Bing* 子 *Zi* Fire Rat	戊 *Wu* 子 *Zi* Earth Rat	庚 *Geng* 子 *Zi* Metal Rat	壬 *Ren* 子 *Zi* Water Rat
▲	✔	✔	✔	▲

★ Excellent   ✔ Auspicious   ● Fair   ▲ Inauspicious   ✗ Dire

董公擇日要覽

子
Rat

董公擇日要覽

十二值神 12 Day Officers	十二地支 Animal Sign of the Day	董公擇日解說 Dong Gong Description
定 *Ding* **Stable**	丑 *Chou* Ox Yin Earth 	辛丑、癸丑、乙丑、丁丑亦次吉,惟己丑不利,諸事不宜,犯之主疾病、生災,凶。 Xin Chou 辛丑, Gui Chou 癸丑, Yi Chou 乙丑 and Ding Chou 丁丑 Days are fairly useable, although Ji Chou 己丑 Days are inauspicious. As such, do not use Ji Chou Days for any important activities or endeavors, for this will result in one being especially susceptible to ailments and miscarriage.

丑
Ox

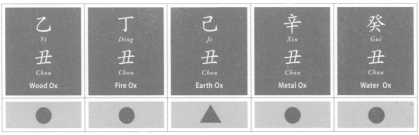

乙 *Yi* 丑 *Chou* Wood Ox	丁 *Ding* 丑 *Chou* Fire Ox	己 *Ji* 丑 *Chou* Earth Ox	辛 *Xin* 丑 *Chou* Metal Ox	癸 *Gui* 丑 *Chou* Water Ox
●	●	▲	●	●

★ Excellent　✔ Auspicious　● Fair　▲ Inauspicious　✕ Dire

董公擇日要覽

Tiger

十二值神 12 Day Officers	十二地支 Animal Sign of the Day	董公擇日解説 Dong Gong Description
執 *Zhi* **Initiate**	寅 *Yin* Tiger Yang Wood 	黃砂。庚寅、天月二德,有黃羅、紫檀、天皇、地皇、金銀寶藏、田塘、庫珠聚、祿帶馬鑾、與官曜眾吉星照臨,宜起造、嫁娶、動土、移居、開張、出行、旺田產、進橫財、增六畜、添人口、與子孫改門庭、家道隆昌。餘寅亦次吉可用,惟甲寅乃正四廢,凶。 The positive Yellow Embrace 黃砂 Star presides over this day. In addition, Geng Yin 庚寅 Day are also supported by the positive energies of the Heavenly 天德 and Earthly Virtue 月德 Stars. The combined presence of other auspicious stars including the Yellow Emperor 黃羅, Purple Sandalwood 紫檀, Heavenly Emperor 天皇, Earthly Emperor 地皇, Golden Ingot 金銀, Precious Treasure 寶藏, Field Pond 田塘, Storage Pearl 庫珠, Converging Wealth and Sky Horse 聚祿帶馬 Stars makes such days most ideal for renovation, marriage, groundbreaking, moving house, launching a business and travel. Their useful energies will contribute to an increase in one wealth, as well as the expansion and growth of one family. In addition, success will be forthcoming in business dealings and all other facets of life. Avoid using a Jia Yin 甲寅 Day, though, as it is one of the inauspicious Four Direct 正四廢 Days.

甲 *Jia* 寅 *Yin* **Wood Tiger**	丙 *Bing* 寅 *Yin* **Fire Tiger**	戊 *Wu* 寅 *Yin* **Earth Tiger**	庚 *Geng* 寅 *Yin* **Metal Tiger**	壬 *Ren* 寅 *Yin* **Water Tiger**
✘	✔	✔	★	✔

★ Excellent ✔ Auspicious ● Fair ▲ Inauspicious ✘ Dire

十二值神 12 Day Officers	十二地支 Animal Sign of the Day	董公擇日解説 Dong Gong Description
破 *Po* **Destruction**	卯 *Mao* **Rabbit** **Yin Wood** 	天賊。癸卯、己卯用事次吉,餘卯不利,有朱雀、勾絞,招官司、口舌,兼犯月厭之凶。乙卯正四廢,亦凶。 The Heavenly Thief 天賊 Star governs this day, thereby rendering only Gui Mao 癸卯 and Ji Mao 己卯 Days fairly useable. The remaining Mao 卯 (Rabbit) Days are, however, inauspicious due to the presence of the negative Red Phoenix 朱雀 and Grappling Hook 勾絞 Stars. These inauspicious stars are the harbingers of lawsuits and malicious gossip. Avoid using a Yi Mao 乙卯 Day in particular, as it is one of the Four Direct 正四廢 Days and hence an extremely inauspicious one.

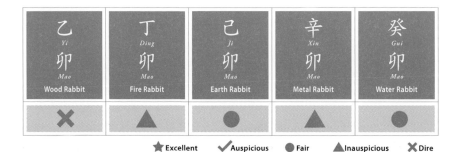

乙 *Yi* 卯 *Mao* **Wood Rabbit**	丁 *Ding* 卯 *Mao* **Fire Rabbit**	己 *Ji* 卯 *Mao* **Earth Rabbit**	辛 *Xin* 卯 *Mao* **Metal Rabbit**	癸 *Gui* 卯 *Mao* **Water Rabbit**
✖	▲	●	▲	●

★ Excellent   ✔ Auspicious   ● Fair   ▲ Inauspicious   ✖ Dire

董公擇日要覽

Dragon

十二值神 12 Day Officers	十二地支 Animal Sign of the Day	董公擇日解説 Dong Gong Description
危 *Wei* **Danger**	辰 *Chen* Dragon Yang Earth	壬辰水潔淨之時，丙辰，宜破土、興工、開張、出行、入宅、婚姻，百事順利，大吉。戊辰，草木凋零，庚辰天地相疑，不吉。甲辰煞入中宮，大凶。 Water Qi on a Ren Chen 壬辰 Day is purely, serene and well-balanced. As such, this day is ideal for renovations, opening a business, travel, moving into a new house or getting married. Bing Chen 丙辰 Days are moderately suitable for groundbreaking, starting a fresh endeavor, opening a business, traveling, enter a new house and marriage. The outcomes of all activities undertaken on these days will be auspicious. Note, however, that Wu Chen 戊辰 Geng Chen 庚辰 and Jia Chen 甲辰 are not useable – particularly Jia Chen Days, when Sha (Killing) Qi can be found in the Central Palace.

甲 *Jia* 辰 *Chen* Wood Dragon	丙 *Bing* 辰 *Chen* Fire Dragon	戊 *Wu* 辰 *Chen* Earth Dragon	庚 *Geng* 辰 *Chen* Metal Dragon	壬 *Ren* 辰 *Chen* Water Dragon
▲	✔	▲	▲	★

 ★ Excellent ✔ Auspicious ● Fair ▲ Inauspicious ✘ Dire

董
公
擇
日
要
覽

Snake

十二值神 12 Day Officers	十二地支 Animal Sign of the Day	董公擇日解說 Dong Gong Description
成 *Cheng* **Success**	巳 *Si* Snake Yin Fire	天喜。乙巳、己巳,有紫檀、帶祿驛馬,集聚曲堂諸星蓋照,宜婚姻、入宅、興工、動工、開張、出行、起造、豬牛羊棧均大吉,百事順利,餘巳日次吉. The presence of the Sky Happiness 天喜 Star further enhances the positive energies on Yi Si 乙巳 and Ji Si 己巳 Days, which already enjoy the auspicious energies of the Purple Sandalwood 紫檀 and Prosperous Sky Horse 帶祿驛馬 Stars. Accordingly, such days are suitable for marriage, moving into a new house, commencing construction work, groundbreaking, launching a business and travel. The remaining Si 巳 (Snake) Days, however, should only be regarded as second-best options.

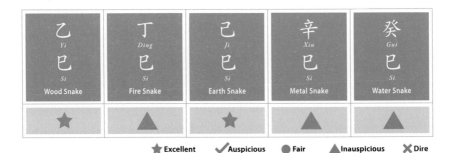

乙 *Yi* 巳 *Si* Wood Snake	丁 *Ding* 巳 *Si* Fire Snake	己 *Ji* 巳 *Si* Earth Snake	辛 *Xin* 巳 *Si* Metal Snake	癸 *Gui* 巳 *Si* Water Snake
★	▲	★	▲	▲

★ Excellent ✓ Auspicious ● Fair ▲ Inauspicious ✗ Dire

十二值神 12 Day Officers	十二地支 Animal Sign of the Day	董公擇日解説 Dong Gong Description
收 *Shou* Receive	午 *Wu* Horse Yang Fire 	福生，可惜建破來沖刑，壬午火星用事次吉。丙午動土、安葬、一切營爲亦次吉。惟戊午有火星，不利，庚午亦不利。犯之損子孫、招官非、冷退，凶。甲午日未詳。 Although the Prosperous Growth 福生 Star is present, the unfortunate occurrence of a Destruction, Clash and Punishment relationship – all simultaneously – tarnish whatever positive energies this day might otherwise have. However, a Ren Wu 壬午 Day is supported by the positive energies of the Fire Star 火星 and is therefore considered above-average in terms of usability. Likewise, Bing Wu 丙午 Days may be used for groundbreaking and burial, while Wu Wu 戊午 Days are also accompanied by the presence of the Fire Star. However, Geng Wu 庚午 Days are inauspicious, and only spell harm for one's descendents as well as the threat of legal problems. Similarly, the Qi on a Jia Wu 甲午 Day is fickle, at best.

甲 *Jia* 午 *Wu* Wood Horse	丙 *Bing* 午 *Wu* Fire Horse	戊 *Wu* 午 *Wu* Earth Horse	庚 *Geng* 午 *Wu* Metal Horse	壬 *Ren* 午 *Wu* Water Horse
▲	✔	✔	▲	★

★ Excellent   ✔ Auspicious   ● Fair   ▲ Inauspicious   ✖ Dire

董公擇日要覽

十二值神 12 Day Officers	十二地支 Animal Sign of the Day	董公擇日解説 Dong Gong Description
開 *Kai* **Open**	 *Wei* **Goat** **Yin Earth** 	丁未、己未、辛未、癸未,均是次吉之日,只宜斬草、開山、掘樹、安葬等事。惟乙未百事不利,凶,內犯棄敗死絕之鄉。 Ding Wei 丁未, Ji Wei 己未, Xin Wei 辛未 and Gui Wei 癸未 Days are fairly usable, but care should be taken to confine their usage to only activities such as burial, cutting trees or excavating mountains. Do not use Yi Wei 乙未 especially for activities of significance, for their resultant outcomes will be disastrous.

未
Goat

乙 *Yi* 未 *Wei* **Wood Goat**	丁 *Ding* 未 *Wei* **Fire Goat**	己 *Ji* 未 *Wei* **Earth Goat**	辛 *Xin* 未 *Wei* **Metal Goat**	癸 *Gui* 未 *Wei* **Water Goat**
▲	✔	✔	✔	✔

★ Excellent ✔ Auspicious ● Fair ▲ Inauspicious ✖ Dire

十二值神 12 Day Officers	十二地支 Animal Sign of the Day	董公擇日解説 Dong Gong Description
閉 *Bi* **Close**	申 *Shen* **Monkey** **Yang Metal** 	戊申天赦,庚申、丙申,天、月二德,宜出行、修方、動土、興工、定磉、拵架、婚姻、入宅、安葬、開張、作倉庫、牛羊豬欄,利子孫、旺田產、進橫財、家門發達,上吉。甲申、壬申次吉。 The Wu Shen 戊申 Day is also known as the Heavenly Pardon 天赦 Day. Other auspicious days include Geng Shen 庚申 and Bing Shen 丙申 Days, which enjoy the positive energies exerted by the Heavenly 天德 and Monthly 月德 Virtue Stars. As such, these days are ideal for travel, groundbreaking, building or moving into a new house, marriage, burial or launching a business. Their positive consequences include an increase in wealth and good descendant luck. Use these days where possible, due to their extremely auspicious energies. Jia Shen 甲申 and Ren Shen 壬申 Days remain second-tier options.

Monkey

甲 *Jia* 申 *Shen* **Wood Monkey**	丙 *Bing* 申 *Shen* **Fire Monkey**	戊 *Wu* 申 *Shen* **Earth Monkey**	庚 *Geng* 申 *Shen* **Metal Monkey**	壬 *Ren* 申 *Shen* **Water Monkey**
	★	★	★	

★ Excellent   ✔ Auspicious   ● Fair   ▲ Inauspicious   ✖ Dire

Ninth Month 九月

October 8th - November 6th

Dog 戌 (Xu) Month

October 8th – November 6th
Dog 戌 (Xu) Month

月德丙、月恩庚，母倉辰戌丑未。天德合辛。

Bing 丙 Days are accompanied by the Monthly Virtue 月德 Star, Geng 庚 Days the Monthly Benevolence 月恩 Star, while Dragon 辰 (Chen), Dog 戌 (Xu), Ox 丑 (Chou) and Goat 未 (Wei) Days are supported by the energies of the Motherly Storage 母倉 Star. Similarly, the Qi of the Heavenly Virtue 天德 Star combines with the energies present on Xin 辛 Days to bring about good outcomes.

寒露：寒露後三煞在北。

'Cold Dew' 寒露 (Han Lu)

When Han Lu 寒露 (Cold Dew) has passed, the Three Killings 三煞 (San Sha) Affliction shall be found in the North sector.

霜降：亥、子、丑方忌修造、動土。

'Frosting' 霜降 (Shuang Jiang)

Shuang Jiang (Frosting) follows in the wake of Han Lu. Do not renovate, dig or disturb the ground in the Northwest 3 亥 (Hai – NW3), North 2 子 (Zi – N2) and Northeast 1 丑 (Chou – NE1) sectors, lest the harmful energies of the Three Killings are unleashed.

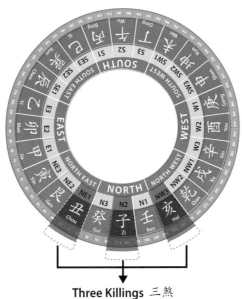

Three Killings 三煞

十二值神 12 Day Officers	十二地支 Animal Sign of the Day	董公擇日解説 Dong Gong Description
建 *Jian* **Establish**	戌 *Xu* **Dog** Yang Earth 	丙戌，天、月二德卻吉。餘戌不利，若用之主損財，貧窮大凶。 Bing Xu 丙戌 Days are supported by the positive energies of the Heavenly Virtue 天德 and Monthly Virtue 月德 Stars. The other Xu 戌 (Dog) days are, however, inauspicious, and embarking on any significant endeavors or activities on such days will only result in one's wealth being lost, in addition to being plagued by catastrophes.

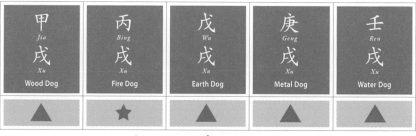

甲 *Jia* 戌 *Xu* Wood Dog	丙 *Bing* 戌 *Xu* Fire Dog	戊 *Wu* 戌 *Xu* Earth Dog	庚 *Geng* 戌 *Xu* Metal Dog	壬 *Ren* 戌 *Xu* Water Dog
▲	★	▲	▲	▲

★ Excellent   ✔ Auspicious   ● Fair   ▲ Inauspicious   ✖ Dire

十二值神 12 Day Officers	十二地支 Animal Sign of the Day	董公擇日解説 Dong Gong Description
除 *Chu* **Remove**	亥 *Hai* **Pig** Yin Water 	天成。乙亥、丁亥,宜起造、開張、嫁娶、入宅、出行、動土,諸事大吉,主子孫興旺,永遠富貴。癸亥六甲窮日,不可用。辛亥純陰之氣,非陽間所用。己亥火星,惟起造嫁娶吉。 The presence of the Heavenly Success 天成 Star renders Yi Hai 乙亥 and Ding Hai 丁亥 Days particularly suitable for renovations, opening a business, marriage, moving into a new house, travel and groundbreaking, as the outcome of all endeavors will be auspicious. Furthermore, using these days augurs well for good descendant luck and long term wealth. However, a Gui Hai 癸亥 Day is considered a Six Jia Weakness Day 六甲窮日, while a Xin Hai 辛亥 Day is overly Yin in Qi. As such, refrain from using both these days. A Ji Hai 己亥 Day is accompanied by the presence of the Fire Star, making it usable for marriage.

乙 *Yi* 亥 *Hai* Wood Pig	丁 *Ding* 亥 *Hai* Fire Pig	己 *Ji* 亥 *Hai* Earth Pig	辛 *Xin* 亥 *Hai* Metal Pig	癸 *Gui* 亥 *Hai* Water Pig
★	★	✔	✖	✖

★ Excellent ✔ Auspicious ● Fair ▲ Inauspicious ✖ Dire

董公擇日要覽

十二值神 12 Day Officers	十二地支 Animal Sign of the Day	董公擇日解説 Dong Gong Description
滿 *Man* **Full**	子 *Zi* Rat Yang Water 	黃砂、天富。丙子,水潔淨之時,兼有天、月二德、黃羅、紫檀、天皇、地皇、層霄連珠、祿馬,諸吉星蓋照,宜嫁娶、開張、出行、入宅、興工、動土、定碻、拴架、安葬、益家門、利子孫、旺田產、進六畜、增橫財,六十日、一百二十日內便驗。壬子木打寶瓶,草木凋零,大凶。餘子日不宜用事。甲子有黃羅、紫檀星蓋照,可用。

Rat

The auspicious Yellow Embrace 黃砂 and Heavenly Fortune 天富 Stars are present throughout the month. Better still, Water Qi on Bing Zi 丙子 Days is serene and pure, further augmented by the presence of the positive Heavenly 天德 and Monthly 月德 Virtue Stars as well as the Yellow Spiral 黃羅, Purple Sandalwood 紫檀, Heavenly Emperor 天皇, Earthly Emperor 地皇, Tiered Clouds 層霄, Linked Pearls 連珠 and Prosperous Horse 祿馬 Stars. This makes Bing Zi Days especially good for marriage, launching a business, travel, moving into or building a new house, groundbreaking and burial. The positive energies on such days augur well for descendant luck and all other endeavors intended to increase and amass material wealth and assets. The favorable results from using them may be seen within 60 to 120 days. Jia Zi 甲子 Days may also be used as a second option, as they harbor positive stars like the Yellow Spiral 黃羅 and Purple Sandalwood 紫檀. Take note, however, that Wood Qi is severely impaired on Ren Zi 壬子 Days, rendering them extremely inauspicious. One should also refrain from using the other Zi 子 (Rat) days.

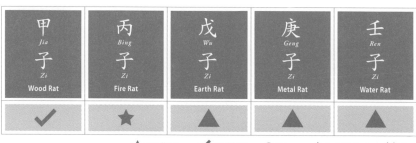

甲 *Jia* 子 *Zi* Wood Rat	丙 *Bing* 子 *Zi* Fire Rat	戊 *Wu* 子 *Zi* Earth Rat	庚 *Geng* 子 *Zi* Metal Rat	壬 *Ren* 子 *Zi* Water Rat
✔	★	▲	▲	▲

★ Excellent ✔ Auspicious ● Fair ▲ Inauspicious ✖ Dire

十二值神 12 Day Officers	十二地支 Animal Sign of the Day	董公擇日解説 Dong Gong Description
平 *Ping* **Balance**	丑 *Chou* Ox Yin Earth	小紅砂。有福生，惜被月建沖破，朱雀、勾絞，招官司、拮据，諸事不利。若小小營爲，内有福生，亦僅可用，然終無利益。大用之立見其凶。丁丑、癸丑，煞入中官，更凶。 The Lesser Red Embrace 小紅砂 Star presides over the day, alongside the Prosperous Growth 福生 Star. Unfortunately, their combined energies are neutralized and clashed away by the inauspicious Yu Jian 月建 Star. The added presence of other negative stars such as the Red Phoenix 朱雀 and Grappling Hook 勾絞 will result in lawsuits arising and strained financial situations, if such days are used for important activities or endeavors. Accordingly, avoid undertaking any major or significant activities on such days, as their outcomes will only be adverse. However, matters of little importance may be undertaken on such days, due to the soothing effect of the Prosperous Growth 福生 Star. The energies on Ding Chou 丁丑 and Gui Chou 癸丑 are particularly detrimental, so avoid using these days at all costs.

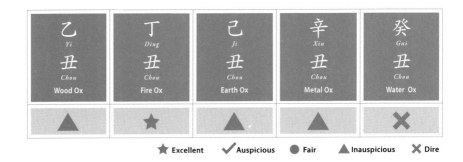

★ **Excellent**　✔ **Auspicious**　● **Fair**　▲ **Inauspicious**　✖ **Dire**

董公擇日要覽

Tiger

十二值神 12 Day Officers	十二地支 Animal Sign of the Day	董公擇日解説 Dong Gong Description
定 *Ding* **Stable**	寅 *Yin* Tiger Yang Wood 	丙寅,天、月二德,庚寅、戊寅,有黃羅、紫檀、天皇、地皇,諸星蓋照,宜起造、嫁娶、出行、入宅、開張,一切諸事,主進財,生貴子、興家道、旺六畜,大吉。壬寅犯月厭,受死無解,但丙寅、戊寅、庚寅三日,雖犯月厭,内有諸吉星蓋照,故大吉。惟甲寅正四廢,凶。 Bing Yin 丙寅 Days are accompanied by the Heavenly 天德 and Monthly Virtue 月德 Stars, while Geng Yin 庚寅 and Wu Yin 戊寅 Days are similarly supported by the positive energies of the auspicious Yellow Spiral 黃羅, Purple Sandalwood 紫檀, Heavenly Emperor 天皇 and Earthly Emperor 地皇 Stars. Such days are hence suitable for renovations, marriage, travel, moving into a new house or opening a business. One who taps into the energies of these days will enjoy an increase in wealth and the birth of noble offspring. However, Ren Yin 壬寅 Days violate the 月厭 Month Detest Star, without the presence of a Relief Star to neutralize this harmful circumstance. Likewise, a Jia Yin 甲寅 Day is also a Direct Abandonment Day 正四廢 and together with a Ren Yin Day, should not be used.

甲 *Jia* 寅 *Yin* **Wood Tiger**	丙 *Bing* 寅 *Yin* **Fire Tiger**	戊 *Wu* 寅 *Yin* **Earth Tiger**	庚 *Geng* 寅 *Yin* **Metal Tiger**	壬 *Ren* 寅 *Yin* **Water Tiger**
▲	★	★	★	▲

★ Excellent   ✔ Auspicious   ● Fair   ▲ Inauspicious   ✗ Dire

十二值神 12 Day Officers	十二地支 Animal Sign of the Day	董公擇日解説 Dong Gong Description
執 *Zhi* **Initiate**	卯 *Mao* **Rabbit** Yin Wood 	辛卯、己卯有黃羅紫檀、天皇地皇諸吉星蓋照。宜開張、出行，入宅，動土，修方，婚姻，起造倉庫。主進財産，增人口，興家進旺六畜大吉，餘卯次吉。惟乙卯正四廢凶。 Xin Mao 辛卯 and Ji Mao 己卯 Days are accompanied by the auspicious Yellow Spiral 黃羅, Purple Sandalwood 紫檀, Heavenly Emperor 天皇 and Earthly Emperor 地皇 Stars; making them ideal for opening a business, travel, moving into a new house, groundbreaking or renovations. Their positive results include an increase in wealth and assets, and an increase in the size of one's family. The Qi on the other Mao 卯 (Rabbit) days however are secondary in strength, at best. Avoid using a Yi Mao 乙卯 Day, as it is one of the Direct Abandonment 正四廢 Days.

董公擇日要覽

Rabbit

十二值神 12 Day Officers	十二地支 Animal Sign of the Day	董公擇日解說 Dong Gong Description
破 *Po* **Destruction**	辰 *Chen* **Dragon** **Yang Earth** 	往亡。丙辰天月二德，修造小吉，但不宜娶親、開張、入宅、移居，主損六畜、耗血財、招口舌。餘辰日更不吉。甲辰、戊辰煞入中宮，大凶。 With the presence of a Death and Emptiness 往亡 Star, even Bing Chen 丙辰 Days, which enjoy the support of the Heavenly and Earthly Virtue 天月二德 Stars may only be suitably used for minor repairs. Major activities such as marriage, launching a business, moving into a new house or migrating to another place should not be undertaken on such days, for violating this rule will only result in livestock and wealth being lost, and gossips troubling the person concerned. The remaining Chen 辰 (Dragon) days are equally inauspicious, although Jia Chen 甲辰 and Wu Chen 戊辰 Days are the worst of the lot.

Dragon

甲 *Jia* 辰 *Chen* Wood Dragon	丙 *Bing* 辰 *Chen* Fire Dragon	戊 *Wu* 辰 *Chen* Earth Dragon	庚 *Geng* 辰 *Chen* Metal Dragon	壬 *Ren* 辰 *Chen* Water Dragon
✖	●	✖	●	▲

★ Excellent   ✔ Auspicious   ● Fair   ▲ Inauspicious   ✖ Dire

董公擇日要覽

巳
Snake

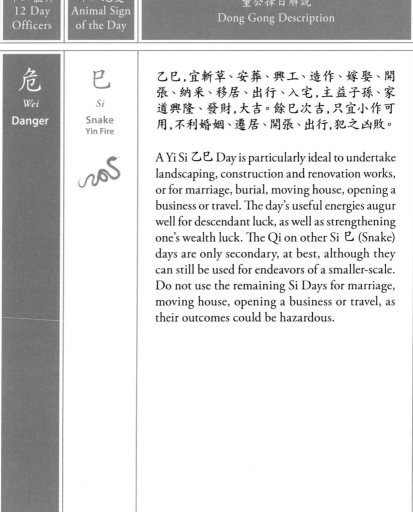

十二值神 12 Day Officers	十二地支 Animal Sign of the Day	董公擇日解説 Dong Gong Description
危 *Wei* **Danger**	巳 *Si* Snake Yin Fire	乙巳，宜斬草、安葬、興工、造作、嫁娶、開張、納采、移居、出行、入宅，主益子孫、家道興隆、發財，大吉。餘巳次吉，只宜小作可用，不利婚姻、遷居、開張、出行，犯之凶敗。 A Yi Si 乙巳 Day is particularly ideal to undertake landscaping, construction and renovation works, or for marriage, burial, moving house, opening a business or travel. The day's useful energies augur well for descendant luck, as well as strengthening one's wealth luck. The Qi on other Si 巳 (Snake) days are only secondary, at best, although they can still be used for endeavors of a smaller-scale. Do not use the remaining Si Days for marriage, moving house, opening a business or travel, as their outcomes could be hazardous.

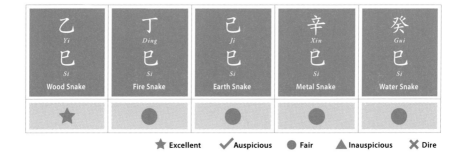

乙 *Yi* 巳 *Si* Wood Snake	丁 *Ding* 巳 *Si* Fire Snake	己 *Ji* 巳 *Si* Earth Snake	辛 *Xin* 巳 *Si* Metal Snake	癸 *Gui* 巳 *Si* Water Snake
★	●	●	●	●

★ Excellent　✓ Auspicious　● Fair　▲ Inauspicious　✗ Dire

十二值神 12 Day Officers	十二地支 Animal Sign of the Day	董公擇日解説 Dong Gong Description
成 *Cheng* **Success**	午 *Wu* Horse Yang Fire 	天喜。丙午天月二德,黃羅、紫檀、天皇、地皇、金銀、庫樓、祿馬諸星拱照,宜婚姻、起造、入宅、出行、開張、倉庫、經商、買賣、動土、斬草、安葬,全吉,大作大發,小作小發,富貴添丁、奴婢自來、謀望勝常。餘午日次吉,可用。 The auspicious Sky Happiness Star exerts its presence throughout the month. Bing Wu 丙午 Days, in particular, also enjoy the useful energies of the Heavenly 天德 and Monthly Virtue 月德 Stars, as well as those of the Yellow Spiral 黃羅, Purple Sandalwood 紫檀、 Heavenly Emperor 天皇 , Earthly Emperor 地皇, Golden Ingot 金銀, Storage 庫樓 and Prosperous Horse 祿馬 Stars. With such a host of auspicious stars governing Bing Wu Days, they are accordingly suitable for renovations, marriage, moving into a new house, travel, opening a business, trade, groundbreaking, landscaping and burial. All endeavors will reap benefits that are proportional to their scale or magnitude, with an increase in wealth and one's family size being the more obvious outcomes. In addition, the other Wu 午 (Horse) days are also auspicious and hence may equally be used.

Horse

甲 *Jia* 午 *Wu* Wood Horse	丙 *Bing* 午 *Wu* Fire Horse	戊 *Wu* 午 *Wu* Earth Horse	庚 *Geng* 午 *Wu* Metal Horse	壬 *Ren* 午 *Wu* Water Horse
✔	★	✔	✔	✔

★ **Excellent**   ✔ **Auspicious**   ● **Fair**   ▲ **Inauspicious**   ✗ **Dire**

十二值神 12 Day Officers	十二地支 Animal Sign of the Day	董公擇日解説 Dong Gong Description
收 *Shou* **Receive**	未 *Wei* **Goat** Yin Earth 	己未,是葬日,辛未、癸未,定磉、拴架,次吉,但不利起造、婚姻、出行、入宅、安葬、開張,倉庫等事,主損血財,遭瘟疫。乙未,朱雀、勾絞、白虎,入中宮,丁未亦凶。 A Ji Wei 己未 Day is also a Burial Day 葬日. Meanwhile, Xin Wei 辛未 and Gui Wei 癸未 Days are considered second-best options for installing beams and columns within a building. They are not suitable to commence major renovations, get married, travel, move into new house, or for burial or opening a business. Ignoring this warning would only result in one's wealth declining and health suffering. Take note that Yi Wei 乙未 Days also harbor the negative Red Phoenix 朱雀, Grappling Hook 勾絞 and White Tiger 白虎 Stars. As such, Yi Wei Days, together with Ding Wei 丁未 Days, are considered inauspicious and hence should not be used.

乙 *Yi* 未 *Wei* **Wood Goat**	丁 *Ding* 未 *Wei* **Fire Goat**	己 *Ji* 未 *Wei* **Earth Goat**	辛 *Xin* 未 *Wei* **Metal Goat**	癸 *Gui* 未 *Wei* **Water Goat**
▲	▲	★	✓	✓

 ★ **Excellent** ✓ **Auspicious** ● **Fair** ▲ **Inauspicious** ✗ **Dire**

董公擇日要覽

十二值神 12 Day Officers	十二地支 Animal Sign of the Day	董公擇日解說 Dong Gong Description
開 *Kai* **Open**	申 *Shen* Monkey Yang Metal	天賊。戊申天赦,甲申水潔淨之時,有黃羅、紫檀、聚祿帶馬星蓋照,宜安葬、作生基,但西沉之日,五行無氣,況當秋暮之候,不宜起造、婚姻、入宅、開張,惟安葬獲吉,益子孫、家門發達。餘申次吉。庚申,乃白虎入中宮,犯之殺人,更凶。

The Heavenly Thief 天賊 Star is present throughout the month. A Wu Shen 戊申 Day is also known as a Heavenly Pardon 天赦 Day; while Water Qi is pure and in perfect balance on a Jia Shen 甲申 Day, augmented by the presence of the auspicious Yellow Spiral 黃羅, Purple Sandalwood 紫檀, Converging Prosperity 聚祿 and Belted Horse 帶馬 Stars. This makes such days particularly ideal for burial or establishing a Yin House. Do note however that by sunset, the positive Qi on such days would have subsided considerably. As such, towards the end of Autumn (when the sun sets earlier), do not undertake renovations, get married, move into new house or open a business on these days. The only suitable activity that one may undertake is burial, which will bring about good descendant luck and prosperity to one family. The remaining Shen 申 (Monkey) days are also auspicious, except for Geng Shen 庚申 Days, when White Tiger Sha enters the Central Palace. One's life and the lives of one's loved ones will be endangered if any activity of significance is undertaken on Geng Shen Days.

甲 *Jia* 申 *Shen* Wood Monkey	丙 *Bing* 申 *Shen* Fire Monkey	戊 *Wu* 申 *Shen* Earth Monkey	庚 *Geng* 申 *Shen* Metal Monkey	壬 *Ren* 申 *Shen* Water Monkey
★	✔	★	▲	✔

★ Excellent   ✔ Auspicious   ● Fair   ▲ Inauspicious   ✘ Dire

十二值神 12 Day Officers	十二地支 Animal Sign of the Day	董公擇日解説 Dong Gong Description
閉 *Bi* **Close**	酉 *You* Rooster Yin Metal 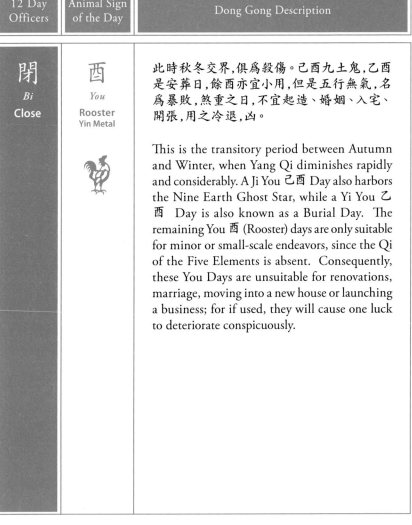	此時秋冬交界,俱爲殺傷。己酉九土鬼,乙酉是安葬日,餘酉亦宜小用,但是五行無氣,名爲暴敗,煞重之日,不宜起造、婚姻、入宅、開張,用之冷退,凶。 This is the transitory period between Autumn and Winter, when Yang Qi diminishes rapidly and considerably. A Ji You 己酉 Day also harbors the Nine Earth Ghost Star, while a Yi You 乙酉 Day is also known as a Burial Day. The remaining You 酉 (Rooster) days are only suitable for minor or small-scale endeavors, since the Qi of the Five Elements is absent. Consequently, these You Days are unsuitable for renovations, marriage, moving into a new house or launching a business; for if used, they will cause one luck to deteriorate conspicuously.

乙 *Yi* 酉 *You* Wood Rooster	丁 *Ding* 酉 *You* Fire Rooster	己 *Ji* 酉 *You* Earth Rooster	辛 *Xin* 酉 *You* Metal Rooster	癸 *Gui* 酉 *You* Water Rooster
●	▲	▲	▲	▲

★ Excellent   ✔ Auspicious   ● Fair   ▲ Inauspicious   ✕ Dire

Tenth Month 十月

November 7th – December 6th

Pig 亥 (Hai) Month

November 7th – December 6th
Pig 亥 (Hai) Month

月德甲、月恩乙，母倉申酉。天德合庚。

The Monthly Virtue 月德 Star presides over Jia 甲 Days, the Monthly Benevolence 月恩 Star influences Yi 乙 Days, the Motherly Storage 母倉 Star exerts its auspicious influence over Monkey 申 (Shen) and Rooster 酉 (You) Days, while the energies of the Heavenly Virtue 天德 Star combine with Geng 庚 Days to make them positive ones.

立冬：立冬前一日爲四絕。

The 'Coming of Winter' 立冬 (Li Dong)

The eve of Li Dong (Coming of Winter) is one of the Four Extinction 四絕 Days.

小雪：立冬後三煞在西，申、酉、戌方忌修造、動土。

'Lesser Snow' 小雪 (Xiao Xue)

The end of Li Dong is marked by the commencement of Xiao Xue (Lesser Snow). With the advent of Xiao Xue, the Three Killings 三煞 (San Sha) Affliction is found in the West. In particular, avoid renovating or digging the ground of the Southwest 3 申 (Shen – SW3), West 2 酉 (You – W2) and Northwest 1 戌 (Xu – NW1) sectors, to prevent the harmful energies of the Three Killings from being unleashed.

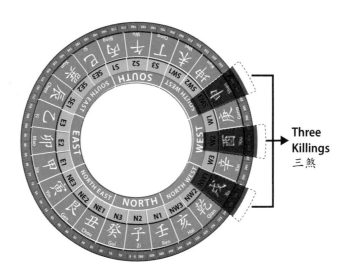

董公擇日要覽

亥
Pig

十二值神 12 Day Officers	十二地支 Animal Sign of the Day	董公擇日解說 Dong Gong Description
建 *Jian* **Establish**	亥 *Hai* Pig Yin Water 	不利起造、開張、嫁娶、入宅、出行、安葬,用之招官司、損家長。即乙亥、己亥,亦只宜小作營爲,緣十月建亥不利。 This is not an auspicious day for renovation, launching a business, marriage, moving into a new house, travel or burial. These activities, if undertaken on this day, will result in one facing legal entanglements and the eldest member of the family being prone to injury. However, Yi Hai 乙亥 and Ji Hai 己亥 Days may be used for activities or endeavors of low significance.

乙 *Yi* 亥 *Hai* Wood Pig	丁 *Ding* 亥 *Hai* Fire Pig	己 *Ji* 亥 *Hai* Earth Pig	辛 *Xin* 亥 *Hai* Metal Pig	癸 *Gui* 亥 *Hai* Water Pig
●	▲	●	▲	▲

★ Excellent　✔ Auspicious　● Fair　▲ Inauspicious　✖ Dire

Rat

十二值神 12 Day Officers	十二地支 Animal Sign of the Day	董公擇日解説 Dong Gong Description
除 *Chu* **Remove**	子 *Zi* Rat Yang Water 	雖是五行旺相,但秋冬交界之初,有轉煞之凶。古云轉煞而傷,未可輕用。甲子天赦不是轉煞。可用。 Even though the Qi of the Five Elements are prosperous on this very day, the transition that separates Autumn from Winter carries with it Heaven and Earth Drilling Sha 轉煞 – thereby rendering this day unusable. However, the Jia Zi 甲子 Days are also Heavenly Pardon 天赦 Days, without the interference of Heaven and Earth Drilling Sha, and can therefore be utilized.

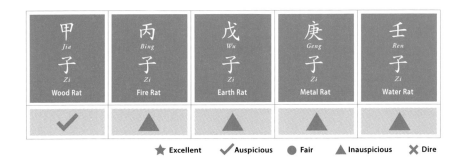

甲 *Jia* 子 *Zi* Wood Rat	丙 *Bing* 子 *Zi* Fire Rat	戊 *Wu* 子 *Zi* Earth Rat	庚 *Geng* 子 *Zi* Metal Rat	壬 *Ren* 子 *Zi* Water Rat
✔	▲	▲	▲	▲

★ **Excellent**　✔ **Auspicious**　● **Fair**　▲ **Inauspicious**　✘ **Dire**

十二值神 12 Day Officers	十二地支 Animal Sign of the Day	董公擇日解説 Dong Gong Description
滿 *Man* **Full**	丑 *Chou* Ox Yin Earth	天富、天成、天賊,丁丑、癸丑,煞入中宮,不利起造、嫁娶,鼓樂喧嘩等事,以及釘門,務驚動神煞損人丁,傷六畜。餘丑日亦不宜用,只可請魂入墓,凡金入丑宮,五行無氣,並犯月厭天賊之凶。 The Heavenly Fortune 天富, Heavenly Success 天成, Heavenly Thief 天賊 Stars preside over this day. On Ding Chou 丁丑 and Gui Chou 癸丑 Days, though, Sha (Killing) Qi enters the Central Palace; making them unsuitable for renovation, marriage, celebrations or even installing doorframes. Violating this rule will only bring harm to both people and livestock. The other Chou 丑 (Ox) days are equally unusable.

丑
Ox

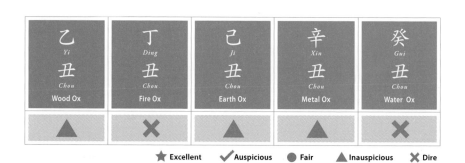

乙 *Yi* 丑 *Chou* Wood Ox	丁 *Ding* 丑 *Chou* Fire Ox	己 *Ji* 丑 *Chou* Earth Ox	辛 *Xin* 丑 *Chou* Metal Ox	癸 *Gui* 丑 *Chou* Water Ox
▲	✖	▲	▲	✖

★ Excellent   ✔ Auspicious   ● Fair   ▲ Inauspicious   ✖ Dire

董公擇日要覽

Tiger

十二值神 12 Day Officers	十二地支 Animal Sign of the Day	董公擇日解説 Dong Gong Description
平 *Ping* **Balance**	寅 *Yin* Tiger Yang Wood 	天富、天成。有到州星，事到官府而後散。惟甲寅乃上吉，壬寅、庚寅次吉，小小修爲則可，大作不宜。餘寅日凶。不可用。 With the auspicious presence of the Heavenly Fortune 天富 and Heavenly Success 天成 Stars, Jia Yin 甲寅 days are good days, with Ren Yin 壬寅 and Geng Yin 庚寅 Days also reasonably usable. Do note however that these days should not be used to undertake any activity or endeavor of great significance. The other Yin 寅 (Tiger) days are inauspicious, and should be avoided.

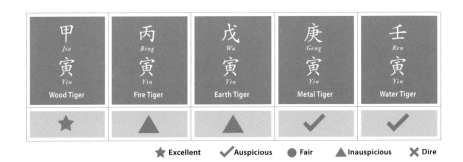

董公擇日要覽

Rabbit

十二值神 12 Day Officers	十二地支 Animal Sign of the Day	董公擇日解說 Dong Gong Description
定 *Ding* **Stable**	卯 *Mao* **Rabbit** Yin Wood 	乙卯天德、辛卯、己卯，宜動土、興工、定磉、上樑、嫁娶、入宅、出行、開張等用之，吉曜照臨，餘卯次吉。 Yi Mao 乙卯 Days are supported by the positive energies of the Heavenly Virtue 天德 Star, while Xin Mao 辛卯 and Ji Mao 己卯 Days are ideal for groundbreaking or commencing construction, building or moving into a new house, getting married, travel or launching a business. The remaining Mao 卯 (Rabbit) Days are secondary, at best, in terms of auspiciousness and usability.

乙 *Yi* 卯 *Mao* Wood Rabbit	丁 *Ding* 卯 *Mao* Fire Rabbit	己 *Ji* 卯 *Mao* Earth Rabbit	辛 *Xin* 卯 *Mao* Metal Rabbit	癸 *Gui* 卯 *Mao* Water Rabbit
✔	✔	★	★	✔

★ Excellent　✔ Auspicious　● Fair　▲ Inauspicious　✘ Dire

辰
Dragon

十二值神 12 Day Officers	十二地支 Animal Sign of the Day	董公擇日解説 Dong Gong Description
執 *Zhi* **Initiate**	**辰** *Chen* Dragon Yang Earth 	甲辰雖有天月二德,只可偷修,若起造、興工、嫁娶、入宅則不利。十月雖不是敗日,然終有凶。餘辰亦不利,惟丙辰日可以開山、斬草、安葬次吉。戊辰煞入中宮,大凶。不可用。 Even with the presence of the positive Heavenly 天德 and Monthly Virtue 月德 Stars, use Jia Chen 甲辰 Days only for minor repairs. They are unsuitable for renovation, commencing construction, marriage or moving into a new house. All other Chen 辰 (Dragon) Days are not useable for activities or endeavors of any sort, with the exception of Bing Chen 丙辰 Days, which are reasonably suitable for excavating, quarrying or building into mountains, landscaping works and burial. Do note that on Wu Chen 戊辰 Days, Sha (Killing) Qi enters the Central Palace; making such days extremely inauspicious and totally useless.

甲 *Jia* 辰 *Chen* Wood Dragon	丙 *Bing* 辰 *Chen* Fire Dragon	戊 *Wu* 辰 *Chen* Earth Dragon	庚 *Geng* 辰 *Chen* Metal Dragon	壬 *Ren* 辰 *Chen* Water Dragon
★	✓	✗	▲	▲

★ Excellent   ✓ Auspicious   ● Fair   ▲ Inauspicious   ✗ Dire

十二值神 12 Day Officers	十二地支 Animal Sign of the Day	董公擇日解説 Dong Gong Description
破 *Po* **Destruction**	巳 *Si* Snake Yin Fire	小紅砂日。亦犯朱雀、勾絞、騰蛇,諸事不宜。惟乙巳有天德,只可小小營爲,用之次吉。丁巳正四廢,凶.犯之雷霆散敗、橫事、失財。 This is known as a Lesser Red Embrace Day 小紅砂日, which is also accompanied and affected by the presence of the negative Red Phoenix 朱雀 and Grappling Hook 勾絞 Stars. As such, avoid using such days for important activities or endeavors. A Yi Si 乙巳 Day with the Heavenly Virtue 天德 Star present may however be used for matters of negligible significance. A Ding Si 丁巳 Day is a Direct Abandonment Day 正四廢 and if used, could result in serious accidents or loss of wealth.

Snake

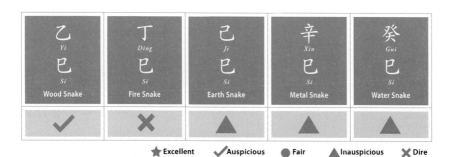

乙 *Yi* 巳 *Si* Wood Snake	丁 *Ding* 巳 *Si* Fire Snake	己 *Ji* 巳 *Si* Earth Snake	辛 *Xin* 巳 *Si* Metal Snake	癸 *Gui* 巳 *Si* Water Snake
✔	✘	▲	▲	▲

★ Excellent ✔ Auspicious ● Fair ▲ Inauspicious ✘ Dire

十二值神 12 Day Officers	十二地支 Animal Sign of the Day	董公擇日解説 Dong Gong Description
危 *Wei* **Danger**	午 *Wu* Horse Yang Fire	黃砂。甲午月德，有黃羅、紫檀、金銀，庫樓，諸吉星蓋照，嫁娶、開張、起造、動土、出行、入宅、安葬，大吉。餘午日次吉，丙午正四廢，凶。 The Yellow Embrace 黃砂 Star exerts its influence throughout the month. Jia Wu 甲午 Days are accompanied by the presence of the Monthly Virtue 月德 and other auspicious stars such as the Yellow Spiral 黃羅, Purple Sandalwood 紫檀, Golden Ingot 金娘 and Storage Star 庫樓. Such days therefore augur well for marriage, launching a business, renovation and groundbreaking works, travel, moving into a new house and burial. All other Wu 午 (Horse) Days remain second-best options; with the exception of a Bing Wu 丙午 Day, which is one of the Direct Abandonment 正四廢 Days and therefore extremely inauspicious if used.

★ Excellent   ✓ Auspicious   ● Fair   ▲ Inauspicious   ✗ Dire

十二值神 12 Day Officers	十二地支 Animal Sign of the Day	董公擇日解説 Dong Gong Description
 成 *Cheng* **Success**	 未 *Wei* Goat Yin Earth 	月建三合,惜乙未煞入中宮,忌出行、安葬、嫁娶、入宅、開張、修造等事.　惟癸未火星,木入秦州,是貴人之星,值黃羅、紫檀、金銀,聯珠星蓋照,宜起造、嫁娶、納財、問名、出行、遇貴,入家宅永安寧,主週年百日、得貴人接引、進田產、生貴子、發福,上吉。餘未次吉。 While this day elegantly forms a Three Harmony 三合 (San He) Formation with the month, Sha (Killing) Qi unfortunately enters the Central Palace on Yi Wei 乙未 Days – making them unsuitable for travel, burial, marriage, moving into a new house, opening a business or even repair work. Gui Wei 癸未 Days contain the Fire Star 火星, where Wood Qi is prosperous and augmented by the simultaneous presence of a Nobleman Star. The presence of positive stars such as the Yellow Spiral 黃羅, Purple Sandalwood 紫檀, Golden Ingot 金銀 and Shining Pearl 聯珠 make this day ideal for repairs, marriage, debt-collection, fame-seeking, travel, meeting people of importance and moving into a new house. Such an auspicious combination also denotes help from noble people in times of need throughout the year, the birth of a noble child, as well as prosperity that heralds an increase in material wealth. However, the other Wei 未 (Goat) Days are only second-tier options.

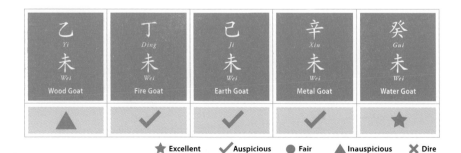

乙未 *Yi* *Wei* Wood Goat	丁未 *Ding* *Wei* Fire Goat	己未 *Ji* *Wei* Earth Goat	辛未 *Xin* *Wei* Metal Goat	癸未 *Gui* *Wei* Water Goat
▲	✔	✔	✔	★

★ Excellent　✔ Auspicious　● Fair　▲ Inauspicious　✖ Dire

十二值神 12 Day Officers	十二地支 Animal Sign of the Day	董公擇日解説 Dong Gong Description
收 *Shōu* **Receive**	申 *Shēn* Monkey Yang Metal	卻犯到州星,用之招官司、損人口。惟甲申水潔淨之時,水土長生居申,利安葬、嫁娶、出行、入宅、動土、開張、起造、營爲,主週年百日貴人自來提拔、諸事得意。庚申受死無氣,又煞入中宮,犯之主殺人,大凶。 This is an inauspicious day to use, as it heralds the advent of legal entanglements and the risk of injury or harm to family members. However, Water Qi on Jia Shen 甲申 Days is pure and serene, with the Qi's growth and advancement potential (長生) found in Shen 申 (Monkey) Days – hence making Jia Shen Days ideal for burial, marriage, travel, moving into a new house, groundbreaking or launching a business. Activating the useful energies of these days will bring about assistance from noble people throughout the year and thereby facilitate all endeavors that they may be smooth-sailing. Avoid Geng Shen 庚申 Days, however, as Qi is dead on such days, rendering them extremely inauspicious.

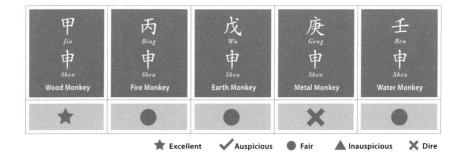

十二值神 12 Day Officers	十二地支 Animal Sign of the Day	董公擇日解說 Dong Gong Description
開 *Kai* **Open**	酉 *You* Rooster Yin Metal	乙酉天德,是葬日,宜娶親、入宅、起造、開張,用之上吉,主增田宅、受職祿、光門戶、奴婢義、僕自來投催、諸事順遂。己酉九土鬼,安葬則可,不宜大用。餘酉日次吉。 A Yi You 乙酉 Day has the Heavenly Virtue 天德 present, and is also a Burial Day 葬日. This makes it an ideal day for marriage, moving into a new home, renovation works or opening a business. Used well, this day will bring about an increase in wealth and assets, and the prospect of a promotion. In short, the outcome of all affairs undertaken on this day will be auspicious. The remaining You 酉 (Rooster) Days are reasonably useable, although a Ji You 己酉 Day harbors the Nine Earth Ghost Star – allowing it to safely serve no other purpose than burial. Where possible, avoid using this day.

酉
Rooster

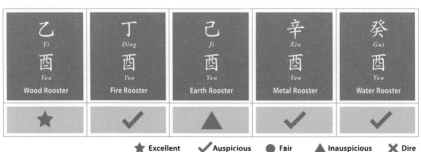

乙 *Yi* 酉 *You* Wood Rooster	丁 *Ding* 酉 *You* Fire Rooster	己 *Ji* 酉 *You* Earth Rooster	辛 *Xin* 酉 *You* Metal Rooster	癸 *Gui* 酉 *You* Water Rooster
★	✓	▲	✓	✓

★ **Excellent**　✓ **Auspicious**　● **Fair**　▲ **Inauspicious**　✗ **Dire**

十二值神 12 Day Officers	十二地支 Animal Sign of the Day	董公擇日解説 Dong Gong Description
閉 *Bi* **Close**	戌 *Xu* Dog Yang Earth 	火星。甲戌月德,宜嫁娶、開張、出行、入宅,但不利動土、起造、埋葬。丙戌、戊戌,百事凶敗。 The Fire Star 火星 is present throughout the month. Jia Xu 甲戌 Days are accompanied by the presence of the Monthly Virtue 月德 Star, rendering them ideal for marriage, opening a business, travel or moving into a new residence. These days are unsuitable, however, for groundbreaking, renovation works and burial. Avoid undertaking major or significant activities on Bing Xu 丙戌 and Wu Xu 戊戌 Days.

甲 *Jia* 戌 *Xu* Wood Dog	丙 *Bing* 戌 *Xu* Fire Dog	戊 *Wu* 戌 *Xu* Earth Dog	庚 *Geng* 戌 *Xu* Metal Dog	壬 *Ren* 戌 *Xu* Water Dog
★	✕	✕	▲	▲

★ Excellent ✔ Auspicious ● Fair ▲ Inauspicious ✕ Dire

Eleventh Month 十一月

December 7th – January 5th (the following year)

Rat 子 (Zi) Month

December 7th – January 5th (the following year)
Rat 子 (Zi) Month

月德壬、月恩甲，母倉申酉。天德合申。

Ren 壬 Days are accompanied by the presence of the Monthly Virtue 月德 Star, Jia 甲 Days are presided over by the Monthly Benevolence 月恩 Star, while the Motherly Storage 母倉 Star exerts its positive influence on Monkey 申 (Shen) and Rooster 申 (You) Days. Monkey Days also enjoy the support of the Heavenly Virtue 天德 Star, which further enhances their usability.

大雪：冬至前一日爲四離。

'Greater Snow' 大雪 (Da Xue)

One day before Dong Zhi 冬至 is one of the Four Abandonment 四離 Days.

冬至：大雪後三煞在南,巳、午、未方忌修造、動土。

'Winter Solstice' 冬至 (Dong Zhi)

Once the 'Greater Snow' 大雪 (Da Xue) period has passed by, the Three Killings 三煞 (San Sha) Affliction can be found in the South. In particular, refrain from digging or 'disturbing' the ground of the Southeast 3 巳 (Si – SE3), South 2 午 (Wu – S2) and Southwest 1 未 (Wei – SW1) sectors, lest the harmful energies of the Three Killings are unleashed.

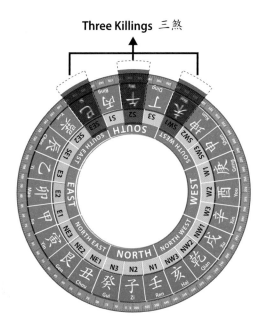

董公擇日要覽

Rat

十二值神 12 Day Officers	十二地支 Animal Sign of the Day	董公擇日解説 Dong Gong Description
建 *Jian* **Establish**	子 *Zi* Rat Yang Water 	火星。甲子天赦日進神,惜被月建沖破,用之主官司、破敗,諸天赦不合之日也。丙子雖值水旺之時,退神爲地轉,亦與月建相沖,其時水斷溪潦力,亦甚減,終是吉中凶兆,主先進益後禍害,正冰消瓦裂之時也。 The Fire Star 火星 present throughout the Day. While Jia Zi 甲子 Days are also marked by the presence of the Heavenly Pardon 天赦 Star, any positive effects are unfortunately negated by the inauspicious Month Establish Star 月建. Hence, using a Jia Zi Day will result in legal issues and other hasslless. Similarly, while Water Qi is prosperous on Bing Zi 丙子 Days, the presence of negative stars causes all positive energies to be neutralized - particularly by the Month Establish 月建 Star. As these positive Qi are significantly stifled, using such days will produce problematic or disastrous outcomes, even though things may appear positive initially.

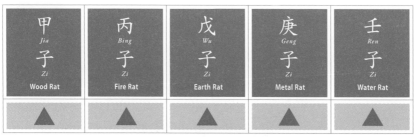

甲 *Jia* 子 *Zi* Wood Rat	丙 *Bing* 子 *Zi* Fire Rat	戊 *Wu* 子 *Zi* Earth Rat	庚 *Geng* 子 *Zi* Metal Rat	壬 *Ren* 子 *Zi* Water Rat
▲	▲	▲	▲	▲

★ Excellent ✔ Auspicious ● Fair ▲ Inauspicious ✖ Dire

十二值神 12 Day Officers	十二地支 Animal Sign of the Day	董公擇日解説 Dong Gong Description
除 *Chu* **Remove**	丑 *Chou* Ox Yin Earth 	天瘟。乙丑金墓之鄉，宜娶親、起造、出行、開張、動土、伐樹、開山，有吉星蓋照，主貴人接引、謀望遂意。餘丑次吉。 The presence of the Heavenly Delicate 天瘟 Star makes Yi Chou 乙丑 Days especially ideal for marriage, renovation, travel, opening a business, groundbreaking, cutting trees, or quarrying or excavating mountains. Such a combination also indicates the availability of assistance from noble people. The remaining Chou 丑 (Ox) Days are only secondary in terms of usability and auspiciousness.

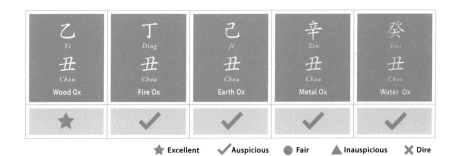

乙 *Yi* 丑 *Chou* Wood Ox	丁 *Ding* 丑 *Chou* Fire Ox	己 *Ji* 丑 *Chou* Earth Ox	辛 *Xin* 丑 *Chou* Metal Ox	癸 *Gui* 丑 *Chou* Water Ox
★	✓	✓	✓	✓

★ **Excellent**　✓ **Auspicious**　● **Fair**　▲ **Inauspicious**　✗ **Dire**

董公擇日要覽

十二值神 12 Day Officers	十二地支 Animal Sign of the Day	董公擇日解説 Dong Gong Description
滿 *Man* **Full**	寅 *Yin* Tiger Yang Wood 	黃砂、天富。是土瘟,但不宜動土.然有福生並黃羅、紫檀、天皇、地皇星蓋照,宜婚姻、入宅、起造、安葬、出行、開張,百事順遂。壬寅、戊寅上吉,丙寅、庚寅次吉、甲寅又次吉。 The presence of the Yellow Sand 黃砂 and Heavenly Fortune 天富 Stars on this day render it unsuitable for groundbreaking. Nevertheless, it is still considered a Prosperous Growth 福生 Day, due to the presence of the auspicious Yellow Spiral 黃羅, Purple Sandalwood 紫檀, Heavenly Emperor 天皇 and Earthly Emperor 地皇 Stars. As such, use this day for marriage, moving into a new house, renovation, burial, travel and opening a business – it augurs well for all significant or large-scale activities. Where possible, use the Ren Yin 壬寅 and Wu Yin 戊寅 Days, as they are the best of the lot. Bing Yin 丙寅 and Geng Yin 庚寅 Days are considered second-grade, with Jia Yin 甲寅 Days being third-grade, in descending order.

Tiger

甲 *Jia* 寅 *Yin* Wood Tiger	丙 *Bing* 寅 *Yin* Fire Tiger	戊 *Wu* 寅 *Yin* Earth Tiger	庚 *Geng* 寅 *Yin* Metal Tiger	壬 *Ren* 寅 *Yin* Water Tiger
●	✔	★	✔	★

 ★ Excellent ✔ Auspicious ● Fair ▲ Inauspicious ✖ Dire

十二值神 12 Day Officers	十二地支 Animal Sign of the Day	董公擇日解說 Dong Gong Description
平 *Ping* **Balance**	卯 *Mao* **Rabbit** **Yin Wood** 	天賊。辛卯火星,卻犯朱雀、勾絞,用之招官司、損財物、好爭鬥、傷情義、多惡疾。凶。惟乙卯一日次吉,餘卯主父子、兄弟不義、爭鬥、自縊,惡人劫害、破敗,大凶。 The Heavenly Thief 天賊 is present throughout the day. A Xin Mao 辛卯 Day is also marked by the presence of the Fire Star 火星, although it also harbors negative stars such as the Red Phoenix 朱雀 and Grappling Hook 勾絞, which make it unsuitable for use. The overall outcomes include legal issues, a decrease in wealth, disputes and quarrels, strained relationships and serious ailments. A Yi Mao 乙卯 Day, however, is considered an above-average day and may be used with care. The remaining Mao 卯 (Rabbit) Days should be avoided, for they cause discord and misunderstanding between fathers and their sons, arguments and failure, as well as give rise to selfishness and provide means for malicious people to harm oneself.

乙 *Yi* 卯 *Mao* **Wood Rabbit**	丁 *Ding* 卯 *Mao* **Fire Rabbit**	己 *Ji* 卯 *Mao* **Earth Rabbit**	辛 *Xin* 卯 *Mao* **Metal Rabbit**	癸 *Gui* 卯 *Mao* **Water Rabbit**
✔	▲	▲	▲	▲

★ Excellent ✔ Auspicious ● Fair ▲ Inauspicious ✘ Dire

董公擇日要覽

辰
Dragon

十二值神 12 Day Officers	十二地支 Animal Sign of the Day	董公擇日解說 Dong Gong Description

 定
Ding
Stable

 辰
Chen
Dragon
Yang Earth

雖云吉。卻有天羅地網之咎，貴人不臨，營爲不利，煞占中宮，犯之殺人，凶。惟壬辰雖犯官符，內有天德、黃羅、紫檀、天皇、地皇星蓋照，宜安葬、安門、娶親、出行、入宅，主家門興旺，生貴子賢孫。甲辰、戊辰似屬吉，然煞入中宮，娶親、入宅等是所宜用。壬辰大宜安葬、安門，上吉。餘事慎之。乃死氣之日，百事不利，犯官符與劫煞，飛宮官符同到此方。

Even though this day is typically regarded as an auspicious day, it nevertheless contains the Heavenly Net 天羅 and Earthly Web 地網 Stars, which 'prevent' the arrival and therefore positive outcomes brought about by Nobleman Stars. The Ren Chen 壬辰 Day also paradoxically violates the Officer Charm 官符 Star while harboring the Heavenly Virtue 天德, Yellow Spiral 黃羅, Purple Sandalwood 紫檀, Heavenly Emperor 天皇 and Earthly Emperor 地皇 Stars. This makes it only suitable for burial, fixing doorframes, marriage or entering a new house. It however also heralds the birth of offspring who will prosper in life. Use the other Chen 辰 (Dragon) Days with care, as the Qi on these days is dead. Adding to their inauspiciousness is the presence of the Officer Charm 官符, Robbery Sha 劫煞 and Flying Palace 飛宮 Stars.

甲 *Jia* 辰 *Chen* Wood Dragon	丙 *Bing* 辰 *Chen* Fire Dragon	戊 *Wu* 辰 *Chen* Earth Dragon	庚 *Geng* 辰 *Chen* Metal Dragon	壬 *Ren* 辰 *Chen* Water Dragon
▲	▲	▲	▲	✓

★ Excellent ✓ Auspicious ● Fair ▲ Inauspicious ✗ Dire

Eleventh Month 十一月

十二值神 12 Day Officers	十二地支 Animal Sign of the Day	董公擇日解說 Dong Gong Description
執 *Zhi* **Initiate**	巳 *Si* Snake Yin Fire	乙巳、癸巳、己巳有黃羅、紫檀、天皇、地皇諸星蓋照,宜安葬、安門、興土、動土、嫁娶、入宅、出行、開張、營爲,諸事用之,添人口、旺家門、生貴子、增田地,大吉。辛巳次吉。丁巳正四廢,凶。 Yi Si 乙巳, Gui Si 癸巳 and Ji Si 己巳 Days are accompanied by the presence of the auspicious Yellow Spiral 黃羅, Purple Sandalwood 紫檀, Heavenly Emperor 天皇 and Earthly Emperor 地皇 Stars. This makes these particular days ideal for burial, positioning a door, groundbreaking, marriage, moving into a new house, travel or opening a business. Utilized well, they will bring about an increase in the number of one family members through the birth of noble children, as well as an increase in wealth and possessions. Likewise, a Xin Si 辛巳 Day may 'only' be second-grade, but it is still auspicious enough to be utilized. Avoid using a Ding Si 丁巳 Day, though, as it is a Direct Abandonment 正四廢 Day.

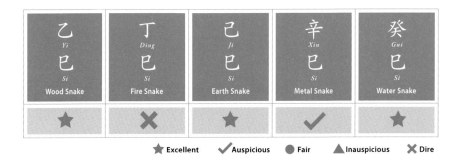

乙 *Yi* 巳 *Si* Wood Snake	丁 *Ding* 巳 *Si* Fire Snake	己 *Ji* 巳 *Si* Earth Snake	辛 *Xin* 巳 *Si* Metal Snake	癸 *Gui* 巳 *Si* Water Snake
★	✖	★	✔	★

★ **Excellent** ✔ **Auspicious** ● **Fair** ▲ **Inauspicious** ✖ **Dire**

董公擇日要覽

十二值神 12 Day Officers	十二地支 Animal Sign of the Day	董公擇日解説 Dong Gong Description
破 *Po* **Destruction**	午 *Wu* Horse Yang Fire 	天賊。壬午火星傍月德,僅可小小急用。餘午 日招瘟疫、害六畜,乃月建沖破之日,凶。丙午 正四廢凶。 The Heavenly Thief 天賊 Star is present throughout the month. On Ren Wu 壬午 Days, the Fire Star 火星 along with the Monthly Virtue 月德 Star exert their influence, making such days only suitable activities of minor importance. The remaining Wu 午 (Horse) Days unsuitable for all important activities or endeavors and if used, will make one more susceptible to sickness and animals and livestock more exposed to harm.

午
Horse

甲 *Jia* 午 *Wu* Wood Horse	丙 *Bing* 午 *Wu* Fire Horse	戊 *Wu* 午 *Wu* Earth Horse	庚 *Geng* 午 *Wu* Metal Horse	壬 *Ren* 午 *Wu* Water Horse
▲	▲	▲	▲	●

 Excellent **Auspicious** ● **Fair** ▲ **Inauspicious** **Dire**

董公擇日要覽

Goat

十二值神 12 Day Officers	十二地支 Animal Sign of the Day	董公擇日解説 Dong Gong Description
危 *Wei* **Danger**	未 *Wei* Goat Yin Earth 	丁未天河水潔淨之時,用之百事全吉。己未日利埋葬最吉。餘事亦吉。此二日用事,主進人口、增田產、得橫財。辛未、癸未諸事不利。乙未煞入中宮,更凶。 On a Ding Wei 丁未 Day, the Heavenly Stream 天河 produces pure and serene Water Qi; making it a very auspicious day that may be suitably used for all matters. Ji Wei 己未 Days are also very good and best suited for burial. Used properly, these two days could lead to one's family expanding and prospering. However, Xin Wei 辛未 and Gui Wei 癸未 Days are unsuitable insofar as important activities are concerned. A Yi Wei 乙未 Day, in particular, is the worst of the 5 types of days, what with the presence of Sha (Killing) Qi in the Central Palace.

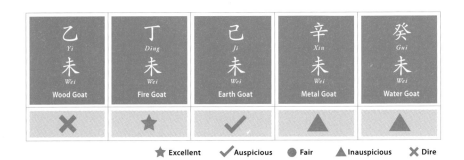

十二值神 12 Day Officers	十二地支 Animal Sign of the Day	董公擇日解説 Dong Gong Description
 成 *Cheng* **Success**	 申 *Shen* Monkey Yang Metal 	天喜。壬申天、月二德、甲申、戊申，五行有氣之時，值黃羅、紫檀、金銀寶藏庫樓，諸吉星蓋照，一切作爲、百福駢臻、諸事順意、生貴子、旺財祿。庚申日只宜安葬，及屋外小小修造則可，若起造若起造大工及婚姻、入宅、開張，立見凶禍，主損家長、傷陰人、小口，謂之五行無氣、煞神聚入中宮，善人不能降福。余自幼年得其文，在江湖選時擇日者四十餘年，無不切中，上年見有人揀用此日，不避齒煩前去攔阻，無如其人不聽，後立見災禍。可知此書擇日，實有應驗不可輕視。丙申日用事，驚犯鬼哭神號，更宜慎之。 The Sky Happiness 天喜 Star is present throughout the day. In addition, Ren Shen 壬申 Days are also accompanied by the Heavenly Virtue 天德 and Monthly Virtue 月德 Stars. Meanwhile, on Jia Shen 甲申 and Wu Shen 戊申 Days, the Qi of the Five Elements are strong and enhanced by the presence of the Yellow Spiral 黃羅, Purple Sandalwood 紫檀, Golden Ingot 金銀, Precious Treasure 寶藏 and Storage 庫樓 Stars. This makes such days perfect for all important activities or endeavors, for if used, they will produce outcomes that increase wealth or result in the birth of a noble child. However, Geng Shen 庚申 Days are only suitable for burial or minor renovation works to the interior of a house. Using a Geng Shen Day for important endeavors or activities such as marriage, entering a new house or opening a business will immediately bring about disastrous outcomes; where elderly family members may be susceptible to poor health, children will tend to get hurt more easily, and one's fortune and sense of harmony will deteriorate. Bing Shen 丙申 Days are the worst of the lot, and should definitely be avoided for all important activities.

申
Monkey

甲 *Jia* 申 *Shen* Wood Monkey	丙 *Bing* 申 *Shen* Fire Monkey	戊 *Wu* 申 *Shen* Earth Monkey	庚 *Geng* 申 *Shen* Metal Monkey	壬 *Ren* 申 *Shen* Water Monkey
★	▲	★	●	★

★ Excellent　✔ Auspicious　● Fair　▲ Inauspicious　✘ Dire

十二值神 12 Day Officers	十二地支 Animal Sign of the Day	董公擇日解説 Dong Gong Description
收 *Shou* **Receive**	酉 *You* Rooster Yin Metal 	小紅砂。有到州星，事到官司而後散，只宜埋葬，次吉，忌起造、開張、出行、入宅、嫁娶等事，犯之官非、冷退、損傷財物，凶。餘酉不利。 With the Lesser Red Embrace 小紅砂 Star governing the day, the only suitable activity that may be done is burial. Do not use this day for renovation, launching a business, travel, moving into a new house or get married. Ignoring this warning will result in lawsuits surfacing, as well as a decrease in wealth and other material assets. Similarly, the other You 酉 (Rooster) Days are not favorable either.

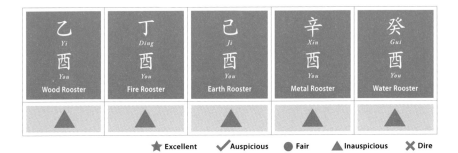

十二值神 12 Day Officers	十二地支 Animal Sign of the Day	董公擇日解説 Dong Gong Description
開 *Kai* **Open**	戌 *Xu* **Dog** Yang Earth 	往亡。小葬亦僅備於急用,乃次吉之日。如丙戌、壬戌煞入中宮,諸事忌用。甲戌八方俱白,二十四向諸神朝天,玄女偷修之日,可用。 As this is an Emptiness Day 往亡, it should only be used for insignificant or minor activities, although burials may be undertaken on this day. Avoid Bing Xu 丙戌 and Ren Xu 壬戌 Days, though, as they are the worst days with Sha (Killing) Qi entering the Central Palace. Jia Xu 甲戌 Days may however be used, as they are supported by the presence of positive day stars.

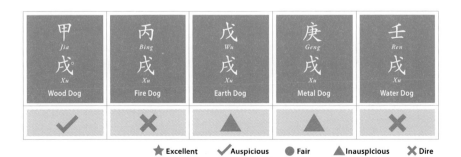

十二值神 12 Day Officers	十二地支 Animal Sign of the Day	董公擇日解説 Dong Gong Description
閉 *Bi* **Close**	亥 *Hai* Pig Yin Water 	乙亥、己亥，文昌貴顯之星，黃羅、紫檀、天皇、地皇、聯珠、天垣、聚祿、帶馬、金銀庫樓、寶藏星蓋照，宜起造、營爲，百事皆吉，八方二十四向皆利，用之家道豐盈、生貴子、進財祿、旺六畜。丁亥次吉之日，癸亥六甲窮日。辛亥婦人之金、陰府決遺之期，一年四季皆不可用.惟二月之辛亥吉，餘亥皆不可用也。 The Yi Hai 乙亥 and Ji Hai 己亥 Days enjoy the support of the Literary Arts 文昌 as well as the Yellow Spiral 黃羅, Purple Sandalwood 紫檀, Heavenly Emperor 天皇, Earthly Emperor 地皇, Stringed Pearl 聯珠, Heavenly Provincial 天垣, Converging Prosperity 聚祿, Sky Horse 帶馬. Golden Ingot 金銀, Storage Wealth 庫樓，Precious Treasure 寶藏 Stars. Such days accordingly produce auspicious outcomes, and are suitable for renovation and trading, in particular. Used well, they will bring about an increase in wealth and assets, and the birth of noble offspring. Meanwhile, a Ding Hai 丁亥 Day is regarded as a 'secondarily' auspicious day. However, a Gui Hai 癸亥 Day is one of the Six Jia Weakness Days 六甲窮日, while a Xin Hai 辛亥 Day is overly Yin in Qi and therefore cannot be used.

乙 *Yi* 亥 *Hai* Wood Pig	丁 *Ding* 亥 *Hai* Fire Pig	己 *Ji* 亥 *Hai* Earth Pig	辛 *Xin* 亥 *Hai* Metal Pig	癸 *Gui* 亥 *Hai* Water Pig
★	✓	★	✗	✗

★ Excellence　✓ Auspicious　● Moderate　▲ Inauspicious　✗ Dire

Twelfth Month 十二月

January 6th - February 3th

Ox 丑 (Chou) Month

January 6th - February 3rd
Ox 丑 (Chou) Month

月德庚、月恩辛，母倉申酉。天德合乙。

The Monthly Virtue 月德 Star accompanies Geng 庚 Days, the Monthly Benevolence 月恩 Star presides over Xin 辛 Days, and the Motherly Storage 母倉 Star exerts its auspicious influence on Monkey 申 (Shen) and Rooster 酉 (You) Days. Similarly, the Heavenly Virtue 天德 Star lends its positive energies to Yi 乙 Days, thereby enhancing them.

小寒：小寒後三煞在東。
'Lesser Cold' 小寒 (Xiao Han)

After the advent of Xiao Han, the Three Killings 三煞 (San Sha) Affliction may be found in the East sector.

大寒：寅、卯、辰方，忌修造、動土。
'Greater Cold' 大寒 (Da Han)

During Da Han, which follows after Xiao Han, refrain from digging, renovating or disturbing the ground in the Northeast 3 寅 (Yin – NE3), East 2 卯 (Mao – E2) and Southeast 1 辰 (Chen – SE1) sectors, to prevent the harmful energies of the Three Killings from being unleashed.

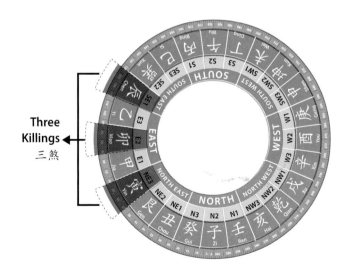

Three Killings
三煞

十二值神 12 Day Officers	十二地支 Animal Sign of the Day	董公擇日解説 Dong Gong Description
建 *Jian* **Establish**	丑 *Chou* Ox Yin Earth 	紅砂、往亡日。乙丑、己丑,宜開山、斬草、興工、動土、嫁娶、開張、出行、入宅,次吉之日也。丁丑煞入中宮,不宜鼓樂、喧嘩、婚姻之事,犯之主刑家長、宅母。癸丑雖旺,乃六煞入中宮,損傷人口,凶。 The presence of the Red Embrace 紅砂 Star makes this an Emptiness Day 往亡日. Yi Chou 乙丑 and Ji Chou 己丑 Days are however suitable for quarrying, excavation, landscaping, construction and groundbreaking works, as well as marriage, opening a business, travel or moving into a new house. On Ding Chou 丁丑 Days, Sha Qi enters the Central Palace, rendering such days unsuitable for celebrations or marriage. Ignoring this warning will only result in elderly family members being more susceptible to illness or injury. Similarly, even though Gui Chou 癸丑 Days are considered prosperous, there is still Sha Qi in the Central Palace, which puts the health and safety of family members at risk. As such, these days should be regarded as inauspicious and hence avoided.

乙 *Yi* 丑 *Chou* Wood Ox	丁 *Ding* 丑 *Chou* Fire Ox	己 *Ji* 丑 *Chou* Earth Ox	辛 *Xin* 丑 *Chou* Metal Ox	癸 *Gui* 丑 *Chou* Water Ox
★	✖	★	●	▲

★ Excellent ✔ Auspicious ● Fair ▲ Inauspicious ✖ Dire

董公擇日要覽

寅
Tiger

十二值神 12 Day Officers	十二地支 Animal Sign of the Day	董公擇日解説 Dong Gong Description
除 *Chu* **Remove**	寅 *Yin* **Tiger** **Yang Wood** 	庚寅火星、天月二德、甲寅、丙寅、壬寅,俱有火星及黃羅、紫檀、天皇、地皇、寶輦,庫珠,金銀、福祿、文昌、祿馬,官蓋眾吉星照臨,宜起造、婚姻、安葬、入宅、開張、出行,百事順利,用之家門發達、動土雙進財產、名登虎榜。戊寅,亦有火星,乃次吉之日,可用。 Geng Yin 庚寅 Days enjoy the supportive energies of the Fire 火星, Heavenly 天德 and Monthly Virtue 月德 Stars. Similarly, Jia Yin 甲寅, Bing Yin 丙寅, and Ren Yin 壬寅 Days are accompanied by the presence of the Fire 火星, Yellow Spiral 黃羅, Purple Sandalwood 紫檀, Heavenly Emperor 天皇, Earthly Emperor 地皇, Precious Carriage 寶輦, Pearl Storage 庫珠, Golden Ingot 金銀, Fortune Prosperity 福祿, Literary Arts 文昌 and Prosperous Horse 祿馬 Stars. This makes all these days ideal for renovations, marriage, burial, moving into a new house, opening a business and travel, with positive outcomes guaranteed for all endeavors. Those who tap into the useful energies of these days will prosper and enjoy an increase in wealth, and the reputation carried by a good name. A Wu Yin 戊寅 Day is also accompanied by the Fire Star 火星, making it a secondary good day to be used.

甲 *Jia* 寅 *Yin* **Wood Tiger**	丙 *Bing* 寅 *Yin* **Fire Tiger**	戊 *Wu* 寅 *Yin* **Earth Tiger**	庚 *Geng* 寅 *Yin* **Metal Tiger**	壬 *Ren* 寅 *Yin* **Water Tiger**
★	★	✓	★	★

★ Excellent   ✓ Auspicious   ● Fair   ▲ Inauspicious   ✗ Dire

十二值神 12 Day Officers	十二地支 Animal Sign of the Day	董公擇日解説 Dong Gong Description
滿 *Man* **Full**	卯 *Mao* **Rabbit** **Yin Wood** 	天富。土瘟，不宜動土，犯之天瘟一年，若用卯日娶親、問名等事小吉，但有六成六不合之疑。惟辛卯造作、興工，乃是次吉之日也。 Despite the presence of the Heavenly Fortune 天富 Star, the threat of an earth-bound disease looms over one's head. Using this day for groundbreaking will only result in one being plagued by health problems throughout the year. It is moderately suitable for marriage, however, with a Xin Mao 辛卯 Day usable for construction purposes.

卯
Rabbit

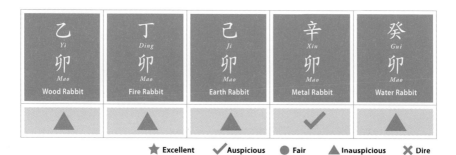

十二値神 12 Day Officers	十二地支 Animal Sign of the Day	董公擇日解説 Dong Gong Description
平 *Ping* **Balance**	辰 *Chen* Dragon Yang Earth 	有到州星,事到官而後散。惟壬辰宜娶親,埋葬、娶親、興工、出行、入宅,次吉。庚辰天、月二德,宜小作,次吉。戊辰草木凋零之時,五行無氣,乃是退星,又兼煞入中宮,諸事不利,凶。 What begins well will end less-than-desirably. As such, while Ren Chen 壬辰 Days harbor good stars, they are only moderately suitable for marriage, burial, commencing work, travel or moving into new premises. One would do better to utilize Geng Chen 庚辰 Days, which are supported by the Heavenly and Earthly Virtue stars and therefore slightly more auspicious. On a Wu Chen 戊辰 Day, however, there is no Qi in the Five Elements, and this scenario, coupled with Sha Qi entering the Central Palace, only makes for an extremely inauspicious day.

甲 *Jia* 辰 *Chen* Wood Dragon	丙 *Bing* 辰 *Chen* Fire Dragon	戊 *Wu* 辰 *Chen* Earth Dragon	庚 *Geng* 辰 *Chen* Metal Dragon	壬 *Ren* 辰 *Chen* Water Dragon
▲	▲	▲	★	✓

 ★ Excellent ✓ Auspicious ● Fair ▲ Inauspicious ✗ Dire

十二值神 12 Day Officers	十二地支 Animal Sign of the Day	董公擇日解説 Dong Gong Description
定 *Ding* **Stable**	巳 *Si* Snake Yin Fire 	天成。一云官符星,非但云是死氣之日,如修方值飛宮州縣官符,立見官事,若其方合吉神眾,集能求其凶,用之亦可。癸巳雖值金水潔淨之時,或可用開山、斬草之事,乃次吉之日,若娶親、開張、出行、入宅、定磉、拴架,卻是天上大空亡納音自絕不宜用也。丁巳正四廢,凶。一年四季凡用巳日,主口舌,雖有喜神化解,亦屬難免。如吉旺凶衰,必須查明年命、向山不犯沖剋,可用。 Although the Heavenly Success Star is present, it is also accompanied by the Officer Charm Star 官符星, which denotes legal matters. As such, this day can only be used if there are other positive stars present to tip the scales towards the more positive side. A Gui Si 癸巳 Day is suitable to excavate mountains or for quarrying and landscaping works, although it remains a less-than-ideal date that should not be used for marriage, opening a business, business-related travel, or moving into or building a new house. On this day, the self Na Yin element is in extinction. Meanwhile, a Ding Si 丁巳 Day is also one of the Direct Abandonment 正四廢 Days, and therefore an inauspicious one that should be avoided. Likewise, those who use the remaining Si 巳(Snake) days subject themselves to the possibility of gossip and slander, even with the presence of favorable stars. To err on the side of caution, only use such days if there are other prosperous stars present, and in tandem with one's birth details (BaZi) and the Facing/Sitting Direction of one's property.

Snake

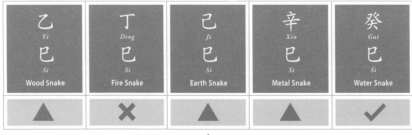

乙 *Yi* 巳 *Si* Wood Snake	丁 *Ding* 巳 *Si* Fire Snake	己 *Ji* 巳 *Si* Earth Snake	辛 *Xin* 巳 *Si* Metal Snake	癸 *Gui* 巳 *Si* Water Snake
▲	✖	▲	▲	✔

★ Excellent   ✔ Auspicious   ● Fair   ▲ Inauspicious   ✖ Dire

十二值神 12 Day Officers	十二地支 Animal Sign of the Day	董公擇日解說 Dong Gong Description
 執 *Zhi* **Initiate**	 午 *Wu* Horse Yang Fire	庚午,天月二德,如庚午年作庚山甲向,宜可收爲納音也,況其日有用庚辰時者,時遇三合照甲庚,而庚祿居申,辰馬又值壬申,此之謂生成祿馬日,龍馬遇祿星,聖人南面星有黃羅、紫檀、天皇、地皇、金銀寶樓,眾吉星蓋照,主益子孫、旺家門、進田產、遷祿位,壬午並吉,餘午次吉,丙午正四廢,凶。 Geng Wu 庚午 Days have the Heavenly 天德 and Monthly Virtue 月德 Stars present. Hence, during a Geng Wu Year 庚午年 year, use the Geng Sitting 庚山, Jia Facing 甲向 setup to receive Na Yin Qi. One can also utilize the Geng Chen 庚辰 Hour, to produce a Three Harmony Shining on Jia and Geng 三合照甲庚 formation, where the Geng Prosperous 祿 Branch resides in the Shen 申 (Monkey) Stem. Such a day is also known as a Prosperous Sky Horse Day 生成祿馬日, which is further supported by a host of auspicious stars including the Yellow Spiral 黃羅, Purple Sandalwood 紫檀, Heavenly Emperor 天皇, Earthly Emperor 地皇, Golden Ingot 金銀 and Precious Building 寶樓. This combination brings about an increase in wealth and good advancement opportunities in life. Do note however that while Ren Wu 壬午 Days are also very auspicious days, the other Wu 午 (Horse) days are only considered second-tier options. Only the Bing Wu 丙午 day is completely unusable, as it is one of the Direct Abandonment 正四廢 Days.

董公擇日要覽

午
Horse

甲 *Jia* 午 *Wu* Wood Horse	丙 *Bing* 午 *Wu* Fire Horse	戊 *Wu* 午 *Wu* Earth Horse	庚 *Geng* 午 *Wu* Metal Horse	壬 *Ren* 午 *Wu* Water Horse
✔	✘	✔	★	★

★ Excellent ✔ Auspicious ● Fair ▲ Inauspicious ✘ Dire

十二值神 12 Day Officers	十二地支 Animal Sign of the Day	董公擇日解説 Dong Gong Description
破 *Po* **Destruction**	未 *Wei* **Goat** Yin Earth	丁未水居巨鰲,癸未水入秦州,内有文昌貴顯之星,宜動土、興工、出行、入宅、娶親、開張,百事大吉。己未、辛未,煞入中宫,凶,乙未亦不利。 Qi is prosperous and thriving on Ding Wei 丁未 and Gui Wei 癸未 Days, which also enjoy the positive energies of the Literary Arts 文昌 Star. As such, these days are suitable groundbreaking, marriage, travel, moving into a new house or opening a business, as all endeavors undertaken will bear fruit. Ji Wei 己未, Xin Wei 辛未 and Yi Wei 乙未 Days, however, harbor Sha Qi, and should hence be avoided.

Goat

乙 *Yi* 未 *Wei* Wood Goat	丁 *Ding* 未 *Wei* Fire Goat	己 *Ji* 未 *Wei* Earth Goat	辛 *Xin* 未 *Wei* Metal Goat	癸 *Gui* 未 *Wei* Water Goat
▲	★	▲	▲	★

★ Excellent ✔ Auspicious ● Fair ▲ Inauspicious ✖ Dire

十二值神 12 Day Officers	十二地支 Animal Sign of the Day	董公擇日解説 Dong Gong Description
危 *Wei* **Danger**	申 *Shen* Monkey Yang Metal 	庚申天月二德,宜修造、安葬、小小營爲,次吉,如大家千百工以上起造、開張、入宅、婚姻等事,卻不宜,其日煞入中宮,不利家長人眷,雖有天、月二德,亦無如之何作,用者損傷手足、匠夫,破失損壞器皿,大作速見、小作緩應,若作牛羊豬圈,六十日、一百二十日內便見虎狼傷害,更生瘟疫。甲申起造、安葬吉。丙申、壬申只宜埋葬吉。戊申日未詳。 Although a Geng Shen 庚申 Day is marked by the presence of the Heavenly and Earthly Virtue 天月二德 Stars, it is only suitable for minor repairs and burial. This day should not be used for major renovations, opening a business, moving into a new house or marriage, as this would result in Sha Qi entering the Central Palace, and harming the eldest member in a family. Worse still, anyone who taps into the energies of this day will be likely attacked by a tiger or wolf, and/or fall ill easily, within 60 to120 days. A Jia Shen 甲申 Day may also be used for minor repairs and burial, while Bing Shen 丙申 and Ren Shen 壬申 Days are especially auspicious days for burial.

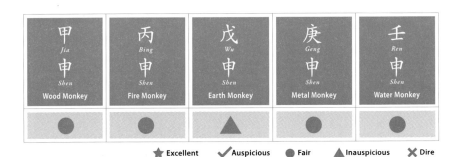

甲 *Jia* 申 *Shen* Wood Monkey	丙 *Bing* 申 *Shen* Fire Monkey	戊 *Wu* 申 *Shen* Earth Monkey	庚 *Geng* 申 *Shen* Metal Monkey	壬 *Ren* 申 *Shen* Water Monkey
● Fair	● Fair	▲ Inauspicious	● Fair	● Fair

★ Excellent　✔ Auspicious　● Fair　▲ Inauspicious　✕ Dire

十二值神 12 Day Officers	十二地支 Animal Sign of the Day	董公擇日解說 Dong Gong Description
成 *Cheng* **Success**	酉 *You* Rooster Yin Metal	天喜。己酉、癸酉,爲金旺之時,乙酉爲水潔淨之時,有黃羅、紫檀、金銀,庫樓、玉堂、庫珠、聚祿,眾祿帶馬,吉星蓋照,利婚姻、起造、開張、入宅、安葬,全吉之日也,主子孫興旺、百事稱心。丁酉亦屬金旺惟,惟埋葬大吉,餘事次之,辛酉金鑾次吉。 With the presence of the Sky Happiness Star, Ji You 己酉 and Gui You 癸酉 Days are further boosted by prosperous Metal Qi. Similarly, Water Qi on a Yi You 乙酉 Day is pure and in perfect balance, with the presence of auspicious stars such as the Yellow Spiral 黃羅, Purple Sandalwood 紫檀, Golden Ingot 金銀, Storage Building 庫樓, Converging Prosperous 聚祿 and Armored Horse 帶馬. Use these days for marriage, renovations, business openings, moving into a new house and burial; their positive energies will produce powerful and prosperous descendents. However, while a Ding You 丁酉 Day, which also harbors prosperous Metal Qi, can be used for burial, the outcome of using such a day for other matters will only bring about moderate results. Similarly, a Xin You 辛酉 Day is only considered a second-grade date, in terms of usability.

Rooster

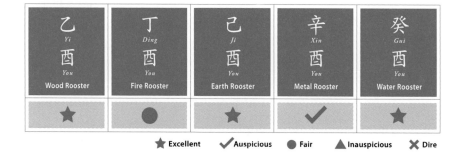

乙 *Yi* 酉 *You* Wood Rooster	丁 *Ding* 酉 *You* Fire Rooster	己 *Ji* 酉 *You* Earth Rooster	辛 *Xin* 酉 *You* Metal Rooster	癸 *Gui* 酉 *You* Water Rooster
★	●	★	✓	★

★ Excellent   ✓ Auspicious   ● Fair   ▲ Inauspicious   ✗ Dire

Twelfth Month 十二月

十二值神 12 Day Officers	十二地支 Animal Sign of the Day	董公擇日解説 Dong Gong Description
收 *Shou* **Receive**	戌 *Xu* **Dog** **Yang Earth** 	有到州星,事到公堂而後散。庚戌有天、月二德、八位魁星有男子之權,先招口舌,而後大吉。甲戌,八方俱白,二十四向諸神朝天,天玄女偷修之日可用。丙戌、壬戌,煞入中宮,壬戌百事皆忌。戊戌日,亦不可用。 One will experience a good start that will unfortunately end in a poor finish. However, Geng Xu 庚戌 Days are accompanied by the Heavenly and Monthly Virtue Stars, which augur well for the authority of males; although they may well have to overcome obstacles first, before reaping the rewards of their labor. Similarly, Jia Xu 甲戌 Days may also be used. Avoid Bing Xu 丙戌 and Ren Xu 壬戌 Days though, as they harbor negative Qi. Wu Xu 戊戌 Day also should not be used.

甲 *Jia* 戌 *Xu* Wood Dog	丙 *Bing* 戌 *Xu* Fire Dog	戊 *Wu* 戌 *Xu* Earth Dog	庚 *Geng* 戌 *Xu* Metal Dog	壬 *Ren* 戌 *Xu* Water Dog
✔	▲	▲	✔	▲

★ Excellent ✔ Auspicious ● Fair ▲ Inauspicious ✖ Dire

十二值神 12 Day Officers	十二地支 Animal Sign of the Day	董公擇日解説 Dong Gong Description
開 *Kai* **Open**	亥 *Hai* Pig Yin Water 	天賊、月厭。乙亥有文昌星,己亥火星,有文昌顯貴星,宜定碓、拵架、婚姻、開張、入宅、出行、營爲,諸事全吉營爲諸事全吉,宜用戊辰時,是日雖犯天賊,卻有天狗護之不妨,故上吉。如遇此日生人,大壞之命。丁亥亦宜用事。辛亥陰氣太甚,非陽間所宜用。癸亥六甲窮日,不可用。己亥因有火星,諸事可用,無不順利,而稱心如意耳。 The Heavenly Thief 天賊 and Month Detest 月厭 Stars are simultaneously present throughout the day. Nevertheless, Yi Hai 乙亥 Days are accompanied by the Literary Arts 文昌 Star, while Ji Hai 己亥 Days harbor the 火星 Fire Star and also the Literary Arts 文昌 Star. Such days are hence ideal for building or moving into a new house, marriage, opening a business, travel etc. Try to use a Ding Hai 丁亥 if possible, as it is suitable for most activities. Yin Qi is overly strong on Xin Hai 辛亥 Days, while a Gui Hai 癸亥 Day is one of the 60 Jia Zi 陰氣太甚 Days. One would be better off using a Ji Hai 己亥 Day, because the presence of the Fire Star 火星 makes it ideal for any type of activity or endeavor.

乙 *Yi* 亥 *Hai* Wood Pig	丁 *Ding* 亥 *Hai* Fire Pig	己 *Ji* 亥 *Hai* Earth Pig	辛 *Xin* 亥 *Hai* Metal Pig	癸 *Gui* 亥 *Hai* Water Pig
★	✔	★	▲	✖

★ Excellent ✔ Auspicious ● Fair ▲ Inauspicious ✖ Dire

十二值神 12 Day Officers	十二地支 Animal Sign of the Day	董公擇日解說 Dong Gong Description
閉 *Bi* **Close**	子 *Zi* Rat Yang Water 	黃砂。庚子雖有天、月二德,卻是天地轉煞之時,壬子、丙子,天轉地煞,不宜興工、動土,犯之大凶。甲子天赦,是進神日,並戊子,宜小可修爲,吉,若大用之則凶禍,纏繞不詳甚莫大焉,納音凶煞,乃北方造之神,純陰黑煞之氣,用事司曹肅令,非大貴不敢用,當用者慎之。 The Yellow Spiral 黃砂 Star is present throughout the day. Geng Zi 庚子 Days are however accompanied by the Heavenly and Earthly Virtues 天月二德 Stars, which clash simultaneously with the negative Heaven and Earth Drilling Sha 天轉地煞 Star. This makes a Geng Zi Day unsuitable for groundbreaking or commencing a new task; for violating this rule would only bring about disaster and catastrophe. Ren Zi 壬子 and Bing Zi 丙子 day also has the Heaven and Earth Drilling Sha 天轉地煞 should not be used. A Jia Zi 甲子 Day is also known as a Heavenly Pardon 天赦 Day, while a Wu Zi 戊子 Day is ideal for activities of minor importance. Do not use such days for major or important events, though.

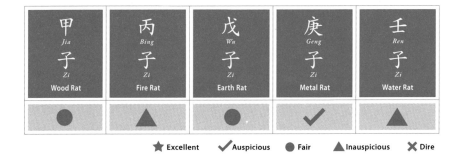

Auxiliary Stars Charts

神煞圖

Grand Duke (Tai Sui) 太歲圖

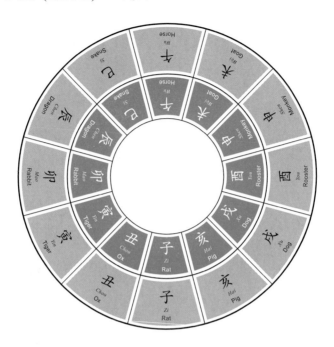

Year Breaker Diagram 歲破圖

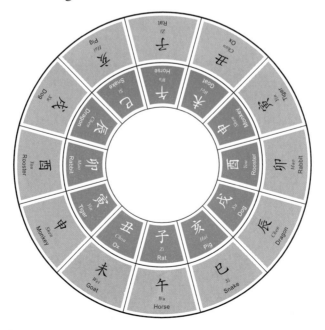

Duke Virtue　歲德圖

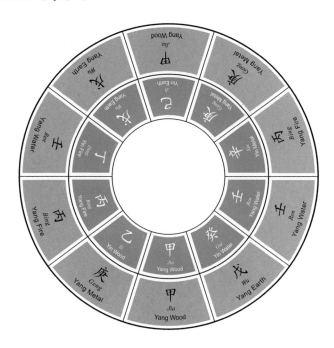

Duke Virtue Combo　歲德合圖

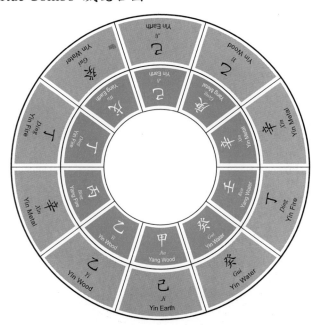

Duke Punishment 歲刑圖

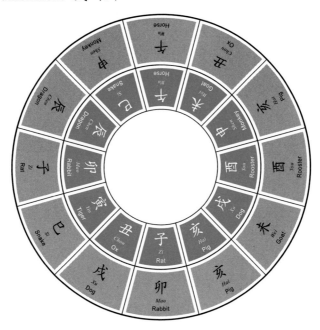

Eight Wealth Diagram 八祿圖

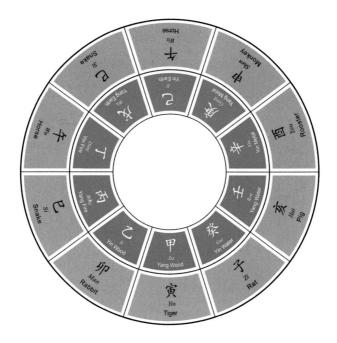

Decree 奏書圖

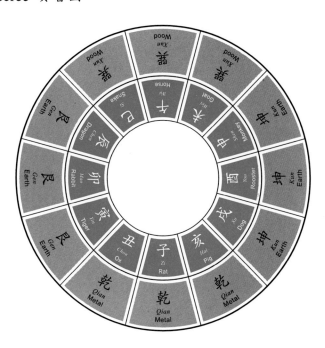

Professor 博士圖

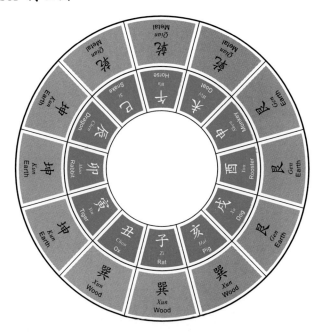

Strongman 力士圖

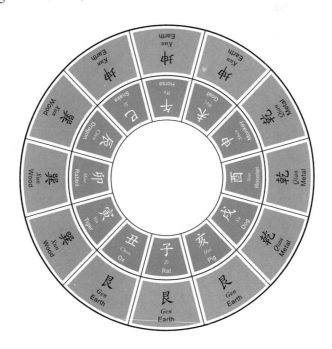

Silkworm Life 蠶命圖

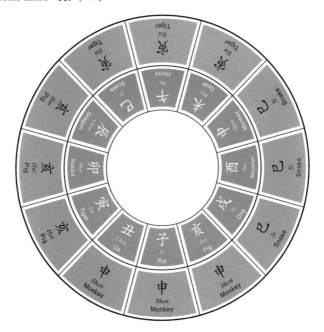

Silkworm Officer　蠶宮圖

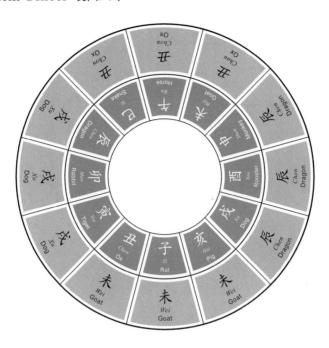

Silkworm Room　蠶室圖

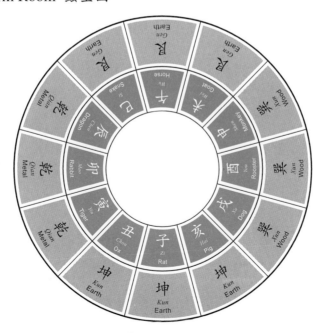

Mountain Patrol Luo Hou Diagram 巡山羅睺圖

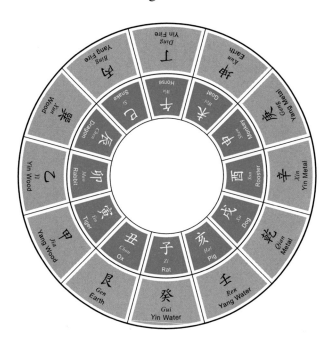

Floating Heaven Emptiness Diagram 浮天空亡圖

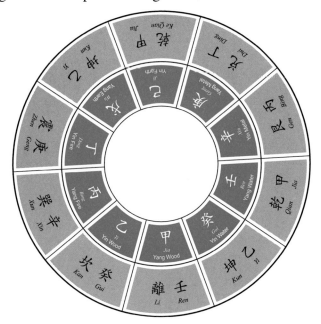

Roasting Star Diagram 炙退圖

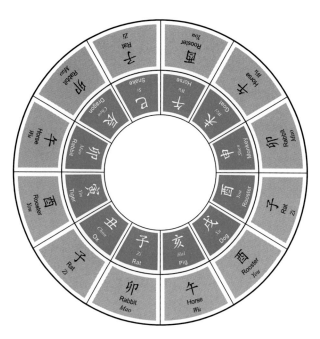

Vast Mold Five Element Diagram 洪範五行圖

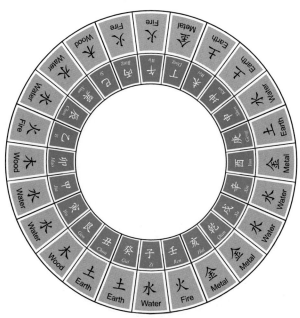

Mountain Covering Yellow Path Diagram 蓋山黃道圖

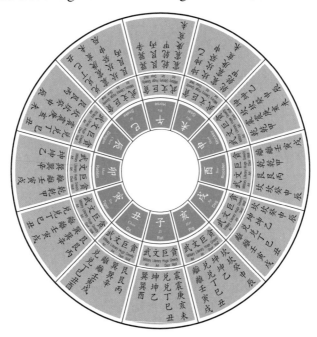

Sitting Sha, Facing Sha Diagram 坐殺向殺圖

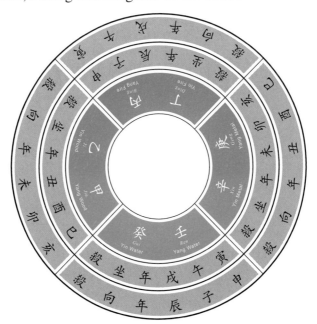

Yin Mansion Diagram 陰府圖

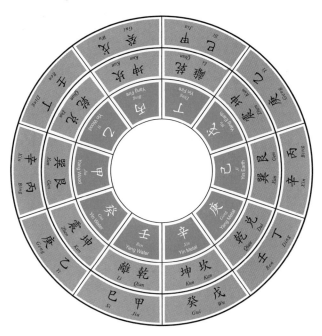

Heavenly Palace Charm Diagram 天宮符圖

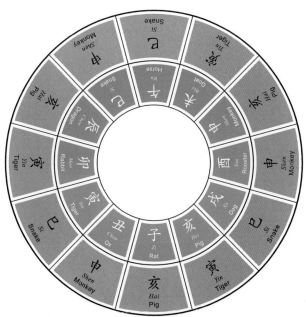

Sole Fire Diagram 燭火圖

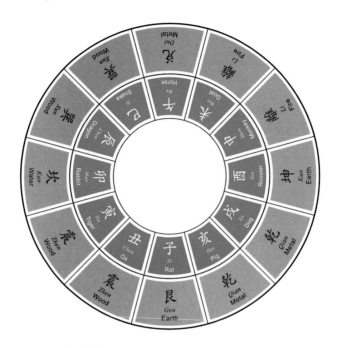

Big General 大將軍圖

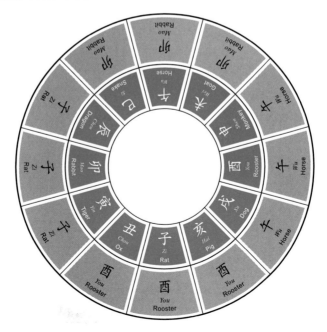

Unsightly Gathering Diagram 群醜圖

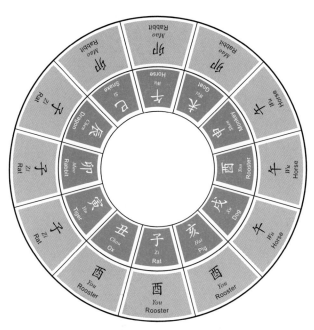

Officer Charm and Livestock Officer 官符畜官圖

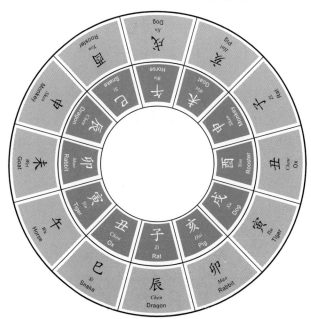

White Tiger 白虎圖

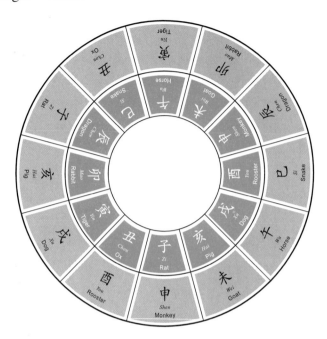

Moon Suspended Guest 太陰吊客圖

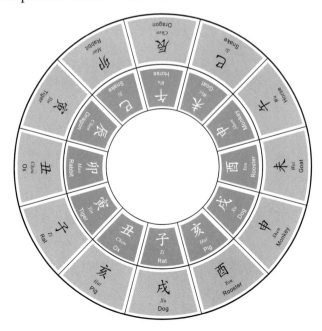

Funeral Door 喪門圖

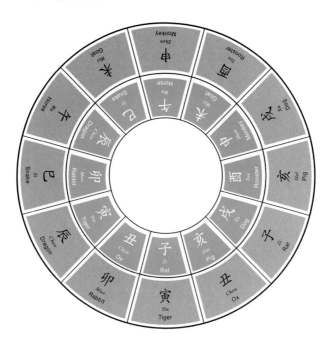

Yellow Flag 黃幡圖

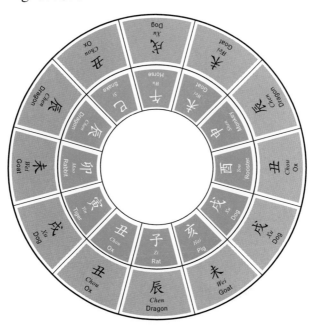

Leopard Tail 豹尾圖

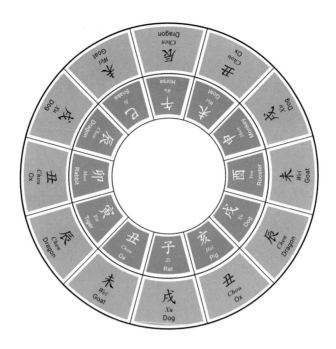

Sickness Charm 病符圖

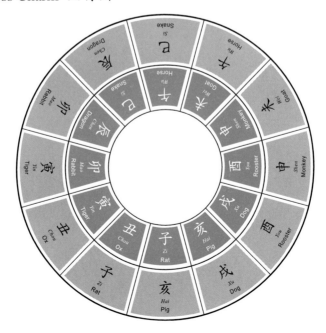

Death Charm 死符小耗圖

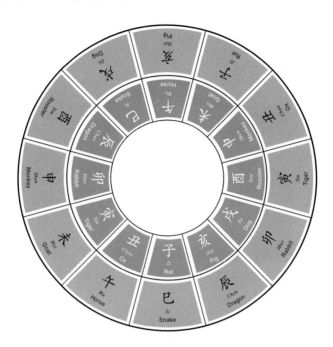

Robbery Sha 劫煞圖

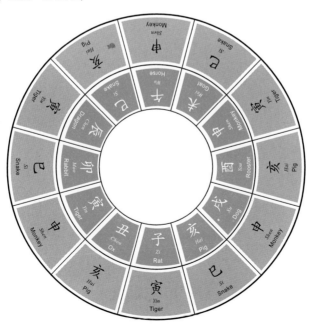

Annual Sha 歲煞圖

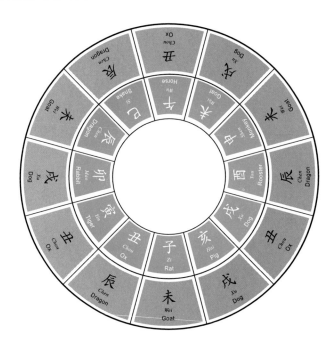

Subsided Army (Great Mishap) 伏兵大禍圖

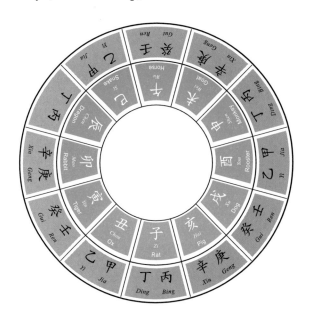

Five Army Assembly Diagram　五兵總圖

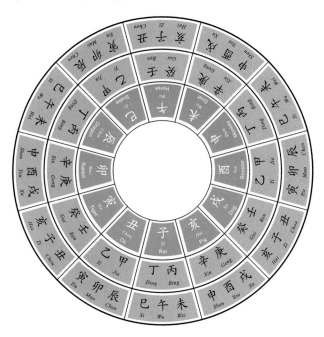

Heavenly Noble　天乙貴人圖

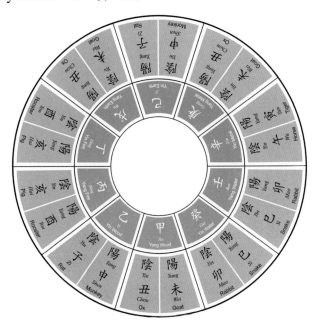

Great Sha 大煞圖

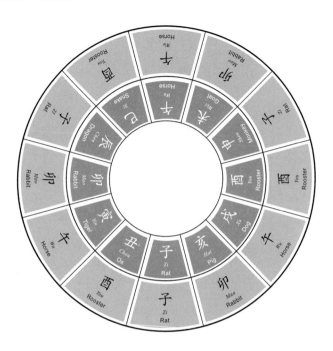

Flying Chaste 飛廉圖

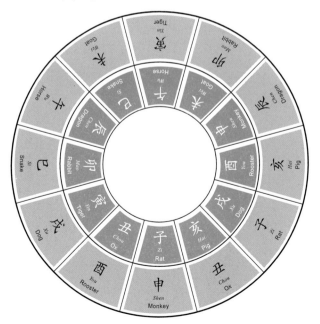

Golden God 金神圖

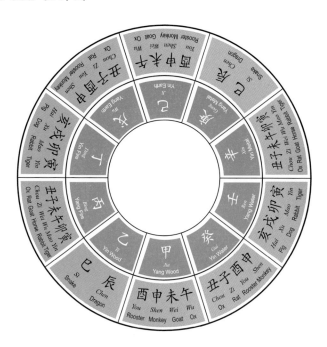

Five Ghost 五鬼圖

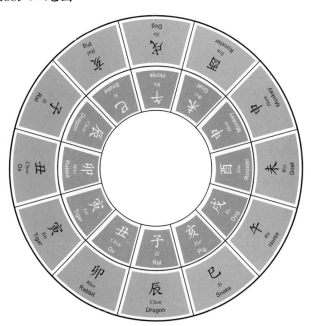

Destructive Five Ghost 破敗五鬼圖

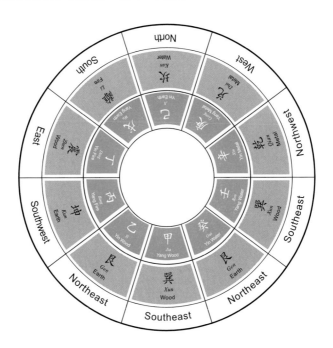

Purple White 12 Annual Star Diagrams

紫白十二歲君圖

Rat Year 1 White 12 Annual Star Diagrams
子年一白十二歲君圖

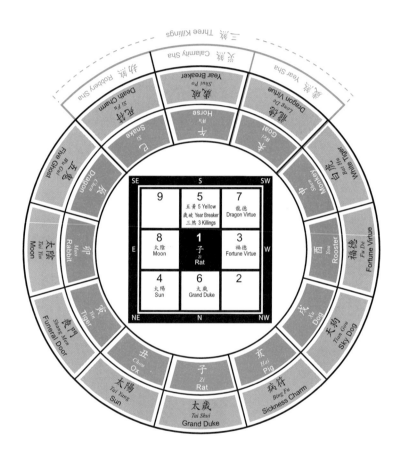

Rat Year 7 Red 12 Annual Star Diagrams
子年七赤十二歲君圖

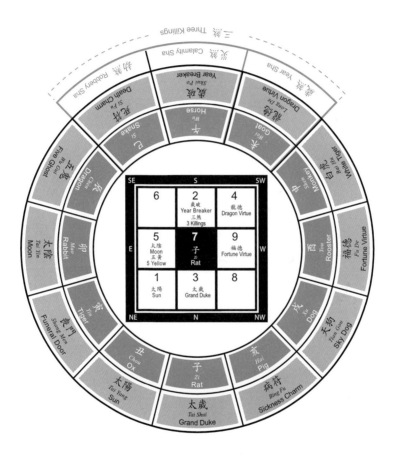

Rat Year 4 Green 12 Annual Star Diagrams
子年四綠十二歲君圖

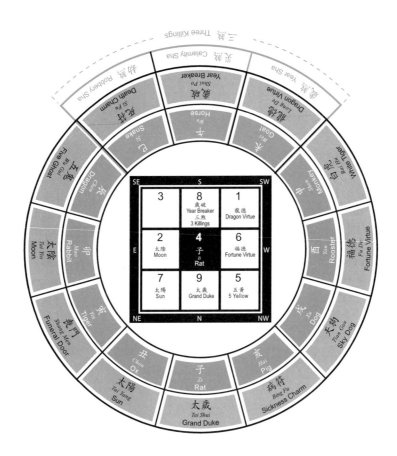

Ox Year 9 Purple 12 Annual Star Diagrams
丑年九紫十二歲君圖

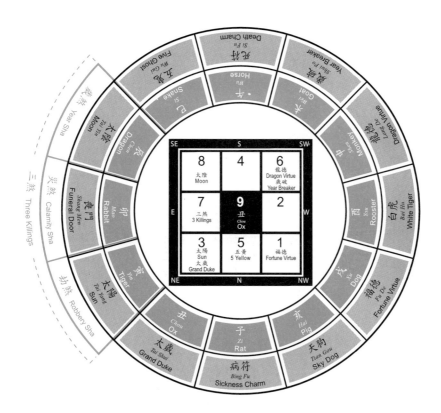

Ox Year 6 White 12 Annual Star Diagrams
丑年六白十二歲君圖

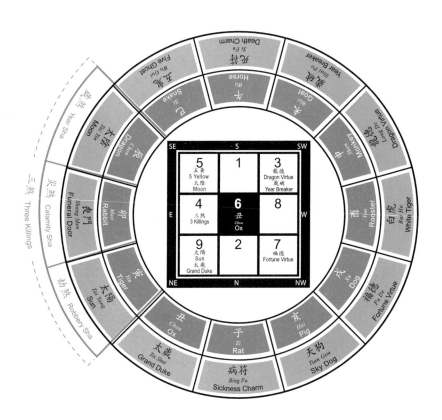

Ox Year 3 Jade 12 Annual Star Diagrams
丑年三碧十二歲君圖

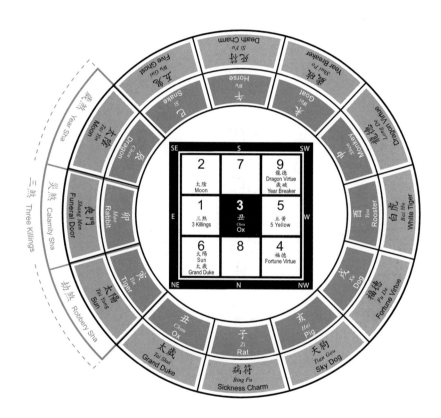

Tiger Year 8 White 12 Annual Star Diagrams
寅年八白十二歲君圖

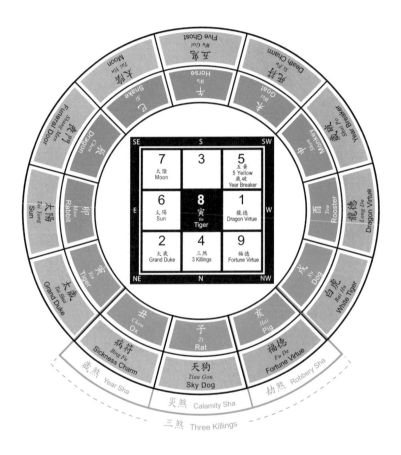

Tiger Year 5 Yellow 12 Annual Star Diagrams
寅年五黃十二歲君圖

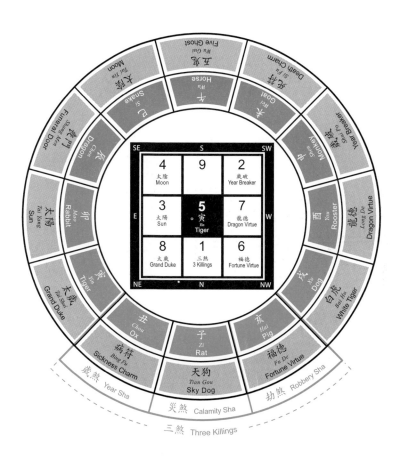

Tiger Year 2 Black 12 Annual Star Diagrams
寅年二黑十二歲君圖

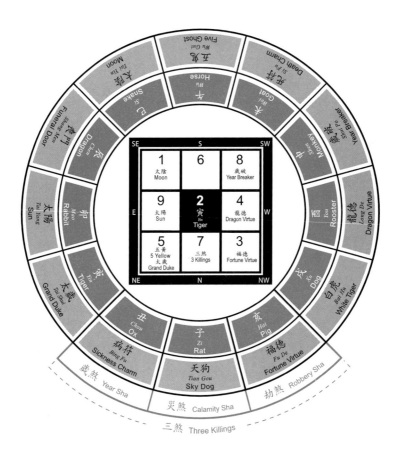

Rabbit Year 1 White 12 Annual Star Diagrams
卯年一白十二歲君圖

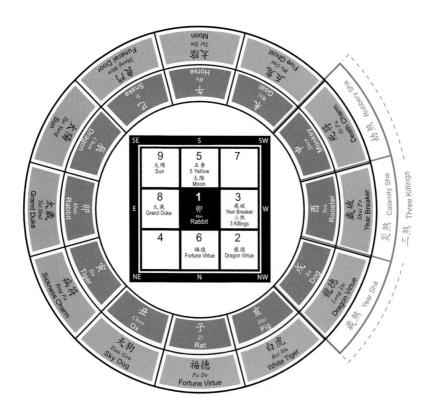

Rabbit Year 4 Green 12 Annual Star Diagrams
卯年四綠十二歲君圖

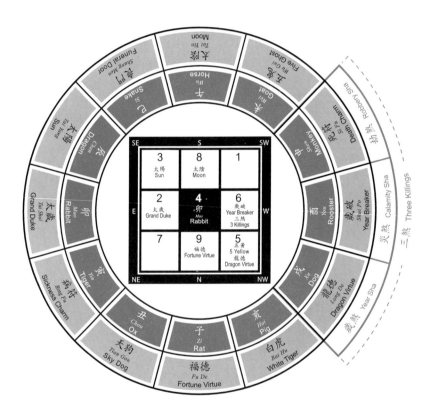

Rabbit Year 7 Red 12 Annual Star Diagrams
卯年七赤十二歲君圖

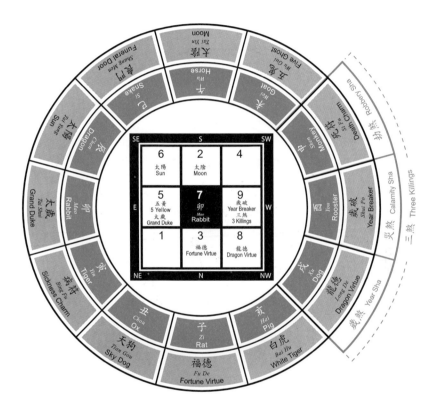

Dragon Year 6 White 12 Annual Star Diagrams
辰年六白十二歲君圖

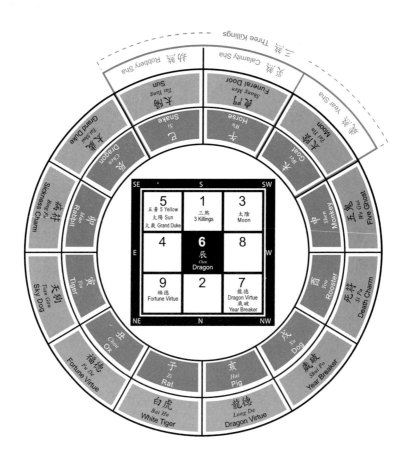

Dragon Year 3 Jade 12 Annual Star Diagrams
辰年三碧十二歲君圖

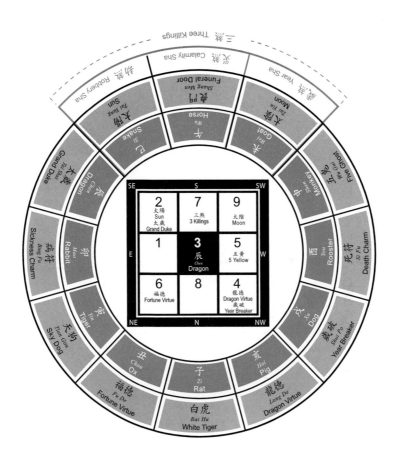

Dragon Year 9 Purple 12 Annual Star Diagrams
辰年九紫十二歲君圖

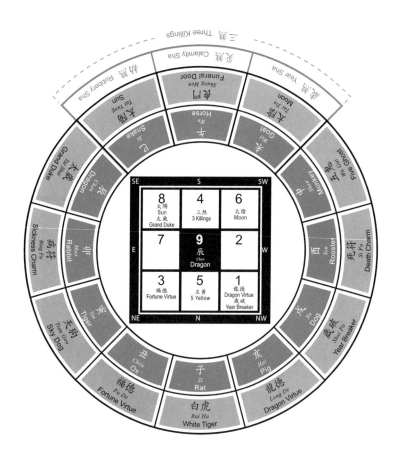

Snake Year 5 Yellow 12 Annual Star Diagrams
巳年五黃十二歲君圖

黃公擇日要覽

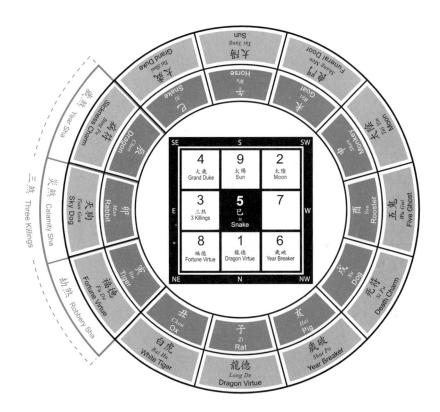

Snake Year 2 Black 12 Annual Star Diagrams
巳年二黑十二歲君圖

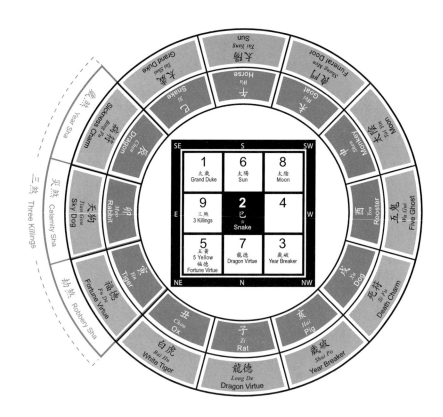

Snake Year 8 White 12 Annual Star Diagrams
巳年八白十二歲君圖

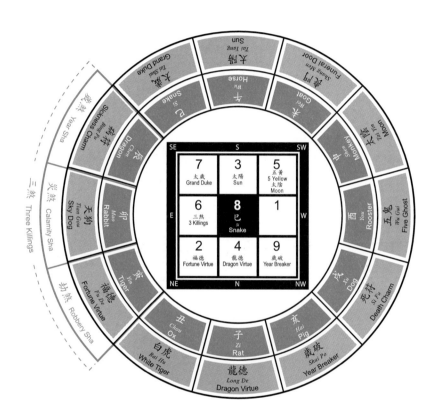

Horse Year 4 Green 12 Annual Star Diagrams
午年四綠十二歲君圖

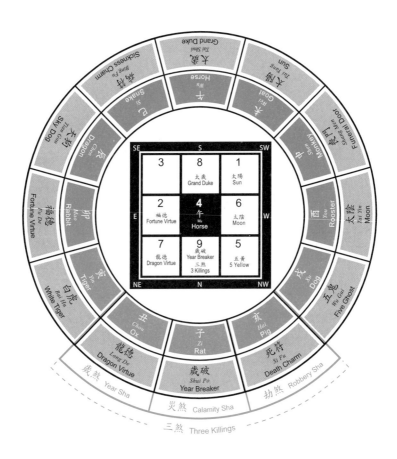

Horse Year 1 White 12 Annual Star Diagrams
午年一白十二歲君圖

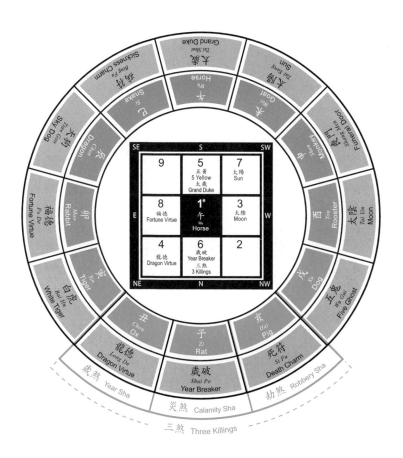

Horse Year 7 Red 12 Annual Star Diagrams
午年七赤十二歲君圖

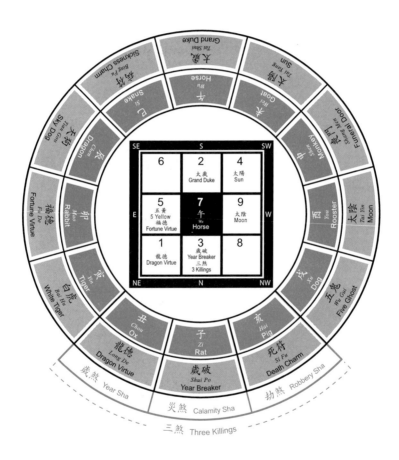

Goat Year 3 Jade 12 Annual Star Diagrams
未年三碧十二歲君圖

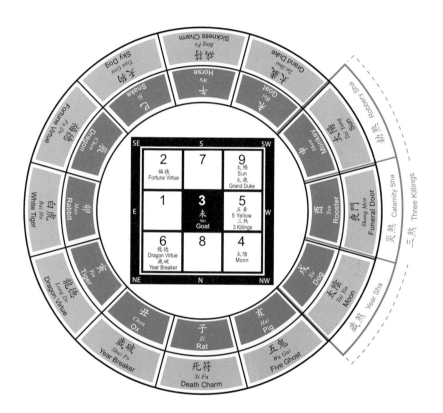

Goat Year 9 Purple 12 Annual Star Diagrams
未年九紫十二歲君圖

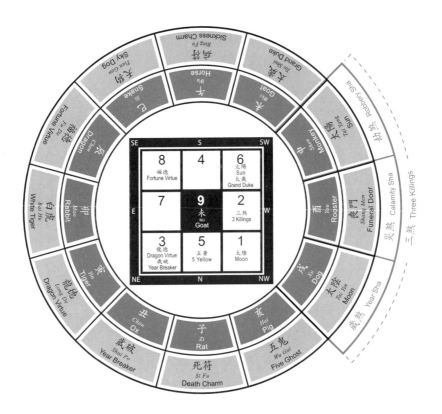

Goat Year 6 White 12 Annual Star Diagrams
未年六白十二歲君圖

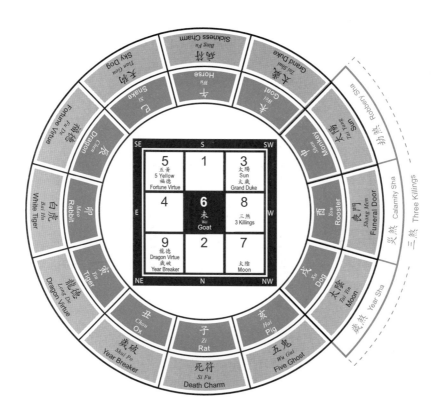

Monkey Year 2 Black 12 Annual Star Diagrams
申年二黑十二歲君圖

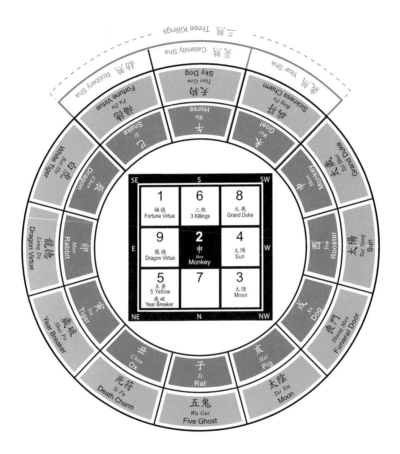

Monkey Year 8 White 12 Annual Star Diagrams
申年八白十二歲君圖

董公擇日要覽

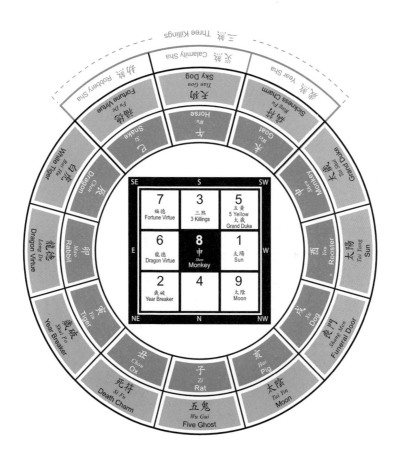

Monkey Year 5 Yellow 12 Annual Star Diagrams
申年五黃十二歲君圖

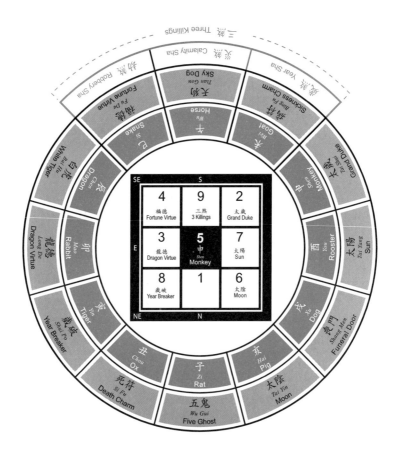

Rooster Year 1 White 12 Annual Star Diagrams
酉年一白十二歲君圖

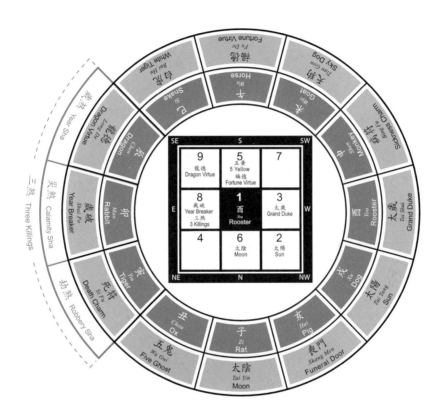

Rooster Year 7 Red 12 Annual Star Diagrams
酉年七赤十二歲君圖

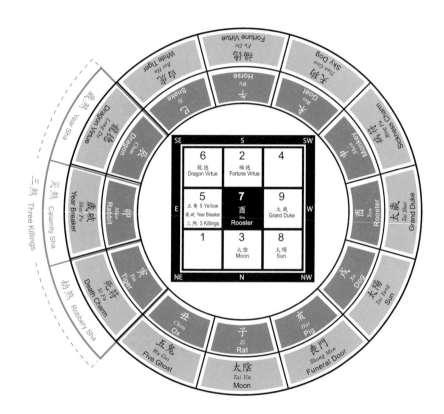

Rooster Year 4 Green 12 Annual Star Diagrams
酉年四綠十二歲君圖

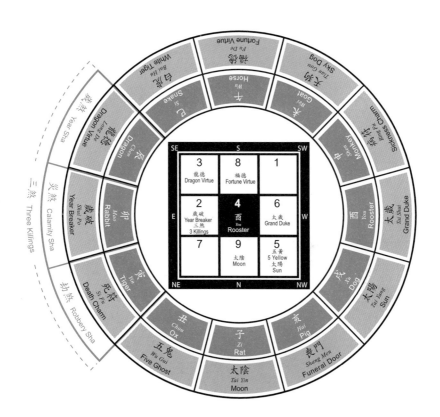

Dog Year 9 Purple 12 Annual Star Diagrams
戌年九紫十二歲君圖

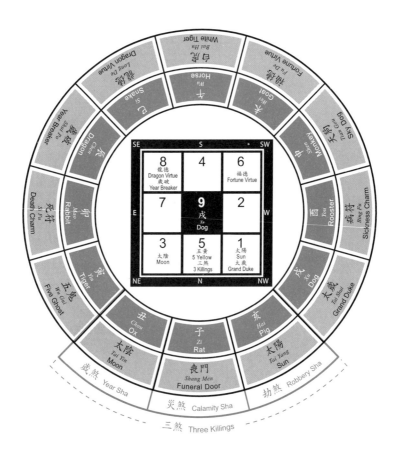

Dog Year 6 White 12 Annual Star Diagrams
戌年六白十二歲君圖

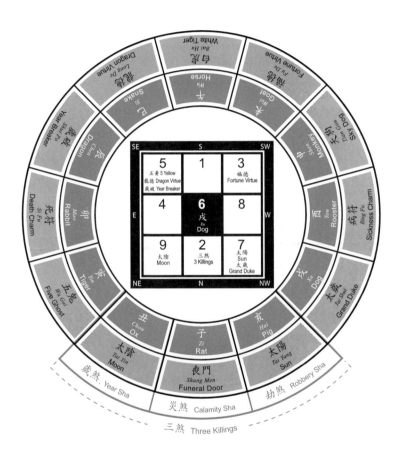

Dog Year 3 Jade 12 Annual Star Diagrams
戌年三碧十二歲君圖

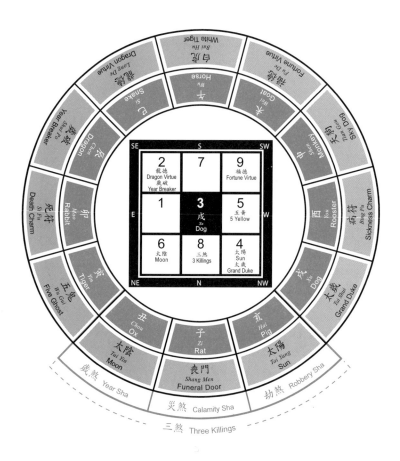

Pig Year 8 White 12 Annual Star Diagrams
亥年八白十二歲君圖

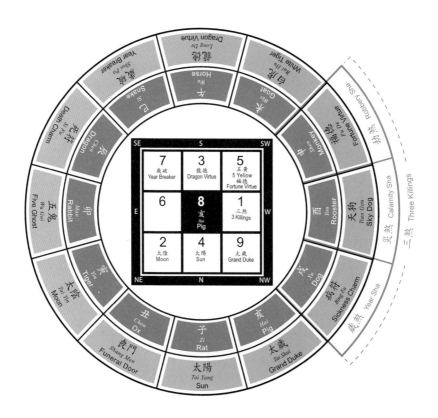

Pig Year 5 Yellow 12 Annual Star Diagrams
亥年五黃十二歲君圖

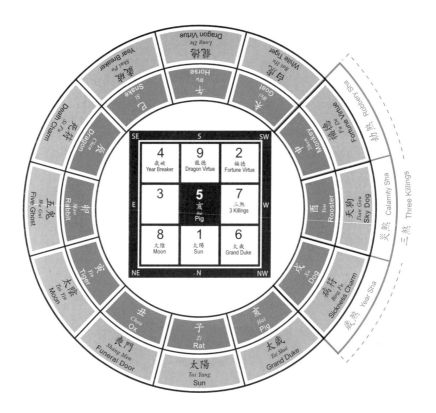

Pig Year 2 Black 12 Annual Star Diagrams
亥年二黑十二歲君圖

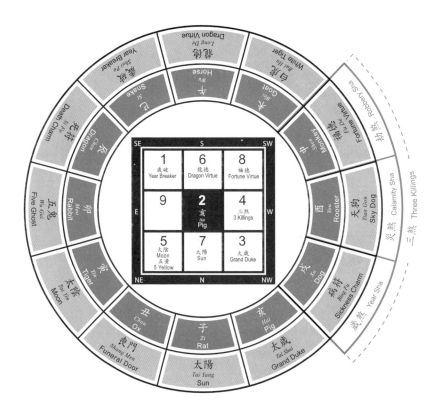

12 Day Officers
建除十二值神

董
公
擇
日
要
覽

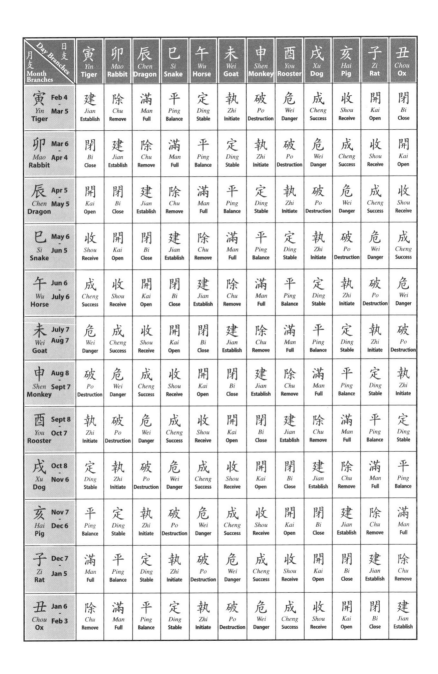

月支 Month Branches \ 日支 Day Branches	寅 Yin Tiger	卯 Mao Rabbit	辰 Chen Dragon	巳 Si Snake	午 Wu Horse	未 Wei Goat	申 Shen Monkey	酉 You Rooster	戌 Xu Dog	亥 Hai Pig	子 Zi Rat	丑 Chou Ox
寅 Yin Tiger Feb 4 - Mar 5	建 Jian Establish	除 Chu Remove	滿 Man Full	平 Ping Balance	定 Ding Stable	執 Zhi Initiate	破 Po Destruction	危 Wei Danger	成 Cheng Success	收 Shou Receive	開 Kai Open	閉 Bi Close
卯 Mao Rabbit Mar 6 - Apr 4	閉 Bi Close	建 Jian Establish	除 Chu Remove	滿 Man Full	平 Ping Balance	定 Ding Stable	執 Zhi Initiate	破 Po Destruction	危 Wei Danger	成 Cheng Success	收 Shou Receive	開 Kai Open
辰 Chen Dragon Apr 5 - May 5	開 Kai Open	閉 Bi Close	建 Jian Establish	除 Chu Remove	滿 Man Full	平 Ping Balance	定 Ding Stable	執 Zhi Initiate	破 Po Destruction	危 Wei Danger	成 Cheng Success	收 Shou Receive
巳 Si Snake May 6 - Jun 5	收 Shou Receive	開 Kai Open	閉 Bi Close	建 Jian Establish	除 Chu Remove	滿 Man Full	平 Ping Balance	定 Ding Stable	執 Zhi Initiate	破 Po Destruction	危 Wei Danger	成 Cheng Success
午 Wu Horse Jun 6 - July 6	成 Cheng Success	收 Shou Receive	開 Kai Open	閉 Bi Close	建 Jian Establish	除 Chu Remove	滿 Man Full	平 Ping Balance	定 Ding Stable	執 Zhi Initiate	破 Po Destruction	危 Wei Danger
未 Wei Goat July 7 - Aug 7	危 Wei Danger	成 Cheng Success	收 Shou Receive	開 Kai Open	閉 Bi Close	建 Jian Establish	除 Chu Remove	滿 Man Full	平 Ping Balance	定 Ding Stable	執 Zhi Initiate	破 Po Destruction
申 Shen Monkey Aug 8 - Sept 7	破 Po Destruction	危 Wei Danger	成 Cheng Success	收 Shou Receive	開 Kai Open	閉 Bi Close	建 Jian Establish	除 Chu Remove	滿 Man Full	平 Ping Balance	定 Ding Stable	執 Zhi Initiate
酉 You Rooster Sept 8 - Oct 7	執 Zhi Initiate	破 Po Destruction	危 Wei Danger	成 Cheng Success	收 Shou Receive	開 Kai Open	閉 Bi Close	建 Jian Establish	除 Chu Remove	滿 Man Full	平 Ping Balance	定 Ding Stable
戌 Xu Dog Oct 8 - Nov 6	定 Ding Stable	執 Zhi Initiate	破 Po Destruction	危 Wei Danger	成 Cheng Success	收 Shou Receive	開 Kai Open	閉 Bi Close	建 Jian Establish	除 Chu Remove	滿 Man Full	平 Ping Balance
亥 Hai Pig Nov 7 - Dec 6	平 Ping Balance	定 Ding Stable	執 Zhi Initiate	破 Po Destruction	危 Wei Danger	成 Cheng Success	收 Shou Receive	開 Kai Open	閉 Bi Close	建 Jian Establish	除 Chu Remove	滿 Man Full
子 Zi Rat Dec 7 - Jan 5	滿 Man Full	平 Ping Balance	定 Ding Stable	執 Zhi Initiate	破 Po Destruction	危 Wei Danger	成 Cheng Success	收 Shou Receive	開 Kai Open	閉 Bi Close	建 Jian Establish	除 Chu Remove
丑 Chou Ox Jan 6 - Feb 3	除 Chu Remove	滿 Man Full	平 Ping Balance	定 Ding Stable	執 Zhi Initiate	破 Po Destruction	危 Wei Danger	成 Cheng Success	收 Shou Receive	開 Kai Open	閉 Bi Close	建 Jian Establish

Special Days

Heaven and Earth Drilling Sha 天地轉煞日

Spring 春	乙卯 *Yi Mao* Wood Rabbit	辛卯 *Xin Mao* Metal Rabbit
Summer 夏	丙午 *Bing Wu* Fire Horse	戊午 *Wu Wu* Earth Horse
Autumn 秋	辛酉 *Xin You* Metal Rooster	癸酉 *Shen You* Water Rooster
Winter 冬	壬子 *Ren Zi* Water Rat	丙子 *Bing Zi* Fire Rat

Four Direct Abandonment Day 正四廢日

Spring 春	庚酉 *Geng You* Metal Rooster	辛酉 *Xin You* Metal Rooster
Summer 夏	壬子 *Ren Zi* Water Rat	癸亥 *Shen Hai* Water Pig
Autumn 秋	甲寅 *Jia Yin* Wood Tiger	辛酉 *Xin You* Metal Rooster
Winter 冬	丙午 *Bing Wu* Fire Horse	丁巳 *Ding Si* Fire Snake

Fire Star Day 火星日

寅 *Yin* Tiger	巳 *Si* Snake	申 *Shen* Monkey	亥 *Hai* Pig	乙丑 *Yi Chou* Wood Ox	甲戌 *Jia Xu* Wood Dog	癸未 *Shen Wei* Water Goat	壬辰 *Ren Chen* Water Dragon
正月 First Month	四月 4th Month	七月 7th Month	十月 10th Month	辛丑 *Xin Chou* Metal Ox	庚戌 *Geng Xu* Metal Dog	己未 *Ji Wei* Earth Goat	
卯 *Mao* Rabbit	午 *Wu* Horse	酉 *You* Rooster	子 *Zi* Rat	甲子 *Jia Zi* Wood Rat	癸酉 *Shen You* Water Rooster	壬午 *Ren Wu* Water Horse	辛卯 *Xin Mao* Metal Rabbit
二月 2nd Month	五月 5th Month	八月 8th Month	十一月 11th Month	庚子 *Geng Zi* Metal Rat	己酉 *Ji You* Earth Rooster	戊午 *Wu Wu* Earth Horse	
丑 *Chou* Ox	辰 *Chen* Dragon	未 *Wei* Goat	戌 *Xu* Dog	壬申 *Ren Shen* Water Monkey	辛巳 *Xin Si* Metal Snake	庚寅 *Geng Yin* Metal Tiger	己亥 *Ji Hai* Earth Pig
三月 3rd Month	六月 6th Month	九月 9th Month	十二月 12th Month	戊申 *Wu Shen* Earth Monkey	丁巳 *Ding Si* Fire Snake		

Yellow Embrace Day 黃砂日

寅 *Yin* Tiger	巳 *Si* Snake	申 *Shen* Monkey	亥 *Hai* Pig	午日 *Wu Ri* Horse Day
正月 First Month	四月 4th Month	七月 7th Month	十月 10th Month	
卯 *Mao* Rabbit	午 *Wu* Horse	酉 *You* Rooster	子 *Zi* Rat	寅日 *Yin Ri* Tiger Day
二月 2nd Month	五月 5th Month	八月 8th Month	十一月 11th Month	
丑 *Chou* Ox	辰 *Chen* Dragon	未 *Wei* Goat	戌 *Xu* Dog	子日 *Zi Ri* Rat Day
三月 3rd Month	六月 6th Month	九月 9th Month	十二月 12th Month	

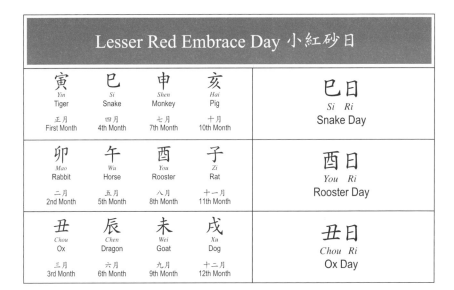

Lesser Red Embrace Day 小紅砂日

寅 *Yin* Tiger 正月 First Month	巳 *Si* Snake 四月 4th Month	申 *Shen* Monkey 七月 7th Month	亥 *Hai* Pig 十月 10th Month	巳 日 *Si Ri* Snake Day
卯 *Mao* Rabbit 二月 2nd Month	午 *Wu* Horse 五月 5th Month	酉 *You* Rooster 八月 8th Month	子 *Zi* Rat 十一月 11th Month	酉 日 *You Ri* Rooster Day
丑 *Chou* Ox 三月 3rd Month	辰 *Chen* Dragon 六月 6th Month	未 *Wei* Goat 九月 9th Month	戌 *Xu* Dog 十二月 12th Month	丑 日 *Chou Ri* Ox Day

Heavenly Thief Day 天賊日

正月 First Month 寅月 Tiger Month	四月 4th Month 巳月 Snake Month	七月 7th Month 申月 Monkey Month	十月 10th Month 亥月 Pig Month
辰 *Chen* Dragon	未 *Wei* Goat	戌 *Xu* Dog	丑 *Chou* Ox
二月 2nd Month 卯月 Rabbit Month	五月 5th Month 午月 Horse Month	八月 8th Month 酉月 Rooster Month	十一月 11th Month 子月 Rat Month
酉 *You* Rooster	子 *Zi* Rat	卯 *Mao* Rabbit	午 *Wu* Horse
三月 3rd Month 辰月 Dragon Month	六月 6th Month 未月 Goat Month	九月 9th Month 戌月 Dog Month	十二月 12th Month 丑月 Ox Month
寅 *Yin* Tiger	巳 *Si* Snake	申 *Shen* Monkey	亥 *Hai* Pig

董公擇日要覽

Month Suppressed Big Mishap 月厭大禍日

正月 First Month 寅月 Tiger Month	四月 4th Month 巳月 Snake Month	七月 7th Month 申月 Monkey Month	十月 10th Month 亥月 Pig Month
戌 *Xu* Dog	未 *Wei* Goat	辰 *Chen* Dragon	丑 *Chou* Ox

二月 2nd Month 卯月 Rabbit Month	五月 5th Month 午月 Horse Month	八月 8th Month 酉月 Rooster Month	十一月 11th Month 子月 Rat Month
酉 *You* Rooster	午 *Wu* Horse	卯 *Mao* Rabbit	子 *Zi* Rat

三月 3rd Month 辰月 Dragon Month	六月 6th Month 未月 Goat Month	九月 9th Month 戌月 Dog Month	十二月 12th Month 丑月 Ox Month
申 *Shen* Monkey	巳 *Si* Snake	寅 *Yin* Tiger	亥 *Hai* Pig

Coldness and Defrosting Day 冰消瓦解日

正月 First Month 寅月 Tiger Month	四月 4th Month 巳月 Snake Month	七月 7th Month 申月 Monkey Month	十月 10th Month 亥月 Pig Month
巳 *Si* Snake	寅 *Yin* Tiger	亥 *Hai* Pig	申 *Shen* Monkey

二月 2nd Month 卯月 Rabbit Month	五月 5th Month 午月 Horse Month	八月 8th Month 酉月 Rooster Month	十一月 11th Month 子月 Rat Month
子 *Zi* Rat	卯 *Mao* Rabbit	午 *Wu* Horse	酉 *You* Rooster

三月 3rd Month 辰月 Dragon Month	六月 6th Month 未月 Goat Month	九月 9th Month 戌月 Dog Month	十二月 12th Month 丑月 Ox Month
丑 *Chou* Ox	戌 *Xu* Dog	未 *Wei* Goat	辰 *Chen* Dragon

Receiving Death Day 受死日

正月 First Month 寅月 Tiger Month	四月 4th Month 巳月 Snake Month	七月 7th Month 申月 Monkey Month	十月 10th Month 亥月 Pig Month
戌 *Xu* Dog	巳 *Si* Snake	丑 *Chou* Ox	申 *Shen* Monkey

二月 2nd Month 卯月 Rabbit Month	五月 5th Month 午月 Horse Month	八月 8th Month 酉月 Rooster Month	十一月 11th Month 子月 Rat Month
辰 *Chen* Dragon	子 *Zi* Rat	未 *Wei* Goat	卯 *Mao* Rabbit

三月 3rd Month 辰月 Dragon Month	六月 6th Month 未月 Goat Month	九月 9th Month 戌月 Dog Month	十二月 12th Month 丑月 Ox Month
亥 *Hai* Pig	午 *Wu* Horse	寅 *Yin* Tiger	酉 *You* Rooster

Emptiness Day 往亡日

正月 First Month 寅月 Tiger Month	四月 4th Month 巳月 Snake Month	七月 7th Month 申月 Monkey Month	十月 10th Month 亥月 Pig Month
寅 *Yin* Tiger	亥 *Hai* Pig	酉 *You* Rooster	未 *Wei* Goat

二月 2nd Month 卯月 Rabbit Month	五月 5th Month 午月 Horse Month	八月 8th Month 酉月 Rooster Month	十一月 11th Month 子月 Rat Month
巳 *Si* Snake	卯 *Mao* Rabbit	子 *Zi* Rat	戌 *Xu* Dog

三月 3rd Month 辰月 Dragon Month	六月 6th Month 未月 Goat Month	九月 9th Month 戌月 Dog Month	十二月 12th Month 丑月 Ox Month
申 *Shen* Monkey	午 *Wu* Horse	辰 *Chen* Dragon	丑 *Chou* Ox

董公擇日要覽

Knife Cut Day 勾絞日

正月 First Month 寅月 Tiger Month	四月 4th Month 巳月 Snake Month	七月 7th Month 申月 Monkey Month	十月 10th Month 亥月 Pig Month
戌 *Xu* Dog	巳 *Si* Snake	丑 *Chou* Ox	申 *Shen* Monkey

二月 2nd Month 卯月 Rabbit Month	五月 5th Month 午月 Horse Month	八月 8th Month 酉月 Rooster Month	十一月 11th Month 子月 Rat Month
辰 *Chen* Dragon	子 *Zi* Rat	未 *Wei* Goat	卯 *Mao* Rabbit

三月 3rd Month 辰月 Dragon Month	六月 6th Month 未月 Goat Month	九月 9th Month 戌月 Dog Month	十二月 12th Month 丑月 Ox Month
亥 *Hai* Pig	午 *Wu* Horse	寅 *Yin* Tiger	酉 *You* Rooster

Red Phoenix Black Path Day 朱雀黑道日

正月 First Month 寅月 Tiger Month	四月 4th Month 巳月 Snake Month	七月 7th Month 申月 Monkey Month	十月 10th Month 亥月 Pig Month
卯 *Mao* Rabbit	酉 *You* Rooster	卯 *Mao* Rabbit	酉 *You* Rooster

二月 2nd Month 卯月 Rabbit Month	五月 5th Month 午月 Horse Month	八月 8th Month 酉月 Rooster Month	十一月 11th Month 子月 Rat Month
巳 *Si* Snake	亥 *Hai* Pig	巳 *Si* Snake	亥 *Hai* Pig

三月 3rd Month 辰月 Dragon Month	六月 6th Month 未月 Goat Month	九月 9th Month 戌月 Dog Month	十二月 12th Month 丑月 Ox Month
未 *Wei* Goat	丑 *Chou* Ox	未 *Wei* Goat	丑 *Chou* Ox

White Tiger Black Path 白虎黑道日

正月 First Month 寅月 Tiger Month	四月 4th Month 巳月 Snake Month	七月 7th Month 申月 Monkey Month	十月 10th Month 亥月 Pig Month
午 *Wu* Horse	子 *Zi* Rat	午 *Wu* Horse	子 *Zi* Rat

二月 2nd Month 卯月 Rabbit Month	五月 5th Month 午月 Horse Month	八月 8th Month 酉月 Rooster Month	十一月 11th Month 子月 Rat Month
申 *Shen* Monkey	寅 *Yin* Tiger	申 *Shen* Monkey	寅 *Yin* Tiger

三月 3rd Month 辰月 Dragon Month	六月 6th Month 未月 Goat Month	九月 9th Month 戌月 Dog Month	十二月 12th Month 丑月 Ox Month
戌 *Xu* Dog	辰 *Chen* Dragon	戌 *Xu* Dog	辰 *Chen* Dragon

Black Tortoise Black Path Day 玄武黑道日

正月 First Month 寅月 Tiger Month	四月 4th Month 巳月 Snake Month	七月 7th Month 申月 Monkey Month	十月 10th Month 亥月 Pig Month
酉 *You* Rooster	卯 *Mao* Rabbit	酉 *You* Rooster	卯 *Mao* Rabbit

二月 2nd Month 卯月 Rabbit Month	五月 5th Month 午月 Horse Month	八月 8th Month 酉月 Rooster Month	十一月 11th Month 子月 Rat Month
亥 *Hai* Pig	巳 *Si* Snake	亥 *Hai* Pig	巳 *Si* Snake

三月 3rd Month 辰月 Dragon Month	六月 6th Month 未月 Goat Month	九月 9th Month 戌月 Dog Month	十二月 12th Month 丑月 Ox Month
丑 *Chou* Ox	未 *Wei* Goat	丑 *Chou* Ox	未 *Wei* Goat

董公擇日要覽

Grappling Hook Black Path Day 勾陳黑道日

正月 First Month 寅月 Tiger Month	四月 4th Month 巳月 .Snake Month	七月 7th Month 申月 Monkey Month	十月 10th Month 亥月 Pig Month
亥 *Hai* Pig	巳 *Si* Snake	亥 *Hai* Pig	巳 *Si* Snake

二月 2nd Month 卯月 Rabbit Month	五月 5th Month 午月 Horse Month	八月 8th Month 酉月 Rooster Month	十一月 11th Month 子月 Rat Month
丑 *Chou* Ox	未 *Wei* Goat	丑 *Chou* Ox	未 *Wei* Goat

三月 3rd Month 辰月 Dragon Month	六月 6th Month 未月 Goat Month	九月 9th Month 戌月 Dog Month	十二月 12th Month 丑月 Ox Month
卯 *Mao* Rabbit	酉 *You* Rooster	卯 *Mao* Rabbit	酉 *You* Rooster

Avoid Visiting The Sick Day 探病忌日

甲寅壬午連庚午，
壬寅乙卯己卯妨，
神仙留下此六日，
探人疾病替人亡。

董公擇日要覽

Summary Table

	正月 First Month	二月 2nd Month	三月 3rd Month	四月 4th Month	五月 5th Month	六月 6th Month	七月 7th Month	八月 8th Month	九月 9th Month	十月 10th Month	十一月 11th Month	十二月 12th Month
黃砂日 Yellow Embrace Day	午 Wu Horse	寅 Yin Tiger	子 Zi Rat	午 Wu Horse	寅 Yin Tiger	子 Zi Rat	午 Wu Horse	寅 Yin Tiger	子 Zi Rat	午 Wu Horse	寅 Yin Tiger	子 Zi Rat
小紅砂日 Lesser Yellow Embrace Day	巳 Si Snake	酉 You Rooster	丑 Chou Ox	巳 Si Snake	酉 You Rooster	丑 Chou Ox	巳 Si Snake	酉 You Rooster	丑 Chou Ox	巳 Si Snake	酉 You Rooster	丑 Chou Ox
天賊日 Heavenly Thief Day	辰 Chen Dragon	酉 You Rooster	寅 Yin Tiger	未 Wei Goat	子 Zi Rat	巳 Si Snake	戌 Xu Dog	卯 Mao Rabbit	申 Shen Monkey	丑 Chou Ox	午 Wu Horse	亥 Hai Pig
月厭大禍日 Month Suppressed Big Mishap Day	戌 Xu Dog	酉 You Rooster	申 Shen Monkey	未 Wei Goat	午 Wu Horse	巳 Si Snake	辰 Chen Dragon	卯 Mao Rabbit	寅 Yin Tiger	丑 Chou Ox	子 Zi Rat	亥 Hai Pig
受死日 Receiving Death Day	戌 Xu Dog	辰 Chen Dragon	亥 Hai Pig	巳 Si Snake	子 Zi Rat	午 Wu Horse	丑 Chou Ox	未 Wei Goat	寅 Yin Tiger	申 Shen Monkey	卯 Mao Rabbit	酉 You Rooster
冰消瓦解日 Coldness and Defrosting Day	巳 Si Snake	子 Zi Rat	丑 Chou Ox	申 Shen Monkey	卯 Mao Rabbit	戌 Xu Dog	亥 Hai Pig	午 Wu Horse	未 Wei Goat	申 Shen Monkey	酉 You Rooster	辰 Chen Dragon
往亡日 Emptiness Day	寅 Yin Tiger	巳 Si Snake	申 Shen Monkey	亥 Hai Pig	卯 Mao Rabbit	午 Wu Horse	酉 You Rooster	子 Zi Rat	辰 Chen Dragon	未 Wei Goat	戌 Xu Dog	丑 Chou Ox
勾絞日 Knife Cut Day	亥 Hai Pig	午 Wu Horse	丑 Chou Ox	申 Shen Monkey	卯 Mao Rabbit	戌 Xu Dog	巳 Si Snake	子 Zi Rat	未 Wei Goat	寅 Yin Tiger	酉 You Rooster	辰 Chen Dragon
朱雀黑道日 Red Phoenix Black Path Day	卯 Mao Rabbit	巳 Si Snake	未 Wei Goat	酉 You Rooster	亥 Hai Pig	丑 Chou Ox	卯 Mao Rabbit	巳 Si Snake	未 Wei Goat	酉 You Rooster	亥 Hai Pig	丑 Chou Ox
白虎黑道日 White Tiger Black Path	午 Wu Horse	申 Shen Monkey	戌 Xu Dog	子 Zi Rat	寅 Yin Tiger	辰 Chen Dragon	午 Wu Horse	申 Shen Monkey	戌 Xu Dog	子 Zi Rat	寅 Yin Tiger	辰 Chen Dragon
玄武黑道日 Black Tortoise Black Path Day	酉 You Rooster	亥 Hai Pig	丑 Chou Ox	卯 Mao Rabbit	巳 Si Snake	未 Wei Goat	酉 You Rooster	亥 Hai Pig	丑 Chou Ox	卯 Mao Rabbit	巳 Si Snake	未 Wei Goat
勾陳黑道日 Grappling Hook Black Path Day	亥 Hai Pig	丑 Chou Ox	卯 Mao Rabbit	巳 Si Snake	未 Wei Goat	酉 You Rooster	亥 Hai Pig	丑 Chou Ox	卯 Mao Rabbit	巳 Si Snake	未 Wei Goat	酉 You Rooster

董公擇日要覽

Luo Hou Days 羅睺日	
Year 年	**Day** 日
子 *Zi* Rat	癸酉 *Shen You* Water Rooster
丑 *Chou* Ox	甲戌 *Jia Xu* Wood Dog
寅 *Yin* Tiger	丁亥 *Ding Hai* Fire Pig
卯 *Mao* Rabbit	甲子 *Jia Zi* Wood Rat
辰 *Chen* Dragon	乙丑 *Yi Chou* Wood Ox
巳 *Si* Snake	甲寅 *Jia Yin* Wood Tiger
午 *Wu* Horse	丁卯 *Ding Mao* Fire Rabbit
未 *Wei* Goat	甲辰 *Jia Chen* Wood Dragon
申 *Shen* Monkey	己巳 *Ji Si* Earth Snake
酉 *You* Rooster	甲午 *Jia Wu* Wood Horse
戌 *Xu* Dog	丁未 *Ding Wei* Fire Goat
亥 *Hai* Pig	甲申 *Jia Shen* Wood Monkey

Yang Gong Disaster Day 楊公忌日	
First Month, 13th Day	正月十三
2nd Month, 11th Day	二月十一
3rd Month, 9th Day	三月初九
4th Month, 7th Day	四月初七
5th Month, 5th Day	五月初五
6th Month, 3rd Day	六月初三
7th Month, 1st Day	七月初一
7th Month, 29th Day	七月二十九
8th Month, 27th Day	八月二十七
9th Month, 25th Day	九月二十五
10th Month, 23th Day	十月二十三
11th Month, 21th Day	十一月二十一
12th Month, 19th Day	十二月十九

The 10 Ferocious Big Disaster Days 十惡大敗

Streams	The 60 Jia Zi 六十甲子					Death & Emptiness Branch 空亡
甲子旬 *Jia Zi Xun* **Wood Rat Stream**	**Year 1984 - 1993**					Dog Pig 戌亥 *Xu Hai*
	甲子， *Jia Zi*	乙丑， *Yi Chou*	丙寅， *Bing Yin*	丁卯， *Ding Mao*	戊辰， *Wu Chen*	
	己巳， *Ji Si*	庚午， *Geng Wu*	辛未， *Xin Wei*	壬申， *Ren Shen*	癸酉 *Gui You*	
甲戌旬 *Jia Xu Xun* **Wood Dog Stream**	**Year 1994 - 2003**					Monkey Rooster 申酉 *Shen You*
	甲戌， *Jia Xu*	乙亥， *Yi Hai*	丙子， *Bing Zi*	丁丑， *Ding Chou*	戊寅， *Wu Yin*	
	己卯， *Ji Mao*	庚辰， *Geng Chen*	辛巳， *Xin Si*	壬午， *Ren Wu*	癸未 *Gui Wei*	
甲申旬 *Jia Shen Xun* **Wood Monkey Stream**	**Year 2004 - 2013**					Horse Goat 午未 *Wu Wei*
	甲申， *Jia shen*	乙酉， *Yi You*	丙戌， *Bing Xu*	丁亥， *Ding Hai*	戊子， *Wu Zi*	
	己丑， *Ji Chou*	庚寅， *Geng Yin*	辛卯， *Xin Mao*	壬辰， *Ren Chen*	癸巳 *Gui Si*	
甲午旬 *Jia Wu Xun* **Wood Horse Stream**	**Year 2014 - 2023**					Dragon Snake 辰巳 *Chen Si*
	甲午， *Jia Wu*	乙未， *Yi Wei*	丙申， *Bing Shen*	丁酉， *Ding You*	戊戌， *Wu Xu*	
	己亥， *Ji Hai*	庚子， *Geng Zi*	辛丑， *Xin Chou*	壬寅， *Ren Yin*	癸卯 *Gui Mao*	
甲辰旬 *Jia Chen Xun* **Wood Dragon Stream**	**Year 2024 - 2033**					Tiger Rabbit 寅卯 *Yin Mao*
	甲辰， *Jia Chen*	乙巳， *Yi Si*	丙午， *Bing Wu*	丁未， *Ding Wei*	戊申， *Wu Shen*	
	己酉， *Ji You*	庚戌， *Geng Xu*	辛亥， *Xin Hai*	壬子， *Ren Zi*	癸丑 *Gui Chou*	
甲寅旬 *Jia Yin Xun* **Wood Tiger Stream**	**Year 2034 - 2043**					Rat Ox 子丑 *Zi Chou*
	甲寅， *Jia Yin*	乙卯， *Yi Mao*	丙辰， *Bing Chen*	丁巳， *Ding Si*	戊午， *Wu Wu*	
	己未， *Ji Wei*	庚申， *Geng Shen*	辛酉， *Xin You*	壬戌， *Ren Xu*	癸亥 *Gui Hai*	

董公擇日要覽

Year	丁亥 Ding Hai Day	己丑 Ji Chou Day
2007	February 22	February 24
	April 23	April 25
	June 22	June 24
	August 21	August 23
	October 20	October 22
	December 19	December 21

Year	丁亥 Ding Hai Day	己丑 Ji Chou Day
2008	February 17	February 19
	April 17	April 19
	June 16	June 18
	August 15	August 17
	October 14	October 16
	December 13	December 15

Year	丁亥 Ding Hai Day	己丑 Ji Chou Day
2009	February 11	February 13
	April 12	April 14
	June 11	June 13
	August 10	August 12
	October 9	October 11
	December 8	December 10

Year	丁亥 Ding Hai Day	己丑 Ji Chou Day
2010	February 6	February 8
	April 7	April 9
	June 6	June 8
	August 5	August 7
	October 4	October 6
	December 3	December 5

董公擇日要覽

Year	丁亥 Ding Hai Day	己丑 Ji Chou Day
2011	February 1	February 3
	April 2	April 4
	June 1	June 3
	July 31	August 2
	September 29	October 1
	November 28	November 30

2012	January 27	January 29
	March 27	March 29
	May 26	May 28
	July 25	July 27
	September 23	September 25
	November 22	November 24

2013	January 21	January 23
	March 22	March 24
	May 21	May 28
	July 20	July 27
	September 18	September 20
	November 17	November 19

2014	March 26	March 28
	May 25	May 27
	July 24	July 26
	September 22	September 24
	November 21	November 23

Year	丁亥 Ding Hai Day	己丑 Ji Chou Day
2015	January 20	January 22
	March 21	March 23
	May 20	May 22
	July 19	July 21
	September 17	September 19
	November 16	November 18
2016	January 15	January17
	March 15	March 17
	May 14	May 16
	July 13	July 15
	September 11	September 13
	November 10	November 12
2017	January 9	January 11
	March 10	March 12
	May 9	May 11
	July 8	July 10
	September 6	September 8
	November 5	November 7

董公擇日要覽

Heavenly Pardon Days 天赫
Spring's 戊寅 Wu Yin Day
Summer's 甲午 Jia Wu Day
Autumn's 戊申 Wu Shen Day
Winter's 甲子 Jia Zi Day

Three Wonder Noble 三奇			
Heavenly Three Noble 天上三奇	甲 *Jia* Wood	戊 *Wu* Earth	庚 *Geng* Metal
Human Three Noble 人中三奇	壬 *Ren* Water	癸 *Shen* Water	辛 *Xin* Metal
Earthly Three Noble 地下三奇	乙 *Yi* Wood	丙 *Bing* Fire	丁 *Ding* Fire

Special Days

Great Separation Day 離別日

Month 月	Day 日
寅 Yin Tiger / 申 Shen Monkey	丙 Bing Fire / 子 Zi Rat

Month 月	Day 日
卯 Mao Rabbit	癸 Gui Water / 丑 Chou Ox

Month 月	Day 日
辰 Chen Dragon	丙 Bing Fire / 寅 Yin Tiger

Month 月	Day 日
巳 Si Snake	丙 Bing Fire / 辰 Chen Dragon

Month 月	Day 日
午 Wu Horse / 未 Wei Goat	丁 Ding Fire / 巳 Si Snake

Month 月	Day 日
酉 You Rooster	庚 Geng Metal / 辰 Chen Dragon

Month 月	Day 日
亥 Hai Pig / 子 Zi Rat	丙 Bing Fire / 午 Wu Horse

Month 月	Day 日
丑 Chou Ox	癸 Gui Water / 巳 Si Snake

Month 月	Day 日
戌 Xu Dog	辛 Xin Metal / 未 Wei Goat

White Tiger Entering Central Palace Day 白虎入中宮

戊寅 Wu Yin Earth Tiger	丁丑 Ding Chou Fire Ox	丙戌 Bing Xu Fire Dog	乙未 Yi Wei Wood Goat	甲辰 Jia Chen Wood Dragon	癸丑 Gui Chou Water Ox	壬戌 Ren Xu Water Dog

Nine Earth Ghost Day 九土鬼日

乙酉 Yi You Wood Rooster	癸巳 Gui Si Water Snake	甲午 Jia Wu Wood Horse	辛丑 Xin Chou Metal Ox	壬寅 Ren Yin Water Tiger	己酉 Ji You Earth Monkey	庚戌 Geng Xu Metal Dog	丁巳 Ding Si Fire Snake	戊午 Wu Wu Earth Horse

董公擇日要覽

248 Dong Gong Date Selection

董公擇日要覽

Four Separation Day 四離日

One Day Before	前一天
Spring Equinox	春分
Summer Solstice	夏至
Autumn Equinox	秋分
Winter Solstice	冬至

Four Extinction Day 四絕日

One Day Before	前一天
Coming of Spring	立春
Coming of Solstice	立夏
Coming of Equinox	立秋
Coming of Solstice	立冬

Day to Move the Bed 設帳安床吉日

Useable Stars :

天德 Heavenly Virtue，月德 Monthly Virtue，天德合 Heavenly Virtue Combo，月德合 Monthly Virtue Combo，三合 Three Harmony，六合 Six Combo，天喜 Sky Happiness，益後 Benefit Descendants，續世 Continuous Descendants，青龍 Green Dragon，黃道 Yellow Path，金匱 Golden Lock，生氣 Life Generating，開 Open，成 Yellow Path，定 Sucess，危 Danger

Day to Move the Bed 設帳安床吉日								
寅 Yin Tiger 正月 First Month	乙卯 Yi Mao	丁酉 Ding You	癸酉 Gui You	乙丑 Yi Chou	丁丑 Ding Chou	癸丑 Gui Chou	己卯 Ji Mao	辛卯 Xing Mao
卯 Mao Rabbit 二月 2nd Month	甲寅 Jia Yin	丙寅 Bing Yin	壬寅 Ren Yin	乙未 Yi Wei	丁未 Ding Wei	己未 Ji Wei	乙亥 Yi Hai	丁亥 Ding Hai
辰 Chen Dragon 三月 3rd Month	甲子 Jia Zi	丙子 Bing Zi	庚子 Geng Zi	壬子 Ren Zi	癸卯 Gui Mao	乙卯 Yi Mao	己卯 Ji Mao	辛卯 Xing Mao	乙巳 Yi Si	丁巳 Ding Si
巳 Si Snake 四月 4th Month	甲子 Jia Zi	丙子 Bing Zi	庚子 Geng Zi	丁丑 Ding Chou	乙卯 Yi Mao	辛卯 Xing Mao	庚午 Geng Wu	甲辰 Jia Chen	丙辰 Bing Chen	丙午 Bing Wu
午 Wu Horse 五月 5th Month	甲寅 Jia Yin	丙寅 Bing Yin	庚寅 Geng Yin	壬寅 Ren Yin	壬辰 Ren Chen	甲辰 Jia Chen	丙辰 Bing Chen
未 Wei Goat 六月 6th Month	甲寅 Jia Yin	丙寅 Bing Yin	壬寅 Ren Yin	乙亥 Yi Hai	丁亥 Ding Hai
申 Shen Monkey 七月 7th Month	甲子 Jia Zi	丙子 Bing Zi	壬子 Ren Zi	庚子 Geng Zi	丙辰 Bing Chen	庚辰 Geng Chen
酉 You Rooster 八月 8th Month	乙丑 Yi Chou	丁丑 Ding Chou	辛丑 Xing Chou	癸丑 Gui Chou	己丑 Ji Chou	甲辰 Jia Chen	丙辰 Bing Chen	壬辰 Ren Chen	庚辰 Geng Chen
戌 Xu Dog 九月 9th Month	甲午 Jia Wu	庚午 Geng Wu	丙午 Bing Wu	辛卯 Xing Mao	辛酉 Xing You	丁酉 Ding You	癸酉 Gui You	乙亥 Yi Hai	丁亥 Ding Hai
亥 Hai Pig 十月 10th Month	甲子 Jia Zi	丙子 Bing Zi	庚子 Geng Zi	乙未 Yi Wei	辛未 Xing Wei
子 Zi Rat 十一月 11th Month	甲寅 Jia Yin	丙寅 Bing Yin	庚寅 Geng Yin	乙巳 Yi Si	己巳 Ji Si	辛未 Xing Wei	乙亥 Yi Hai	丁亥 Ding Hai
丑 Chou Ox 十二月 12th Month	甲子 Jia Zi	丙子 Bing Zi	壬子 Ren Zi	甲寅 Jia Yin	丙寅 Bing Yin

Auspicious Hours Chart 吉時

日支 Day Branch	子 Zi Rat	丑 Chou Ox	寅 Yin Tiger	卯 Mao Rabbit	辰 Chen Dragon	巳 Si Snake	午 Wu Horse	未 Wei Goat	申 Shen Monkey	酉 You Rooster	戌 Xu Dog	亥 Hai Pig
福德 Fortune Virtue	子 Zi Rat	寅 Yin Tiger	辰 Chen Dragon	午 Wu Horse	申 Shen Monkey	戌 Xu Dog	子 Zi Rat	寅 Yin Tiger	辰 Chen Dragon	午 Wu Horse	申 Shen Monkey	戌 Xu Dog
鳳輦 Phoenix Carriage	午 Wu Horse	申 Shen Monkey	戌 Xu Dog	子 Zi Rat	寅 Yin Tiger	辰 Chen Dragon	午 Wu Horse	申 Shen Monkey	戌 Xu Dog	子 Zi Rat	寅 Yin Tiger	辰 Chen Dragon
寶光 Precious Light	丑 Chou Ox	卯 Mao Rabbit	巳 Si Snake	未 Wei Goat	酉 You Rooster	亥 Hai Pig	丑 Chou Ox	卯 Mao Rabbit	巳 Si Snake	未 Wei Goat	酉 You Rooster	亥 Hai Pig
太乙 Great Yi	申 Shen Monkey	戌 Xu Dog	子 Zi Rat	寅 Yin Tiger	辰 Chen Dragon	午 Wu Horse	申 Shen Monkey	戌 Xu Dog	子 Zi Rat	寅 Yin Tiger	辰 Chen Dragon	午 Wu Horse
少微 Lesser Petite	卯 Mao Rabbit	巳 Si Snake	未 Wei Goat	酉 You Rooster	亥 Hai Pig	丑 Chou Ox	卯 Mao Rabbit	巳 Si Snake	未 Wei Goat	酉 You Rooster	亥 Hai Pig	丑 Chou Ox
貴人 Noble-man	酉 You Rooster	亥 Hai Pig	丑 Chou Ox	卯 Mao Rabbit	巳 Si Snake	未 Wei Goat	酉 You Rooster	亥 Hai Pig	丑 Chou Ox	卯 Mao Rabbit	巳 Si Snake	未 Wei Goat

時支 Hour Branch

董公擇日要覽

About Joey Yap

Joey Yap is the Founder and Master Trainer of the Mastery Academy of Chinese Metaphysics, a global organisation devoted to the worldwide teaching of Feng Shui, BaZi, Mian Xiang, Yi Jing and other Chinese Metaphysics subjects. Joey is also the Founder of Yap Global Consulting, an international Feng Shui and Chinese Astrology consulting firm offering audit and consultation services to corporations and individuals all over the world.

Joey received his formal education in Malaysia and Australia. He has combined the best of Eastern learning and Western education systems in the teaching methodology practiced at the Academy. Students of the Mastery Academy study traditional syllabuses of Chinese Metaphysics but through Western-style modular programs that are structured and systematic, enabling individuals to easily and quickly learn, grasp and master complex Chinese Metaphysics subjects like Feng Shui and BaZi. These unique structured learning systems are also utilized by Mastery Academy instructors all over the world to teach BaZi and Feng Shui.

The Mastery Academy is also the first international educational organisation to fully utilize the benefits of the Internet to promote continuous education, encourage peer-to-peer learning, enable mentoring and distance learning. Students interact with each other live, and continue to learn and improve their knowledge.

Despite his busy schedule, Joey continues to write for the Mastery Journal, a monthly eZine on Feng Shui and Astrology devoted for world-wide readers and the production of the world's first bilingual *Ten Thousand Year Calendar*. He is also the best selling author of *Stories and Lessons on Feng Shui, Mian Xiang- Discover Face Reading, Tong Shu Diary, BaZi - The Destiny Code, BaZi - The Destiny Code Revealed, Feng Shui for Homebuyers-Interior, Feng Shui for Homebuyers-Exterior* and the *Mini Feng Shui Compass*. Besides being a regular guest of various radio and TV talk shows, Joey is also a regular columnist for a national newspaper and various magazines in Malaysia. In fact, he hosted his own *TV series, Discover Feng Shui with Joey Yap*, on Malaysia's 8TV channel in 2005; a popular program that focused on heightening awareness of Feng Shui and Chinese Metaphysics.

A firm believer in innovation being the way forward, Joey recently released the BaZi Ming Pan 2.0 software, which allows users to generate configurable, detailed BaZi charts.

Author's personal website: www.joeyyap.com
Academy website: www.masteryacademy.com | www.masteryjournal.com
| www.maelearning.com

EDUCATION
The Mastery Academy of Chinese Metaphysics:
the first choice for practitioners and aspiring students of the art and science of Chinese Classical Feng Shui and Astrology.

For thousands of years, Eastern knowledge has been passed from one generation to another through the system of discipleship. A venerated master would accept suitable individuals at a young age as his disciples, and informally through the years, pass on his knowledge and skills to them. His disciples in turn, would take on their own disciples, as a means to perpetuate knowledge or skills.

This system served the purpose of restricting the transfer of knowledge to only worthy honourable individuals and ensuring that outsiders or Westerners would not have access to thousands of years of Eastern knowledge, learning and research.

However, the disciple system has also resulted in Chinese Metaphysics and Classical Studies lacking systematic teaching methods. Knowledge garnered over the years has not been accumulated in a concise, systematic manner, but scattered amongst practitioners, each practicing his/her knowledge, art and science, in isolation.

The disciple system, out of place in today's modern world, endangers the advancement of these classical fields that continue to have great relevance and application today.

At the Mastery Academy of Chinese Metaphysics, our Mission is to bring Eastern Classical knowledge in the fields of metaphysics, Feng Shui and Astrology sciences and the arts to the world. These Classical teachings and knowledge, previously shrouded in secrecy and passed on only through the discipleship system, are adapted into structured learning, which can easily be understood, learnt and mastered. Through modern learning methods, these renowned ancient arts, sciences and practices can be perpetuated while facilitating more extensive application and understanding of these classical subjects.

The Mastery Academy espouses an educational philosophy that draws from the best of the East and West. It is the world's premier educational institution for the study of Chinese Metaphysics Studies offering a wide range and variety of courses, ensuring that students have the opportunity to pursue their preferred field of study and enabling existing practitioners and professionals to gain cross-disciplinary knowledge that complements their current field of practice.

Courses at the Mastery Academy have been carefully designed to ensure a comprehensive yet compact syllabus. The modular nature of the courses enables students to immediately begin to put their knowledge into practice while pursuing continued study of their field and complementary fields. Students thus have the benefit of developing and gaining practical experience in tandem with the expansion and advancement of their theoretical knowledge.

Students can also choose from a variety of study options, from a distance learning program, the Homestudy Series, that enables study at one's own pace or intensive foundation courses and compact lecture-based courses, held in various cities around the world by Joey Yap or our licensed instructors. The Mastery Academy's faculty and make-up is international in nature, thus ensuring that prospective students can attend courses at destinations nearest to their country of origin or with a licensed Mastery Academy instructor in their home country.

The Mastery Academy provides 24x7 support to students through its Online Community, with a variety of tools, documents, forums and e-learning materials to help students stay at the forefront of research in their fields and gain invaluable assistance from peers and mentoring from their instructors.

TM

MASTERY ACADEMY
OF CHINESE METAPHYSICS

www.masteryacademy.com

MALAYSIA
19-3, The Boulevard
Mid Valley City
59200 Kuala Lumpur, Malaysia
Tel   : +603-2284 8080
Fax   : +603-2284 1218
Email : info@masteryacademy.com

SINGAPORE
14, Robinson Road # 13-00
Far East Finance Building
Singapore 048545
Tel   : +65-6722 8775
Fax   : +65-3125 7131
Email : singapore@masteryacademy.com

AUSTRALIA
PO Box 692,
Bentley WA 6982, Australia
Tel   : +618-9262 0468
Fax   : +618-9262 0469
Email : australia@masteryacademy.com

Represented in:
Australia, Austria, Brazil, Canada, China, Cyprus, France, Germany, Greece, Hungary, India, Japan, Indonesia, Italy, Malaysia, Mexico, Netherlands, New Zealand, Philippines, Russian Federation, Poland, Singapore, South Africa, Switzerland, Turkey, U.S.A., Ukraine, United Kingdom

Introducing...
The Mastery Academy's E-Learning Center!

The Mastery Academy's goal has always been to share authentic knowledge of Chinese Metaphysics with the whole world.

Nevertheless, we do recognize that distance, time, and hotel and traveling costs – amongst many other factors – could actually hinder people from enrolling for a classroom-based course. But with the advent and amazing advance of IT today, NOT any more!

With this in mind, we have invested heavily in IT, to conceive what is probably the first and only E-Learning Center in the world today that offers a full range of studies in the field of Chinese Metaphysics.

Convenient   Study from Your   Easy Enrollment
                  Own Home

The Mastery Academy's E-Learning Center

Now, armed with your trusty computer or laptop, and Internet access, knowledge of classical Feng Shui, BaZi (Destiny Analysis) and Mian Xiang (Face Reading) are but a literal click away!

Study at your own pace, and interact with your Instructor and fellow students worldwide, from anywhere in the world. With our E-Learning Center, knowledge of Chinese Metaphysics is brought DIRECTLY to you in all its clarity – topic-by-topic, and lesson-by-lesson; with illustrated presentations and comprehensive notes expediting your learning curve!

Your education journey through our E-Learning Center may be done via any of the following approaches:

1. Online Courses

There are 3 Programs available: our Online Feng Shui Program, Online BaZi Program, and Online Mian Xiang Program. Each Program consists of several Levels, with each Level consisting of many Lessons in turn. Each Lesson contains a pre-recorded video session on the topic at hand, accompanied by presentation-slides and graphics as well as downloadable tutorial notes that you can print and file for future reference.

| Video Lecture | Presentation Slide | Downloadable Notes |

2. MA Live!

MA Live!, as its name implies, enables LIVE broadcasts of Joey Yap's courses and seminars – right to your computer screen. Students will not only get to see and hear Joey talk on real-time `live', but also participate and more importantly, TALK to Joey via the MA Live! interface. All the benefits of a live class, minus the hassle of actually having to attend one!

How It Works

Our Live Classes   You at Home

3. Video-On-Demand (VOD)

Get immediate streaming-downloads of the Mastery Academy's wide range of educational DVDs, right on your computer screen. No more shipping costs and waiting time to be incurred!

Instant VOD Online

Choose From Our list of Available VODs!   Click "Play" on Your PC

Welcome to **www.maelearning.com**; the web portal of our E-Learning Center, and YOUR virtual gateway to Chinese Metaphysics!

Mastery Academy around the world

Canada

United States

Mexico

Brazil

United Kingdom
Switzerland
Netherlands
France
Italy
Cyprus

Austria
Germany

Poland
Hungary
Greece

Russian
Federation

Ukraine

Turkey

China

Japan

India

South Africa

Philippines
Kuala Lumpur
Malaysia

Indonesia

Singapore

Australia

New Zealand

YAP GLOBAL CONSULTING

Joey Yap & Yap Global Consulting

Headed by Joey Yap, Yap Global Consulting (YGC) is a leading international consulting firm specializing in Feng Shui, Mian Xiang (Face Reading) and BaZi (Destiny Analysis) consulting services worldwide. Joey - an internationally renowned Master Trainer, Consultant, Speaker and best-selling Author - has dedicated his life to the art and science of Chinese Metaphysics.

YGC has its main offices in Kuala Lumpur and Australia, and draws upon its diverse reservoir of strength from a group of dedicated and experienced consultants based in more than 30 countries, worldwide.

As the pioneer in blending established, classical Chinese Metaphysics techniques with the latest approach in consultation practices, YGC has built its reputation on the principles of professionalism and only the highest standards of service. This allows us to retain the cutting edge in delivering Feng Shui and Destiny consultation services to both corporate and personal clients, in a simple and direct manner, without compromising on quality.

Across Industries: Our Portfolio of Clients

Our diverse portfolio of both corporate and individual clients from all around the world bears testimony to our experience and capabilities.

Virtually every industry imaginable has benefited from our services - ranging from academic and financial institutions, real-estate developers and multinational corporations, to those in the leisure and tourism industry. Our services are also engaged by professionals, prominent business personalities, celebrities, high-profile politicians and people from all walks of life.

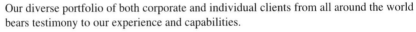

YAP GLOBAL GONSULTING

Name (Mr./Mrs./Ms.): _____

Contact Details _____

Tel: _____ Fax: _____

Mobile : _____

E-mail: _____

What Type of Consultation Are You Interested In?

☐ Feng Shui   ☐ BaZi   ☐ Date Selection   ☐ Yi Jing

Please tick if applicable:

☐ Are you a Property Developer looking to engage Yap Global Consulting?

☐ Are you a Property Investor looking for tailor-made packages to suit your investment requirements?

Please attach your name card here.

Thank you for completing this form.
Please fax it back to us at:

Singapore	**Australia**	**Malaysia & the rest of the world**
Fax: +65-3125 7131	Fax: +618-9262 0469	Fax: +603-2284 2213
Tel : +65-6722 8775	Tel : +618-9262 0468	Tel : +603-2284 1213

Feng Shui Consultations

For Residential Properties
• Initial Land/Property Assessment
• Residential Feng Shui Consultations
• Residential Land Selection
• End-to-End Residential Consultation

For Commercial Properties
• Initial Land/Property Assessment
• Commercial Feng Shui Consultations
• Commercial Land Selection
• End-to-End Commercial Consultation

For Property Developers
• End-to-End Consultation
• Post-Consultation Advisory Services
• Panel Feng Shui Consultant

For Property Investors
• Your Personal Feng Shui Consultant
• Tailor-Made Packages

For Memorial Parks & Burial Sites
• Yin House Feng Shui

BaZi Consultations

Personal Destiny Analysis
• Personal Destiny Analysis for Individuals
• Children's BaZi Analysis
• Family BaZi Analysis

Strategic Analysis for Corporate Organizations
• Corporate BaZi Consultations
• BaZi Analysis for Human Resource Management

Entrepreneurs & Business Owners
• BaZi Analysis for Entrepreneurs

Career Pursuits
• BaZi Career Analysis

Relationships
• Marriage and Compatibility Analysis
• Partnership Analysis

For Everyone
• Annual BaZi Forecast
• Your Personal BaZi Coach **Personal Destiny Analysis**
• Personal Destiny Analysis for Individuals

• **Marriage Date Selection**
• **Caesarean Birth Date Selection**
• **House-Moving Date Selection**
• **Renovation & Groundbreaking Dates**

• **Signing of Contracts**
• **Official Openings**
• **Product Launches**

A Time-Tested, Accurate Science

• With a history predating 4 millennia, the Yi Jing - or Classic of Change - is one of the oldest Chinese texts surviving today. Its purpose as an oracle, in predicting the outcome of things, is based on the variables of Time, Space and Specific Events.

• A Yi Jing Assessment provides specific answers to any specific questions you may have about a specific event or endeavor. This is something that a Destiny Analysis would not be able to give you.

Basically, what a Yi Jing Assessment does is focus on only ONE aspect or item at a particular point in your life, and give you a calculated prediction of the details that will follow suit, if you undertake a particular action. It gives you an insight into a situation, and what course of action to take in order to arrive at a satisfactory outcome at the end of the day.

Please Contact YGC for a personalized Yi Jing Assessment!

INVITING US TO YOUR CORPORATE EVENTS

Many reputable organizations and institutions have worked closely with YGC to build a synergistic business relationship by engaging our team of consultants, led by Joey Yap, as speakers at their corporate events. Our seminars and short talks are always packed with audiences consisting of clients and associates of multinational and public-listed companies as well as key stakeholders of financial institutions.

We tailor our seminars and talks to suit the anticipated or pertinent group of audience. Be it a department, subsidiary, your clients or even the entire corporation, we aim to fit your requirements in delivering the intended message(s).

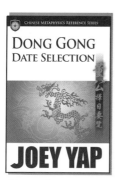

**Dong Gong
Date Selection**

**Xuan Kong Da Gua
Ten Thousand
Year Calendar**

**The Ten Thousand
Year Calendar**
(Professional Edition)

**Xuan Kong Da Gua
Reference Book 1**

**Xuan Kong Da Gua
Reference Book 2**

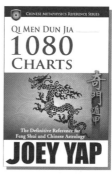

**Qi Men Dun Jia
1080 Charts**

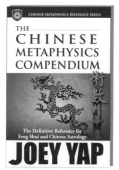

**The Chinese
Metaphysics
Compendium**

**Earth Study
Discern Truth
Volume One**

Latest DVDs Release by Joey Yap
Feng Shui for Homebuyers DVD Series

Best-selling Author, and international Master Trainer and Consultant Joey Yap reveals in these DVDs the significant Feng Shui features that every homebuyer should know when evaluating a property.

Joey will guide you on how to customise your home to maximise the Feng Shui potential of your property and gain the full benefit of improving your health, wealth and love life using the 9 Palace Grid. He will show you how to go about applying the classical applications of the Life Gua and House Gua techniques to get attuned to your Sheng Qi (positive energies).

In these DVDs, you will also learn how to identify properties with good Feng Shui features that will help you promote a fulfilling life and achieve your full potential. Discover how to avoid properties with negative Feng Shui that can bring about detrimental effects to your health, wealth and relationships.

Joey will also elaborate on how to fix the various aspects of your home that may have an impact on the Feng Shui of your property and give pointers on how to tap into the positive energies to support your goals.

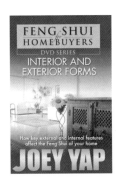

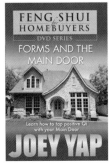

Feng Shui for Homebuyers Series

Feng Shui For Homebuyers - Exterior

Best selling Author and international Feng Shui Consultant, Joey Yap, will guide you on the various important features in your external environment that have a bearing on the Feng Shui of your home. For homeowners, those looking to build their own home or even investors who are looking to apply Feng Shui to their homes, this book provides valuable information from the classical Feng Shui theories and applications.

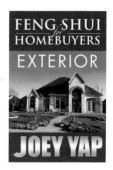

This book will assist you in screening and eliminating unsuitable options with negative FSQ (Feng Shui Quotient) should you acquire your own land or if you are purchasing a newly built home. It will also help you in determining which plot of land to select and which to avoid when purchasing an empty parcel of land.

Feng Shui for Homebuyers - Interior

A book every homeowner or potential house buyer should have. The Feng Shui for Homebuyers (Interior) is an informative reference book and invaluable guide written by best selling Author and international Feng Shui Consultant, Joey Yap.

This book provides answers to the important questions of what really does matter when looking at the internal Feng Shui of a home or office. It teaches you how to analyze your home or office floor plans and how to improve their Feng Shui. It will answer all your questions about the positive and negative flow of Qi within your home and ways to utilize them to your maximum benefit.

Providing you with a guide to calculating your Life Gua and House Gua to fine-tune your Feng Shui within your property, Joey Yap focuses on practical, easily applicable ideas on what you can implement internally in a property.

Discover Feng Shui with Joey Yap (TV Series)

Discover Feng Shui with Joey Yap: Set of 4 DVDs

Informative and entertaining, classical Feng Shui comes alive in *Discover Feng Shui with Joey Yap!*

Dying to know how you can use Feng Shui to improve your house or office, but simply too busy attend for formal classes?

You have the questions. Now let Joey personally answer them in this 4-set DVD compilation! Learn how to ensure the viability of your residence or workplace, Feng Shui-wise, without having to convert it into a Chinese antiques' shop. Classical Feng Shui is about harnessing the natural power of your environment to improve quality of life. It's a systematic and subtle metaphysical science.

And that's not all. Joey also debunks many a myth about classical Feng Shui, and shares with viewers Face Reading tips as well!

Own the series that national channel 8TV did a re-run of in 2005, today!

Educational Tools & Software

Mini Feng Shui Compass

This Mini Feng Shui Compass with the accompanying Companion Booklet written by leading Feng Shui and Chinese Astrology Master Trainer Joey Yap is a must-have for any Feng Shui enthusiast.

The Mini Feng Shui Compass is a self-aligning compass that is not only light at 100gms but also built sturdily to ensure it will be convenient to use anywhere. The rings on the Mini Feng Shui Compass are bi-lingual and incorporate the 24 Mountain Rings that is used in your traditional Luo Pan.

The comprehensive booklet included will guide you in applying the 24 Mountain Directions on your Mini Feng Shui Compass effectively and the 8 Mansions Feng Shui to locate the most auspicious locations within your home, office and surroundings. You can also use the Mini Feng Shui Compass when measuring the direction of your property for the purpose of applying Flying Stars Feng Shui.

BaZi Ming Pan Software Version 2.0
Professional Four Pillars Calculator for Destiny Analysis

The BaZi Ming Pan Version 2.0 Professional Four Pillars Calculator for Destiny Analysis is the most technically advanced software of its kind in the world today. It allows even those without any knowledge of BaZi to generate their own BaZi Charts, and provides virtually every detail required to undertake a comprehensive Destiny Analysis.

This Professional Four Pillars Calculator allows you to even undertake a day-to-day analysis of your Destiny. What's more, all BaZi Charts generated by this software are fully printable and configurable! Designed for both enthusiasts and professional practitioners, this state-of-the-art software blends details with simplicity, and is capable of generating 4 different types of BaZi charts: **BaZi Professional Charts, BaZi Annual Analysis Charts, BaZi Pillar Analysis Charts and BaZi Family Relationship Charts.**

Additional references, configurable to cater to all levels of BaZi knowledge and usage, include: • Dual Age & Bilingual Option (Western & Chinese) • Na Yin narrations • 12 Life Stages evaluation • Death & Emptiness • Gods & Killings • Special Days • Heavenly Virtue Nobles

This software also comes with a Client Management feature that allows you to save and trace clients' records instantly, navigate effortlessly between BaZi charts, and file your clients' information in an organized manner.

The BaZi Ming Pan Version 2.0 Calculator sets a new standard by combining the best of BaZi and technology.

Accelerate Your Face Reading Skills With Joey Yap's Face Reading Revealed DVD Series

Mian Xiang, the Chinese art of Face Reading, is an ancient form of physiognomy and entails the use of the face and facial characteristics to evaluate key aspects of a person's life, luck and destiny. In his Face Reading DVDs series, Joey Yap shows you how the facial features reveal a wealth of information about a person's luck, destiny and personality.

Mian Xiang also tell us the talents, quirks and personality of an individual. Do you know that just by looking at a person's face, you can ascertain his or her health, wealth, relationships and career? Let Joey Yap show you how the 12 Palaces can be utilised to reveal a person's inner talents, characteristics and much more.

Each facial feature on the face represents one year in a person's life. Your face is a 100-year map of your life and each position reveals your fortune and destiny at a particular age as well as insights and information about your personality, skills, abilities and destiny.

Using Mian Xiang, you will also be able to plan your life ahead by identifying, for example, the right business partner and knowing the sort of person that you need to avoid. By knowing their characteristics through the facial features, you will be able to gauge their intentions and gain an upper hand in negotiations.

Do you know what moles signify? Do they bring good or bad luck? Do you want to build better relationships with your partner or family members or have your ever wondered why you seem to be always bogged down by trivial problems in your life?

In these highly entertaining DVDs, Joey will help you answer all these questions and more. You will be able to ascertain the underlying meaning of moles, birthmarks or even the type of your hair in Face Reading. Joey will also reveal the guidelines to help you foster better and stronger relationships with your loved ones through Mian Xiang.

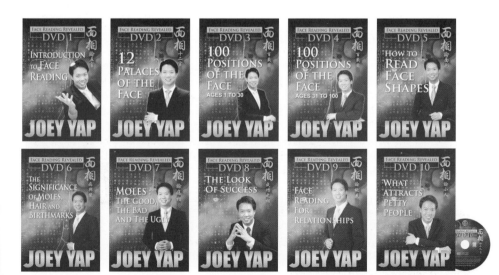

Continue Your Journey with Joey Yap's Books

BaZi - The Destiny Code (English & Chinese versions)

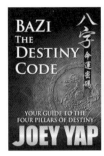

Leading Chinese Astrology Master Trainer Joey Yap makes it easy to learn how to unlock your Destiny through your BaZi with this book. BaZi or Four Pillars of Destiny is an ancient Chinese science which enables individuals to understand their personality, hidden talents and abilities as well as their luck cycle, simply by examining the information contained within their birth data. *The Destiny Code* is the first book that shows readers how to plot and interpret their own Destiny Charts and lays the foundation for more in-depth BaZi studies. Written in a lively entertaining style, the Destiny Code makes BaZi accessible to the layperson. Within 10 chapters, understand and appreciate more about this astoundingly accurate ancient Chinese Metaphysical science.

BaZi - The Destiny Code Revealed

In this follow up to Joey Yap's best-selling *The Destiny Code*, delve deeper into your own Destiny chart through an understanding of the key elemental relationships that affect the Heavenly Stems and Earthly Branches. Find out how Combinations, Clash, Harm, Destructions and Punishments bring new dimension to a BaZi chart. Complemented by extensive real-life examples, *The Destiny Code Revealed* takes you to the next level of BaZi, showing you how to unlock the Codes of Destiny and to take decisive action at the right time, and capitalise on the opportunities in life.

The Ten Thousand Year Calendar

The Ten Thousand Year Calendar or 萬年曆 Wan Nian Li is a regular reference book and an invaluable tool used by masters, practitioners and students of Feng Shui, BaZi (Four Pillars of Destiny), Chinese Zi Wei Dou Shu Astrology (Purple Star), Yi Jing (I-Ching) and Date Selection specialists.

JOEY YAP's *Ten Thousand Year Calendar* provides the Gregorian (Western) dates converted into both the Chinese Solar and Lunar calendar in both the English and Chinese language.

It also includes a comprehensive set of key Feng Shui and Chinese Astrology charts and references, including Xuan Kong Nine Palace Flying Star Charts, Monthly and Daily Flying Stars, Water Dragon Formulas Reference Charts, Zi Wei Dou Shu (Purple Star) Astrology Reference Charts, BaZi (Four Pillars of Destiny) Heavenly Stems, Earthly Branches and all other related reference tables for Chinese Metaphysical Studies.

Annual Releases

Chinese Astrology for 2008

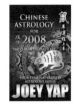

This information-packed annual guide to the Chinese Astrology for 2008 goes way beyond the conventional 'animal horoscope' book. To begin with, author Joey Yap includes a personalized outlook for 2008 based on the individual's BaZi Day Pillar (Jia Zi) and a 12-month micro-analysis for each of the 60 Day Pillars – in addition to the annual outlook for all 12 animal signs and the 12-month outlook for each animal sign in 2008. Find out what awaits you in 2008 from the four key aspects of Health, Wealth, Career and Relationships… with Joey Yap's **Chinese Astrology for 2008**!

Feng Shui for 2008

Maximize the Qi of the Year of the Earth Rat for your home and office, with Joey Yap's **Feng Shui for 2008** book. Learn how to tap into the positive sectors of the year, and avoid the negative ones and those with the Annual Afflictions, as well as ascertain how the annual Flying Stars affect your property by comparing them against the Eight Mansions (Ba Zhai) for 2008. Flying Stars enthusiasts will also find this book handy, as it includes the monthly Flying Stars charts for the year, accompanied by detailed commentaries on what sectors to use and avoid – to enable you to optimize your Academic, Relationships and Wealth Luck in 2008.

Tong Shu Diary 2008

Organize your professional and personal lives with the **Tong Shu Diary 2008**, with a twist… it also allows you to determine the most suitable dates on which you can undertake important activities and endeavors throughout the year! This compact Diary integrates the Chinese Solar and Lunar Calendars with the universal lingua franca of the Gregorian Calendar.

Tong Shu Monthly Planner 2008

Tailor-made for the Feng Shui or BaZi enthusiast in you, or even professional Chinese Metaphysics consultants who want a compact planner with useful information incorporated into it. In the **Tong Shu Monthly Planner 2008**, you will find the auspicious and inauspicious dates for the year marked out for you, alongside the most suitable activities to be undertaken on each day. As a bonus, there is also a reference section containing all the monthly Flying Stars charts and Annual Afflictions for 2008.

Tong Shu Desktop Calendar 2008

Get an instant snapshot of the suitable and unsuitable activities for each day of the Year of the Earth Rat, with the icons displayed on this lightweight Desktop Calendar. Elegantly presenting the details of the Chinese Solar Calendar in the form of the standard Gregorian one, the **Tong Shu Desktop Calendar 2008** is perfect for Chinese Metaphysics enthusiasts and practitioners alike. Whether it a business launching or meeting, ground breaking ceremony, travel or house-moving that you have in mind, this Calendar is designed to fulfill your information needs.

Tong Shu Year Planner 2008

This one-piece Planner presents you all the essential information you need for significant activities or endeavors…with just a quick glance! In a nutshell, it allows you to identify the favorable and unfavorable days, which will in turn enable you to schedule your year's activities so as to make the most of good days, and avoid the ill-effects brought about by inauspicious ones.

Continue Your Journey with Joey Yap's Books

Mian Xiang - Discover Face Reading

Need to identify a suitable business partner? How about understanding your staff or superiors better? Or even choosing a suitable spouse? These mind boggling questions can be answered in Joey Yap's introductory book to Face Reading titled *Mian Xiang – Discover Face Reading*. This book will help you discover the hidden secrets in a person's face.

Mian Xiang – Discover Face Reading is comprehensive book on all areas of Face Reading, covering some of the most important facial features, including the forehead, mouth, ears and even the philtrum above your lips. This book will help you analyse not just your Destiny but help you achieve your full potential and achieve life fulfillment.

Stories and Lessons on Feng Shui (English & Chinese versions)

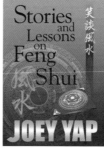

Stories and Lessons on Feng Shui is a compilation of essays and stories written by leading Feng Shui and Chinese Astrology trainer and consultant Joey Yap about Feng Shui and Chinese Astrology.

In this heart-warming collection of easy to read stories, find out why it's a myth that you should never have Water on the right hand side of your house, the truth behind the infamous 'love' and 'wealth' corners and that the sudden death of a pet fish is really NOT due to bad luck!

More Stories and Lessons on Feng Shui

Finally, the long-awaited sequel to *Stories & Lessons on Feng Shui*!

If you've read the best-selling Stories & Lessons on Feng Shui, you won't want to miss this book. And even if you haven't read *Stories & Lessons on Feng Shui*, there's always a time to rev your Feng Shui engine up.

The time is NOW.

And the book? *More Stories & Lessons on Feng Shui* – the 2nd compilation of the most popular articles and columns penned by Joey Yap; **specially featured in national and international publications, magazines and newspapers.**

All in all, *More Stories & Lessons on Feng Shui* is a delightful chronicle of Joey's articles, thoughts and vast experience - as a professional Feng Shui consultant and instructor - that have been purposely refined, edited and expanded upon to make for a light-hearted, interesting yet educational read. And with Feng Shui, BaZi, Mian Xiang and Yi Jing all thrown into this one dish, there's something for everyone…so all you need to serve or accompany *More Stories & Lessons on Feng Shui* with is your favorite cup of tea or coffee!

Continue Your Journey with Joey Yap's Books

Xuan Kong: Flying Stars Feng Shui

Xuan Kong Flying Stars Feng Shui is an essential introductory book to the subject of Xuan Kong Fei Xing, a well-known and popular system of Feng Shui, written by International Feng Shui Master Trainer Joey Yap.

In his down-to-earth, entertaining and easy to read style, Joey Yap takes you through the essential basics of Classical Feng Shui, and the key concepts of Xuan Kong Fei Xing (Flying Stars). Learn how to fly the stars, plot a Flying Star chart for your home or office and interpret the stars and star combinations. Find out how to utilise the favourable areas of your home or office for maximum benefit and learn 'tricks of the trade' and 'trade secrets' used by Feng Shui practitioners to enhance and maximise Qi in your home or office.

An essential integral introduction to the subject of Classical Feng Shui and the Flying Stars System of Feng Shui!

Xuan Kong Flying Stars: Structures and Combinations

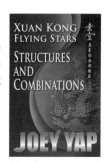

Delve deeper into Flying Stars through a greater understanding of the 81 Combinations and the influence of the Annual and Monthly Stars on the Base, Sitting and Facing Stars in this 2nd book in the Xuan Kong Feng Shui series. Learn how Structures like the Combination of 10, Up the Mountain and Down the River, Pearl and Parent String Structures are used to interpret a Flying Star chart.

(Available in 2008)

Xuan Kong Flying Stars: Advanced Techniques

Take your knowledge of Xuan Kong Flying Stars to a higher level and learn how to apply complex techniques and advanced formulas such as Castle Gate Technique, Seven Star Robbery Formation, Advancing the Dragon Formation and Replacement Star technique amongst others. Joey Yap also shows you how to use the Life Palace technique to combine Gua Numbers with Flying Star numbers and utilise the predictive facets of Flying Stars Feng Shui.

(Available in 2009)

Continue Your Journey with Joey Yap's Books

The Art of Date Selection: Personal Date Selection

In today's modern world, it is not good enough to just do things effectively – we need to do them efficiently, as well. From the signing of business contracts and moving into a new home, to launching a product or even tying the knot; everything has to move, and move very quickly too. There is a premium on Time, where mistakes can indeed be costly.

The notion of doing the Right Thing, at the Right Time and in the Right Place is the very backbone of Date Selection. Because by selecting a suitable date specially tailored to a specific activity or endeavor, we infuse it with the most positive energies prevalent in our environment during that particular point in time; and that could well make the difference between 'make-and-break'! With the *Art of Date Selection: Personal Date Selection*, learn simple, practical methods you can employ to select not just good dates, but personalized good dates. Whether it's a personal activity such as a marriage or professional endeavor such as launching a business, signing a contract or even acquiring assets, this book will show you how to pick the good dates and tailor them to suit the activity in question, as well as avoid the negative ones too!

The Art of Date Selection: Feng Shui Date Selection

Date Selection is the Art of selecting the most suitable date, where the energies present on the day support the specific activities or endeavors we choose to undertake on that day. Feng Shui is the Chinese Metaphysical study of the Physiognomy of the Land – landforms and the Qi they produce, circulate and conduct. Hence, anything that exists on this Earth is invariably subject to the laws of Feng Shui. So what do we get when Date Selection and Feng Shui converge?

Feng Shui Date Selection, of course! Say you wish to renovate your home, or maybe buy or rent one. Or perhaps, you're a developer, and wish to know WHEN is the best date possible to commence construction works on your project. In any case – and all cases – you certainly wish to ensure that your endeavors are well supported by the positive energies present on a good day, won't you? And this is where Date Selection supplements the practice of Feng Shui. At the end of the day, it's all about making the most of what's good, and minimizing what's bad.

(Available in 2008)

Elevate Your Feng Shui Skills With Joey Yap's Home Study Course And Educational DVDs

Xuan Kong Vol.1
An Advanced Feng Shui Home Study Course

Learn the Xuan Kong Flying Star Feng Shui system in just 20 lessons! Joey Yap's specialised notes and course work have been written to enable distance learning without compromising on the breadth or quality of the syllabus. Learn at your own pace with the same material students in a live class would use. The most comprehensive distance learning course on Xuan Kong Flying Star Feng Shui in the market. Xuan Kong Flying Star Vol. 1 comes complete with a special binder for all your course notes.

Feng Shui for Period 8 - (DVD)

Don't miss the Feng Shui Event of the next 20 years! Catch Joey Yap LIVE and find out just what Period 8 is all about. This DVD boxed set zips you through the fundamentals of Feng Shui and the impact of this important change in the Feng Shui calendar. Joey's entertaining, conversational style walks you through the key changes that Period 8 will bring and how to tap into Wealth Qi and Good Feng Shui for the next 20 years.

Xuan Kong Flying Stars Beginners Workshop - (DVD)

Take a front row seat in Joey Yap's Xuan Kong Flying Stars workshop with this unique LIVE RECORDING of Joey Yap's Xuan Kong Flying Stars Feng Shui workshop, attended by over 500 people. This DVD program provides an effective and quick introduction of Xuan Kong Feng Shui essentials for those who are just starting out in their study of classical Feng Shui. Learn to plot your own Flying Star chart in just 3 hours. Learn 'trade secret' methods, remedies and cures for Flying Stars Feng Shui. This boxed set contains 3 DVDs and 1 workbook with notes and charts for reference.

BaZi Four Pillars of Destiny Beginners Workshop - (DVD)

Ever wondered what Destiny has in store for you? Or curious to know how you can learn more about your personality and inner talents? BaZi or Four Pillars of Destiny is an ancient Chinese science that enables us to understand a person's hidden talent, inner potential, personality, health and wealth luck from just their birth data. This specially compiled DVD set of Joey Yap's BaZi Beginners Workshop provides a thorough and comprehensive introduction to BaZi. Learn how to read your own chart and understand your own luck cycle. This boxed set contains 3 DVDs and 1 workbook with notes and reference charts.

Interested in learning MORE about Feng Shui? Advance Your Feng Shui Knowledge with the Mastery Academy Courses.

Feng Shui Mastery Series™
LIVE COURSES (MODULES ONE TO FOUR)

Feng Shui Mastery – Module One

Beginners Course

Designed for students seeking an entry-level intensive program into the study of Feng Shui , Module One is an intensive foundation course that aims not only to provide you with an introduction to Feng Shui theories and formulas and equip you with the skills and judgments to begin practicing and conduct simple Feng Shui audits upon successful completion of the course. Learn all about Forms, Eight Mansions Feng Shui and Flying Star Feng Shui in just one day with a unique, structured learning program that makes learning Feng Shui quick and easy!

Feng Shui Mastery – Module Two

Practitioners Course

Building on the knowledge and foundation in classical Feng Shui theory garnered in M1, M2 provides a more advanced and in-depth understanding of Eight Mansions, Xuan Kong Flying Star and San He and introduces students to theories that are found only in the classical Chinese Feng Shui texts. This 3-Day Intensive course hones analytical and judgment skills, refines Luo Pan (Chinese Feng Shui compass) skills and reveals 'trade secret' remedies. Module Two covers advanced Forms Analysis, San He's Five Ghost Carry Treasure formula, Advanced Eight Mansions and Xuan Kong Flying Stars and equips you with the skills needed to undertake audits and consultations for residences and offices.

Feng Shui Mastery – Module Three

Advanced Practitioners Course

Module Three is designed for Professional Feng Shui Practitioners. Learn advanced topics in Feng Shui and take your skills to a cutting edge level. Be equipped with the knowledge, techniques and confidence to conduct large scale audits (like estate and resort planning). Learn how to apply different systems appropriately to remedy situations or cases deemed inauspicious by one system and reconcile conflicts in different systems of Feng Shui. Gain advanced knowledge of San He (Three Harmony) systems and San Yuan (Three Cycles) systems, advanced Luan Tou (Forms Feng Shui) and specialist Water Formulas.

Feng Shui Mastery – Module Four

Master Course

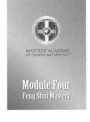

The graduating course of the Feng Shui Mastery (FSM) Series, this course takes the advanced practitioner to the Master level. Power packed M4 trains students to 'walk the mountains' and identify superior landform, superior grade structures and make qualitative evaluations of landform, structures, Water and Qi and covers advanced and exclusive topics of San He, San Yuan, Xuan Kong, Ba Zhai, Luan Tou (Advanced Forms and Water Formula) Feng Shui. Master Internal, External and Luan Tou (Landform) Feng Shui methodologies to apply Feng Shui at every level and undertake consultations of every scale and magnitude, from houses and apartments to housing estates, townships, shopping malls and commercial districts.

BaZi Mastery Series™

BaZi Mastery – Module One
Intensive Foundation Course

This Intensive One Day Foundation Course provides an introduction to the
principles and fundamentals of BaZi (Four Pillars of Destiny) and Destiny
Analysis methods such as Ten Gods, Useful God and Strength of Qi. Learn how
to plot a BaZi chart and interpret your Destiny and your potential. Master
BaZi and learn to capitalize on your strengths, minimize risks and downturns
and take charge of your Destiny.

BaZi Mastery – Module Two
Practical BaZi Applications

BaZi Module Two teaches students advanced BaZi analysis techniques and
specific analysis methods for relationship luck, health evaluation, wealth
potential and career potential. Students will learn to identify BaZi chart
structures, sophisticated methods for applying the Ten Gods, and how to read
Auxiliary Stars. Students who have completed Module Two will be able to
conduct professional BaZi readings.

BaZi Mastery – Module Three
Advanced Practitioners Program

Designed for the BaZi practitioner, learn how to read complex cases and unique
events in BaZi charts and perform Big and Small assessments. Discover how to
analyze personalities and evaluate talents precisely, as well as special formulas
and classical methodologies for BaZi from classics such as Di Tian Sui and
Qiong Tong Bao Jian.

BaZi Mastery – Module Four
Master Course in BaZi

The graduating course of the BaZi Mastery Series, this course takes the
advanced practitioner to the Masters' level. BaZi M4 focuses on specialized
techniques of BaZi reading, unique special structures and advance methods
from ancient classical texts. This program includes techniques on date selection
and ancient methodologies from the Qiong Tong Bao Jian and Yuan Hai Zi
Ping classics.

Xuan Kong Mastery – Module One
Advanced Foundation Program

This course is for the experienced Feng Shui professionals who wish to expand their knowledge and skills in the Xuan Kong system of Feng Shui, covering important foundation methods and techniques from the Wu Chang and Guang Dong lineages of Xuan Kong Feng Shui.

Xuan Kong Mastery – Module Two A
Advanced Xuan Kong Methodologies

Designed for Feng Shui practitioners seeking to specialise in the Xuan Kong system, this program focuses on methods of application and Joey Yap's unique Life Palace and Shifting Palace Methods, as well as methods and techniques from the Wu Chang lineage.

Xuan Kong Mastery – Module Two B
Purple White

Explore in detail and in great depth the star combinations in Xuan Kong. Learn how each different combination reacts or responds in different palaces, under different environmental circumstances and to whom in the property. Learn methods, theories and techniques extracted from ancient classics such as Xuan Kong Mi Zhi, Xuan Kong Fu, Fei Xing Fu and Zi Bai Jue.

Xuan Kong Mastery – Module Three
Advanced Xuan Kong Da Gua

This intensive course focuses solely on the Xuan Kong Da Gua system covering the theories, techniques and methods of application of this unique 64-Hexagram based system of Xuan Kong including Xuan Kong Da Gua for landform analysis.

MIAN XIANG MASTERY SERIES™
LIVE COURSES (MODULES ONE AND TWO)

Mian Xiang Mastery – Module One
Basic Face Reading

A person's face is their fortune – learn more about the ancient Chinese art of Face Reading. In just one day, be equipped with techniques and skills to read a person's face and ascertain their character, luck, wealth and relationship luck.

Mian Xiang Mastery – Module Two
Practical Face Reading

Mian Xiang Module Two covers face reading techniques extracted from the ancient classics Shen Xiang Quan Pian and Shen Xiang Tie Guan Dau. Gain a greater depth and understanding of Mian Xiang and learn to recognize key structures and characteristics in a person's face.

Yi Jing Mastery Series™
LIVE COURSES

Traditional Yi Jing

'Yi', relates to change. Change is the only constant in life and the universe, without exception to this rule. The Yi Jing is hence popularly referred to as the Book or Classic of Change. Discoursed in the language of Yin and Yang, the Yi Jing is one of the oldest Chinese classical texts surviving today. With Traditional Yi Jing, learn how this Classic is used to divine the outcomes of virtually every facet of life; from your relationships to seeking an answer to the issues you may face in your daily life.

Plum Blossom Numerology

Shao Yong, widely regarded as one of the greatest scholars of the Sung Dynasty, developed Mei Hua Yi Shu (Plum Blossom Numerology) as a more advanced means for divination purposes using the Yi Jing. In Plum Blossom Numerology, the results of a hexagram are interpreted by referring to the Gua meanings, where the interaction and relationship between the five elements, stems, branches and time are equally taken into consideration. This divination method, properly applied, allows us to make proper decisions whenever we find ourselves in a predicament.

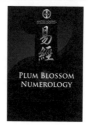

Ze Ri Mastery Series™
LIVE COURSES (MODULES ONE AND TWO)

Ze Ri Mastery Series Module 1

The Mastery Academy's Date Selection Mastery Series Module 1 is specifically structured to provide novice students with an exciting introduction to the Art of Date Selection. Learn the rudiments and tenets of this intriguing metaphysical science. What makes a good date, and what makes a bad date? What dates are suitable for which activities, and what dates simply aren't? And of course, the mother of all questions: WHY aren't all dates created equal. All in only one Module – Module 1!

Ze Ri Mastery Series Module 2

In Module 2, discover advanced Date Selection techniques that will take your knowledge of this Art to a level equivalent to that of a professional's! This is the Module where Date Selection infuses knowledge of the ancient metaphysical science of Feng Shui and BaZi (Chinese Astrology, or Four Pillars of Destiny). Feng Shui, as a means of maximizing Human Luck (i.e. our luck on Earth), is often quoted as the cure to BaZi, which allows us to decipher our Heaven (i.e. inherent) Luck. And one of the most potent ways of making the most of what life has to offer us is to understand our Destiny, know how we can use the natural energies of our environment for our environments and MOST importantly, WHEN we should use these energies and for WHAT endeavors!

You will learn specific methods on how to select suitable dates, tailored to specific activities and events. More importantly, you will also be taught how to suit dates to a person's BaZi (Chinese Astrology, or Four Pillars of Destiny), in order to maximize his or her strengths, and allow this person to surmount any challenges that lie in wait. Add in the factor of 'place', and you would have satisfied the notion of `doing the right thing, at the right time and in the right place'! A basic knowledge of BaZi and Feng Shui will come in handy in this Module, although these are not pre-requisites to successfully undergo Module 2.

Walk the Mountains! Learn Feng Shui in a Practical and Hands-on Program.

 Feng Shui Mastery Excursion Series™ : CHINA

Learn landform (Luan Tou) Feng Shui by walking the mountains and chasing the Dragon's vein in China. This Program takes the students in a study tour to examine notable Feng Shui landmarks, mountains, hills, valleys, ancient palaces, famous mansions, houses and tombs in China. The Excursion is a 'practical' hands-on course where students are shown to perform readings using the formulas they've learnt and to recognize and read Feng Shui Landform (Luan Tou) formations.

Read about China Excursion here:
http://www.masteryacademy.com/Education/schoolfengshui/fengshuimasteryexcursion.asp

Mastery Academy courses are conducted around the world. Find out when will Joey Yap be in your area by visiting **www.masteryacademy.com** or call our office at +603-2284 8080.